Y0-AGC-242

Frontier deserves the wide audience for which it is written. The reader is persuaded by diligent and exhaustive research to accept the conclusion that 'White Australians have generally failed to appreciate the great weight of history which presses the land rights movement forward'. Reynolds' account also points to ways in which the history can be understood —and even re-made.

Donald Denoon, Historical Studies

...a remarkable book, not just because it is bulging with new factual material but because Reynolds brings all his scholarship to bear on a single focus... This is history with a moral and urgent purpose.

Peter Read, Aboriginal History

In telling the story of the European occupation of Australia and the violence on the frontier, Henry Reynolds has done what the good historian should do: he gives us the very stuff of colonial occupation, life on the out-stations and in the townships where, right from the start, the blacks were feared and despised—even by compassionate men whose hearts became hardened by the exigencies of occupation and husbandry.

John Hooker, The Age

If the direction of Australian thinking and Australian policy ever substantially changes it will be to Reynolds that much of the credit must go.

Don Watson, Times on Sunday

OTHER BOOKS BY HENRY REYNOLDS

The Other Side of the Frontier
The Law of the Land
Dispossession
With the White People
Fate of a Free People
Aboriginal Sovereignty

Frontier

Aborigines, Settlers and Land

Henry Reynolds

ALLEN & UNWIN

For Margaret
Who puts the theory into practice

First published in 1987
Reprinted 5 times
Reissued in new format 1996

Allen & Unwin Pty Ltd
9 Atchison Street, St Leonards, NSW 2065 Australia
Phone: (61 2) 9901 4088
Fax: (61 2) 9906 2218
E-mail: 100252.103@compuserve.com

National Library of Australia
Cataloguing-in-publication entry:

Reynolds, Henry, 1938–
Frontier: Aborigines, settlers and land.

Bibliography.
Includes index.
ISBN 1 86448 191 9

1. Frontier and pioneer life—Australia. 2. Aborigines,
Australian—Treatment. 3. Land settlement—Australia—
History. 4. Racism—Australia—History.
5. Australia—Race relations. I. Title

994.0049915

Typeset 11/13pt Garamond by Setrite Typesetters
Printed by Australian Print Group, Maryborough, Victoria

10 9 8 7 6 5 4 3 2 1

Contents

v

Acknowledgements

Many people have provided me with encouragement and assistance during the years that I have been accumulating evidence and developing a picture of the history of white—Aboriginal relations. I am especially grateful to the Australian Research Grants Committee for providing me, over ten years or so, with the means to conduct research in the libraries and archives in all parts of Australia and overseas. Without such help research in Townsville would be very difficult indeed. I have to thank the inter-library loans staff of James Cook University and many other institutions for providing innumerable books and articles. Colleagues in my own university and others scattered all over Australia have provided advice, stimulation and encouragement. Val Hicks and Sue Baulch were competent, and patient, typists. John Iremonger and Venetia Nelson have been efficient and helpful as publisher and editor and—much more importantly—have believed in the book throughout its growth and development.

Introduction

This book is a sequel to *The Other Side of the Frontier* which dealt with the Aboriginal response to the European invasion and settlement of Australia. It covers much the same ground but is concerned with the attitudes and the behaviour of the settlers and their reaction to the blacks they were dispossessing. While the books share similar themes they stand alone and can be read as separate works, although each will illuminate the other. Neither book is designed to be a general, or comprehensive, history of white—Aboriginal relations. They are selective in focus, concentrating on a number of major themes, tracing them from the first settlement until the early decades of the twentieth century and exploring evidence from every part of Australia, overleaping colonial/State boundaries and passing back and forth through the first 150 years of white settlement.

The research was conducted over twelve years in all parts of Australia and in Britain. The need to cover the whole continent meant that many issues were examined over and over again in their different regional settings. The quotations of contemporary material represent a very small selection of evidence that has been collected and an even smaller sample of the vast amount of material turned over during innumerable hours of dogged research. Without much difficulty many paragraphs could have been expanded into chapters and chapters into books. The aim throughout has been to present, in a form accessible to the non-specialist, a distillation of the Australian frontier experience as it was manifested in the relations between whites and Aborigines. Direct quotations have been widely used in order to allow the settlers to tell their own story. Many major themes have been left over for what I hope will be a third book dealing with the incorporation of the Aborigines into the European economy, the linked issues of assimilation and segregation, and the blacks who, from the earliest years of settlement, assisted the expansion of the frontier as guides, trackers, police-troopers and stockmen.

Three central themes run through the book: frontier conflict, racial ideology and land ownership. Each fully warrants the attention devoted to it. No one who reads colonial newspapers, speeches, letters or books can overlook the persistent racial violence without grossly distorting the truth. Three chapters out of seven are not an overemphasis on conflict given its ubiquity and longevity and its continuing influence in many parts of Australia. If anything the treatment of frontier violence is restrained. Little attention has been given to details of punitive expeditions, to poisoning and other atrocities committed in all parts of the continent. Much could have been made of these horror stories, but the temptation was avoided so as better to pursue the central issues.

The second major theme is the development and expression of racial ideas and their impact on colonial society including the neglected humanitarians and missionaries who took up the Aboriginal cause and struggled against the strong mainstream of behaviour and opinion. The third theme is the question of land ownership and how conflicting claims and theories about tenure have been at the centre of relations between white and black since the beginnings of European settlement.

Research in libraries and archives has not been the only source of information and inspiration. Alongside traditional scholarship must be placed the experience of twenty years spent in northern Australia during which time I have seen the daily interaction of white and black Australians. Personal experience illustrated better than books how powerful the past was, how important the frontier experience, how persistent the basic theories of nineteenth-century racism, how resentful Europeans often were at Aboriginal advancement, how fear still haunted black communities. Many small incidents brought these facts home. There was, for instance, the young primary school headmaster who told me some years ago that while he was very fond of his Aboriginal pupils there was nothing that could be done for them because they had smaller brains than did Europeans. At a dinner party I overheard a progressive and liberal-minded barrister confessing that no matter how hard he tried he could not bring himself to believe that killing a black was as serious as killing a white man. An Aboriginal woman, elegant and self-confident, told me that until she had gone to work in Sydney in her early twenties she had never once dared to look a white man straight in the eye. Several black activists have explained to me at various times that their parents and grandparents are ever fearful that by speaking out the young people will be imprisoned or killed or will have their children taken away from them. A police superintendent of the Cairns district told a local television audience some years ago that his men had to be tough on the blacks because they had the task of holding down 20 000 of them. At a restaurant recently a group of young men and women spent half an hour or so trying to outdo one another in the vehemence of their hatred of the blacks and in suggesting bizarre and brutal schemes to 'get rid of them'. Yet beside these and many similar incidents, there has been an extraordinary transformation of the Aboriginal situation in the last ten years—a black renaissance—and a significant growth of understanding and tolerance among the whites. But the past is still alive, is dangerously alive, in many parts of Australia.

Like *The Other Side of the Frontier* this book is about the present as well as our colonial heritage. While based on sound scholarship it is inspired by passion about the past and concern for the future of that multi-racial society which, while small in numbers, still occupies half the continent.

—PART I—
Conflict

– 1 –

Unrecorded Battlefields

Was Australia settled or invaded? pioneered or conquered? won by sweat or won by blood? Was it the fruit of industry or a prize of war? These are questions which have reverberated through Australian history, the cause of argument and anguish since the early years of settlement. One of the first histories of New South Wales, published in 1816, expressed the view that colonisation in the antipodes was uniquely peaceful:

> for here there are no scenes...of desolating war and bloodshed to contemplate, no peaceable inhabitants driven from their smiling dwellings, and deprived of the comforts of life, by means of the destroying invader. Our settlers have not established themselves by the sword, nor willingly done injury to the naked miserable stragglers, who were found on these barren shores.

It was an appealing interpretation of colonial history which gained many followers. Writing half a century later, at a time of escalating frontier conflict, Queensland's Governor Bowen hailed the 'triumph of peaceful progress...victories without injustice or bloodshed, conquests not over man, but over nature'.

The opposing view of colonisation was strongly argued in a letter written to a Launceston paper in 1831 at the end of three years of intense conflict with the Tasmanian Aborigines. The correspondent, J.E., asked rhetorically:

> Are these unhappy people, the subjects of our King, in a state of rebellion or are they an injured people, whom we have invaded and with whom we are at war?
> Are they within the reach of our laws; or are they to be judged by the

3

law of nations? Are they to be viewed in the light of murderers, or as prisoners of war?

Have they been guilty of any crime under the laws of nations which is punishable by death, or have they only been carrying on a war *in their way*?

Are they British subjects at all, or a foreign enemy who has never yet been subdued and which resists our usurped authority and domination...

We are at war with them: they look upon us as enemies—as invaders—as oppressors and persecutors—they resist our invasion. They have never been subdued, therefore they are not rebellious subjects, but an injured nation, defending in their own way, their rightful possessions, which have been torn from them by force.

The legal situation was clear from the beginning. Australia was a colony of settlement not of conquest. The common law arrived with the First Fleet; the Aborigines became instant subjects of the King, amenable to, and in theory protected by, that law. They could be murdered, outlawed or made subject to martial law but they could not be treated as enemies of the state. Lord Glenelg, the Secretary of State for the Colonies, issued a definitive statement of the situation in 1837 when informing Governor Bourke that the blacks were protected by the law and that it was impossible to regard them as aliens 'with whom a war can exist, and against whom Her Majesty's troops may exercise belligerent rights'. But few of those who had lived on the frontier thought of Australia as a uniquely peaceful society, legal theory or historical interpretation notwithstanding. Neither theory nor interpretation could satisfactorily account for the violence which haunted the pioneer fringe for 150 years. Writing in 1880, the ethnographers Fison and Howitt summed up the experience of a century of conflict:

It may be stated broadly that the advance of settlement has, upon the frontier at least, been marked by a line of blood. The actual conflict of the two races has varied in intensity and in duration, as the various native tribes have themselves in mental and physical character...But the tide of settlement has advanced along an ever widening line, breaking the tribes with its first waves and overwhelming their wrecks with its flood.

Was it warfare?

Frontier skirmishing felt like a form of warfare. Those who had experienced it said so in books and newspapers, letters and speeches, in public statement and private conversations, in every colony and throughout the nineteenth century. Before the settlement at Sydney was a year old, Governor Phillip and his officers were complaining about a 'state of petty warfare'; an 'open war' started with Hawkesbury River clans as the settlers began to farm the valley in 1795. In 1826, with the Europeans edging along the Hunter River, the missionary L.E. Threlkeld wrote home to England: 'You will be grieved to hear that war has commenced and still continues against the Aborigines of this land.' Two years later a troubled Tasmanian settler wrote to the Governor with suggestions about how to 'stop the ferocious warfare which now reigns in this Island'; a week later the Governor himself communicated with all the magistrates deploring the 'lawless and cruel warfare'. A naval captain visiting the Swan River in 1832 noted in his diary that there was 'really a most awful warfare' in progress; a pioneer West Australian settler declared: 'We are at war with the original owners, we have never known them in any capacity but as enemies.' In northern New South Wales in the late 1830s Europeans felt they were 'in an enemy's country'; the whole region was in 'a state of warfare'. Twenty years later the Queensland parliament heard that the colonists 'must be considered to be, as they always have been, at open war with the Aborigines'. In 1879 the editor of the *Queenslander* informed his readers: 'we are today at open war with every tribe of wild blacks on the frontier'; a colleague writing for the *Queensland Figaro* referred to the 'constant border warfare on the verge line of settlement'. Black killed by the Queensland Native Police, a parliamentary committee was told, 'were shot in battle' on what a retired officer of the force termed 'the unrecorded battlefields of Queensland'.

Martyrs of their country

While Europeans often attributed Aboriginal resistance to their adversaries' savage nature, there were many settlers who regarded it as the natural, if unwelcome, response to invasion. 'They consider every injury they can inflict upon white men as an act of duty and patriotic [*sic*],' a Tasmanian colonist wrote in 1828, 'and however they may dread the punishment which our laws inflict upon them, they consider the sufferers...as martyrs of their country.' A contemporary wrote to a Hobart paper two years later observing that every day afforded 'some proof of their determination to destroy, and their declaration to war with the whites'. It was absurd to see the blacks 'in the light of occasional rioters', a New South Wales settler argued in 1839; they were 'enemies arrayed in arms and waging war against Europeans as their invaders'. A visitor to the colony in the 1840s argued: 'It must not be forgotten, while we are meditating on the treatment of the natives...that their country is occupied by force—that they attempted, but in vain, to beat off the English settlers.' The editor of the *Northern Territory Times* remarked in 1875: 'We are invading their country and they have a perfect right to—and it is but natural that they should—do their best to obstruct our passage through it.' The Government Resident in Darwin agreed. 'Entry into their country is an act of invasion', he observed, and 'they will halt at no opportunity of attacking the white invaders.'

The enemy of everyday

Frontier settlers compared their circumstances with those of other colonists in different parts of the Empire. In the late 1850s Queenslanders drew parallels with the Indian Mutiny, the editor of the *Moreton Bay Courier* arguing that conflict with central Queensland clans had cost 'more white victims than the massacre at Cawnpore'; the Dawson River blacks had committed atrocities 'only equalled by the Sepoys of India'. A few years later a resident in the pioneer township of Bowen compared the local situation with the Jamaica Rebellion. Writing in the *Port Denison Times* he observed: 'We know the storm that was raised in England against the Jamaica riots, yet it is estimated that the whole sacrifice of life in Jamaica at that time did not exceed 400. What then will the people of England say when they learn that more than this number of natives falls each year in Queensland?' In 1885 a north Queensland settler argued that the local blacks were 'just as difficult to deal with as the savage hordes in the Sudan'; in fact 'war should be declared against them until they are subdued'. Defending punitive expeditions in the Northern Territory a local politician and newspaper proprietor argued that it was 'looked upon as heroism in other countries...for a white man to conquer the natives'. Similar justification was urged in Western Australia; settlers on punitive expeditions were as justified as were British soldiers when they 'shot at either Kaffirs, Zulus, Abyssinians or any other inferior race'. Summing up the folk wisdom of the frontier, the editor of the *Rockhampton Bulletin* wrote that there was

> no way of treating them, except as belligerents when they commit outrages has yet been found efficacious in the back tracks. They may be tolerated and treated kindly so long as they refrain from mischievous acts, but when they rob, steal, or murder, they must be treated as enemies to the state and shot down with as little compunction as soldiers shoot each other in battles amongst civilized men. That this is a deplorable necessity we admit, but is it more deplorable than the practice in modern civilized warfare?

Queenslanders compared expenditure on external defence in the 1870s and 1880s with money spent on the Native Police Force, the cost of which, they argued, 'should be a parliamentary vote of equal consideration with coastal defences or volunteer corps'. 'We have', a writer explained in the *Queenslander* in 1879, 'not grudged a large outlay on national defence with but a very doubtful prospect of foreign attack'; why then should the Government 'stint the funds necessary for the repression of the enemy within our gates?' An embattled selector on the Atherton Tableland wrote to a Brisbane paper observing,

> there are thousands, that can be spent on Defence Forces, to protect the inhabitants of this country from the invisible, perhaps imaginary, but for certain distant enemies; but we cannot afford to keep an efficient body of police to keep in check the enemy we have at our door, the enemy of every day, the one that slowly but surely robs us and impoverishes us.

The guerilla mode of warfare

Settlers were keenly aware of the special nature of frontier conflict, referring variously to a 'kind of war', a 'sort of warfare', a 'species of warfare'. They frequently talked of guerilla warfare. The term 'guerilla' was apparently first used in the 1830s when it was still comparatively new to English, having been introduced into the language during the Peninsula War. In 1833 a West Australian settler assessed Aboriginal tactics by reference to the 'guerilla mode of warfare'; Henry Melville wrote a history of Tasmania in which he depicted the problems of island colonists who were 'suffering from a guerilla war'.

Many features of the conflict were new to the British, even to those who had been in the armed forces in Europe and other parts of the Empire. Their Aboriginal adversaries were constantly on the move; they had no villages, fields or fortifications which could be captured. They lived off the land, exploiting an ancient and sophisticated bushcraft. Their movements were unpredictable, groups waxing and waning for no apparent reason, adopting the classical stratagems of the weak when pitted against the strong—stealth, surprise, secrecy. After making a detailed study of the tactics of Tasmanian Aborigines Calder observed that they never attacked at a disadvantage and 'invariably retired directly when overmatched which was part of their system of warfare'. Aboriginal clans rarely contested the first entry of Europeans. They either avoided them altogether or attempted to establish friendly relations with them. Even when conflict broke out they tried to remain on or near their own country. The wave of settlement did not always thrust them aside, but sometimes engulfed them where they stood. Fighting typically broke out months or years after the Europeans had established themselves. Even then it was scattered and sporadic, not necessarily involving all whites or all resident clans. There were no front lines, no clear demarcations between the territory of opposing forces, no distinctions between combatants and civilians. While commiserating with beleaguered Port Fairy settlers, C.J. La Trobe, the Government Resident at Port Phillip, wrote:

> The evils you complain of are those which have every where accompanied the occupation of a new country inhabited by savage tribes, even under circumstances far more favourable both to the settler who seeks for protection, and the Government desiring to afford it, for instance, where a well

defined frontier and neutral ground could be interposed between the civilized and uncivilized, I need scarcely remind you, how little real security has been enjoyed. Here there is not even such a line. The savage tribes are not only upon our borders, but intermingle with us in every part of the district.

The scattered, uneven nature of the conflict, which allowed some contemporary observers and many later historians to overlook it altogether, intensified rather than allayed European insecurity. Violence was sporadic but no one knew when and where it would break out. It could occur anywhere, at any time. No one could feel safe. Writing when memories of conflict were still fresh, the Tasmanian historian West observed:

The crimes were fearful, and the effect of their outrage on the colonial mind can only by imagined. The fierce robbers of European origin (the bushrangers) who had infested the land, were not half so terrible; these were at least restrained by early association and national sympathies; often by conscience, even by each other. But the natives... united the antipathy of a national foe, and the rapacity of a banditti, with the spite of individual revenge: they were at once a people in arms and a distributed band of assassins.

Constant dread

Fear smouldered for years in some frontier districts; anxiety became habitual. A Tasmanian farmer observed in 1830 that even the reaper in the field was in 'constant dread', so much so that his work suffered because half his time was 'taken up looking about for fear of a sudden attack'. Island settlers who were 'compelled to travel, left their families prey to inexpressible anxiety'. On the McIntyre River in the 1840s stockmen found that for years 'not one of them could stir from his hut unarmed; when one milked or went for a bucket of water, another fully armed stood over him; the horses in the paddocks were killed and the calves in the pens also close to the huts where the men lived'. A central Queensland squatter told a Rockhampton meeting in 1865 that he and his men 'had lived five years contantly in arms'. In the 1880s north Queensland selectors felt they were 'liable to be speared or tomahawked at any moment'; the northern miner found his movements 'dogged and hemmed in one every side and his life menaced every time he set foot out of doors'.

The unpredictability of Aboriginal movements was possibly the greatest cause of alarm; they might appear at any moment; even when not visible they could be hovering silently in the shadows. While reminiscing about life on the fringes of settlement in New South Wales in the 1820s, an old pioneer recalled that his servants were in 'mortal terror' of the Aborigines whose stealth 'got on to their nerves'. They were appalled by the horror of 'waiting, waiting, waiting for the creeping stealthy, treacherous blacks'. A Tasmanian settler complained that Aboriginal movements were 'so uncertain and conducted with so much uncertainty and secrecy that we seldom hear of them but their acts of aggression and cruelty'. 'They are hovering close around us,' wrote another anxious islander, 'I live in constant anxiety fearing some murder or other dreadful accident.' 'As to the Blacks,' a young Queensland squatter wrote in his diary in 1863, 'one cannot tell how near they may be—an odd spear may at any unsuspecting moment be whizzed into one's vitals.' A drover with long experience of the frontier observed that a lizard running over dry grass would wake one 'when always on the watch for darkies'. A young man visiting Gladstone soon after its foundation wrote in his diary, 'the dreaded danger generally consists in blacks keeping in the background, out of sight, pouncing upon you at night unawares, the fearful Myall tribes do this, and are never seen to approach the white man's camp unless to murder or burn'.

Frontier settlers made no secret of their insecurity. Patrick Leslie wrote from the Darling Downs in the early 1840s of his 'constant dread of the blacks'; the West Australian Bessie Bussell explained in 1837 that the word native was 'fraught with fatigue, fear and anxiety'. Tasmanian farmers were said to tremble at the sight of a fire in the bush. 'We are in daily dread' one explained in 1828, 'expecting every hour to be again attacked'. A pioneer venturing into new country in the Maranoa in the 1840s found that his men were 'frightened into convulsions'; in these same years Brisbane Valley squatters lived in 'perpetual suspense... ever on the tiptoe of expectation and indeed sometimes in a state of high mental tension'. Farther north and later in the century selectors worked with a 'feverish expectancy', their minds 'always on the rack'. A shepherd on an isolated north Queensland station left a graphic account of his fears on his first night alone out on the run:

> I then turned my attention to going to bed. I arranged my blankets in a corner of the hut, and lay down (as I thought) to sleep. But sleep would not come. First of all, I began to think what a long way off I was from my fellow-men, at least from men of my own colour, cut off entirely from all assistance, should I require it. Supposing I was taken ill, suppose the blacks attacked me, I might shout for help, no one could hear me. Then I began to argue that this was all nonsense, I was well and strong, and there were probably no blacks anywhere near. It was foolish to annoy myself with such idle speculations, I had better go to sleep, but it was no use; all the horrible stories that I had ever heard thronged to my recollection: of men attacked by savages and murdered, of ghastly corpses subjected to frightful mutilations, of dead men lying unregarded and found days after in lonely huts. Then I began to picture to myself the dreary bush outside, and the forms that might even then be creeping up in silence, shortly to be broken by unearthly yells. I lay now broad awake, and the perspiration streamed from every pore. My hearing seemed unnaturally sharpened, and the Bush seemed as noisy as it had before been silent: all round the hut I fancied I heard the cracking of dry sticks, and the rustling of grass.

Some of the most detailed accounts of the demoralisation of frontier settlers were provided by Edward Curr, the manager of the Van Diemen's Land Company in north-west Tasmania. In dispatches to his board in London he described the morale of men in the outlying camps who were in 'a dreadful state of alarm'. One or two of them were 'so reduced and altered by the state of constant dread in which they had existed that they were no longer the same men'. He wrote of another hutkeeper who was:

> in a state of very great alarm. He told me the Natives had surrounded the hut and had been there the whole morning: that the first thing he saw in the morning as he looked out of the door was a blackfellow standing protected by a little fowl house about fifteen paces from the hut door, with a spear poised in his hand which he pointed towards him. The sight he said struck him motionless, and he had scarcely presence of mind sufficient to step back into the hut. The natives he said had been about all day and he and the shepherd had never dared in consequence to move out, and that they expected every minute that the hut would be rushed by them...Mackenzie was very much alarmed by Innes' spirit which was completely extinguished. He entreated me to remove him from so dangerous a station, that he would do anything he was set to anywhere else, only let him be where he was not

in constant dread of his life. He wished himself in Newgate for there he said his life would be safe.

The blacks are coming

At times individual fears merged and became communal. The most common cause of panic was the belief that the Aborigines were about to combine and advance en masse, determined to kill all the Europeans or drive them away. There was one such incident before European settlement was a year old. Early in the morning on 18 December 1788, word was brought into the main settlement at Sydney Cove that the blacks were assembling in force. The marine captain Watkin Tench explained that the terror of the messengers who 'brought the first intelligence magnified the number to two thousand; a second messenger diminished it to four hundred'. A detachment was ordered out to meet the 50 or so 'Indians' who scattered before the soldiers arrived on the scene. At the Swan River in the 1830s Governor Stirling was concerned that any Aboriginal success in skirmishes with the settlers would encourage them to 'eventually combine together for the extermination of the whites'. During the winter of 1838 Port Phillip settlers thought the blacks would combine and 'make a general attack on the settlers and drive them from the country'. In the following year the Commissioner of Crown Lands on the Liverpool Plains reported that there was a 'general impression among Overseers and Stockmen' that the local clans would 'unite and make a general attack on the Herds and Stations'. At Moreton Bay in 1852 it was expected that there would be 'a general rising amongst the Aborigines in this part of the country this winter'. West Kimberley settlers petitioned the West Australian Governor in 1889, warning him that for some time past the blacks had been 'planning a descent' on the settlements 'with the object of killing all the Europeans'. In 1887 whites on the Daly River were full of anguish, believing that with the onset of the wet season the local Aborigines were going to 'wipe out all the white settlers'.

The Aboriginal threat seemed to add to, even conspire with, the dangers of a strange and hostile environment. Anxiety, bad enough in daylight, grew alarmingly at night. 'However alarming such occurrences by day appear,' a Tasmanian settler wrote in 1828, 'how much more awful are their attacks by night.' Reminiscing in later life, a Gippsland pioneer recalled the fears of frontier nights. Cases of sudden death, he wrote,

> and much more a death by violence, make a much deeper impression on the mind of a person living in the solitary wilds of a new country, than in a crowded and populous one like home, where the bustle and gaiety of life have a tendency to withdraw the mind from continually brooding over the common lot of humanity. But here, although the missing man might be a stranger, he is missed at every turn; and the solitary occupation of a stockman and shepherd, not only in the daytime, but in the stillness of the night, conduces much to serious reflection, heightened by the certainty of continued risk and exposure to the same danger from an enemy who is most often encountered when least expected.

From the barrel of the gun

Frontier society bristled with guns. Men—and sometimes women as well—carried guns when out of doors and kept them loaded and close to hand at home. When anxiety intensified they were put under the pillow or beside the bed, were grasped in the night at the slightest unexplained sound and were picked up again when venturing out in the morning. In some places this routine was followed for months, even years on end. A British scientist visiting Australia in the 1840s explained that after meeting Aborigines on many parts of the coast 'watchfulness becomes habitual; an unusual sound or motion strikes upon your ear or eye unconsciously as it were; your gun is always ready to your hand, and your hand ready to act instinctively'. Many bushmen came to believe that 'to relinquish your gun for a minute might cost you your life'. Expeditions went heavily armed into new country. George Leslie reassured his parents in 1839 about precautions taken by his brother Patrick on his journey to the Darling Downs, explaining that the party was 'taking plenty of firearms for fear of the blacks and we are to build our huts in a square and have all the windows looking into the square and have the outside walls double slabbed and portholes [sic] and if we find the blacks disagreeable we will get a ten pounder and I expect that will astonish them'. At much the same time Macmillan's party was pushing south from the settled districts into Gippsland. Each member had two double-barrelled guns, a brace of pistols and 60 rounds of cartridges for each gun. They were told that no shots were to be fired in camp, but every member of the party was 'to have his gun beside him covered with his blanket to be ready at a moment's warning'. Firearms were just as common in districts settled earlier in the 1820s and 1830s. While on his 'friendly mission' to the Tasmanian Aborigines G.A. Robinson met a stockman on an outlying property who carried a musket as tall as himself, a brace of large pistols, a bayonet at his side as well as cartridge and powder boxes. A visitor to the infant Swan River settlement thought it laughable to see shepherds carrying guns instead of crooks; Port Phillip shepherds all carried guns and had 'the appearance of soldiers on duty'. On the Ovens River in 1840 shepherds would not leave the head station without being provided with a carbine or fowling piece, and a brace of pistols. An old pioneer later recalled that in the early days at Port Phillip, 'the blacks being so tretchrous it took us to be watshful to ourselves, for no one durst steer out without a loaded gun in his hand [*sic*]'. As to the natives, a Tasmanian settler wrote in 1830:

> I can assure you we are all now so fearful of their being near us, that we never move, without a gun, if the Cart has to go to the Mill or elsewhere, we lose the services of one man at home, being obliged to send two, one as driver, the other as Convoy—[my wife] is uneasy if I even go so far as the barn, and even to that short distance I always carry a gun, the trouble and loss they have and will still cause us is quite paralysing.

Insecurity persisted during the settlement of north Australia in the second half of the nineteenth century although the weapons used, usually Colt revolvers and repeating rifles, were far more efficient than those available a generation earlier. Miners, small farmers, sheep and cattle men, all carried guns with them wherever they went. Diggers heading for the north Queensland goldfields were warned not to travel in groups of less than eight and to keep their rifles ready for action, revolvers being no use as the blacks could kill with their spears at 80 yards. The *Cooktown Courier* noted that as a consequence of the general insecurity hundreds of men had learned to use firearms. 'Now every man travels well armed,' the editor wrote and 'a carrier's camp at eventide is a regular school of musketry.' The typical wagon travelling to and from the Palmer River goldfield was a 'perfect arsenal in the matter of Snider rifles, double barrelled guns, Colt's revolvers and all kinds of ball cartridge'. In the more remote areas of the north guns were still worn in the first decades of the twentieth century. A royal commissioner reported that in the 1920s it was considered essential to carry firearms in the Kimberleys and it was the 'practice of men to always go armed'. A visitor to Wyndham in the years before the First World War was amazed to see a hotel full of men wearing revolvers and cartridge-studded belts. It was curious, he wrote, 'to see men in rough moleskin pants and crimean shirts quietly playing billiards in an Australian hotel with a Colt or a Webley in a weather-beaten leather holster hanging on their hips. The right, openly to carry arms, did not extend to the local residents, but only to those men who came in from the back-country where every man was armed as a safeguard against the Aborigines'.

Surviving accounts of outback stations provide graphic illustration of the importance of guns on the frontier. A Victorian pioneer described his hut near Swan Hill which was constructed of logs and was 'loopholed for musketry'. The guns were always kept loaded and ready for use. J.F. Mann, who travelled with Leichhardt in southern Queensland in the 1840s, described conditions on a remote cattle station where they stopped for a night. One man had to keep continual watch, gun in hand, while the squatter had 'nearly a dozen guns in the corner of his hut within reach, ready for use'. In his unpublished reminiscences A.C. Grant recalled that in his parents' central Queensland homestead every room had a couple of freshly loaded guns hanging in convenient places in case of surprise attack. At Westmoreland on the Queensland–Northern Territory border, 'everywhere one could see loaded rifles and revolvers strewn carelessly about', while at Retreat Station in the Mackay hinterland there were twelve square portholes cut in the slab walls and a gun and ammunition hung alongside each one. While describing the interior of his hut in the

Murchison district in a letter to his absent fiancé in 1881, Alexander Crawford provided an inventory of his possessions illustrating the firearms available to the two occupants. On the shelves made from boxes stood the food as well as two or three pistols, half a dozen revolvers, six guns, powder and caps. Two revolvers lay on the table where he was writing.

On some stations the women carried guns as well as the men. Lucy Gray of Hughenden station had her own gun and in the Dawson country in the 1850s Mrs Scott practised with her revolver for half an hour a day. She recalled later that in 'those times I should never have dreamed of going along the covered way from the house to the kitchen without my loaded revolver in my belt'. Guns were carried even on those stations which experienced no conflict with the blacks. The Archer brothers had a record of peaceful contact on several properties in southern Queensland, yet on Durundur, although there was no apparent danger, they rode fully armed with a brace of pistols and rifles 'slung light cavalry fashion'. Mary McManus recalled in later life that her parents had never had any difficulty with the Maranoa clans, yet they 'always had guns ready'. A clergyman who travelled widely in southern Queensland in the 1870s noted: 'In the districts now settled are many signs of the dangers, men had always to encounter from the natives. In stations where life is safer than in the streets of London there are racks of old fashioned muskets, relics of our first military occupation.' Guns were kept in fear of Aborigines in the pioneer townships of north Australia. Revolvers were 'a necessary article of everyday wear' in the Northern Territory's small settlements. Every second man in Rockhampton in the 1850s had a revolver slung at his belt. In 1874 the police magistrate at Normanton reported that it was 'positively unsafe to be out of doors, after nightfall unless provided with firearms'. The Georgetown correspondent of the *Queenslander* wondered, in 1878, when townspeople would be able to look after their houses 'without being loaded with firearms'. Both Cardwell and Mackay knew periods of anxiety when men had guns standing beside them when working out of doors, while even in Ipswich and Brisbane people kept firearms for fear of the blacks. Thomas

Welsby recalled in later life how in 1862 a skirmish between opposing groups of Aborigines on the outskirts of Ipswich prompted two neighbouring families to crowd fearfully into his parents' house. The men had their rifles and revolvers loaded and ready for use. In 1846 the Brisbane paper the *Moreton Bay Courier* reported that no one 'now ventures to trust himself unarmed beyod the precincts of the town'. In 1857 the Moreton Bay correspondent in the Sydney *Empire* noted that it was generally thought unwise to travel far out of town without a gun. While reminiscing in 1922 about his early life in Brisbane, John Wilson recalled that the town blacks caused little trouble. 'They made no difference,' he said, 'beyond keeping our firearms always handy.'

Fear comes to town

It is not surprising that Europeans, isolated on a vast frontier and often outnumbered by neighbouring clans, should suffer from periods of acute anxiety. The fear of town-dwellers is less easy to account for. Yet even in the major colonial towns people stirred uneasily in their sleep. The *Perth Gazette* reported that in June 1832 'a sudden discharge of firearms' started by some 'drunken idlers to celebrate the anniversary of the Battle of Waterloo' spread complete panic through the town. Five years later when soldiers from the local garrison had been sent into the country the editor of the *Swan River Guardian* observed: 'There are only a few soldiers left in Perth, and the settlers in the towns are thus in rather an alarming predicament; if a general combination amongst the native tribes should take place. We should therefore advise every householder to provide himself with firearms.' Adelaide, too, had its nights of fear. In his reminiscences Pastor Finlayson recalled: 'the natives were then in considerable numbers, and there were frequent alarms. On one night the whole colony was awake and under arms...our great fear arose from what we supposed were the tribes beyond the hills, but we soon found out that there were fewer there than among the settlers.'

In Brisbane during the 1840s news of Aboriginal attacks on outlying farms 'created much alarm' in the town. One evening in

December 1849 a rumour swept the community. The local Aborigines, it was said, were arming ready to advance on the settlement. Feelings ran high. A military party marched off and fired a volley into the sleeping and unsuspecting camp at Breakfast Creek. While justifying the action the *Moreton Bay Courier* argued that the excitement of the townspeople was not surprising. 'At the late hour of eleven o'clock', the paper reported, 'a rumour that the natives were in arms for hostile purposes, on the outskirts of town was sufficiently alarming' to justify the military action.

Many small towns experienced similar, if more frequent, moments of alarm. This was particularly so in Queensland with its widely dispersed settlement and history of frontier violence. In 1861 Rockhampton residents heard that the blacks were gathering near the town. Concern spiralled when a woman was attacked on the outskirts of the settlement. Demands for protection led to an ineffectual sortie by the town police. With that the Native Police Force was called in. They dispersed the local camp and while driving the occupants over the river shot five of them. In neighbouring Gladstone anxiety grew after a successful Aboriginal attack on Mt Larcomb Station in the hinterland. Townspeople became convinced the blacks would 'ultimately assemble in overwhelming numbers and rush the township itself'. The Government Resident, sharing their concern, reported to his superiors in Sydney in 1856 that he was 'extremely anxious' for the safety of the settlement. Normanton, Cloncurry and Ravenswood all experienced moments of fear when residents thought the blacks were coming to drive them out of the country. In 1874 Cooktown citizens slept fitfully after Aboriginal attacks on travellers and stock near the settlement. The editor of the local paper wrote:

> it is in no drivelling tone that we say our houses and our wives and children are at the mercy of these black rascals, who if they in broad daylight will drive in white men and then cooly [sic] massacre their horses and bullocks, only five miles from Cooktown we may reasonably expect that in the absence of the native police they will some fine night or day either slaughter us when we are quite unprepared, or burn us out of their territory.

Three towns—Port Lincoln in South Australia, Cardwell and

Maryborough in Queensland—suffered so severely from prolonged anxiety that they were nearly abandoned. Port Lincoln, at
the bottom of Eyre Peninsula, was extremely isolated and was
only readily accessible by sea. The pattern of events there was a
familiar one. Aboriginal attacks on sheep and cattle stations in the
interior created concern in the town. During one month in 1842
five people were speared in the hinterland. Stations were abandoned and their owners moved into town. Rumor had it that
several hundred black warriors were massing and that they had
sworn to kill all the Europeans. Those who could left the settlement or moved to an offshore island. Several men shipped in a
passing whaler. The population fell during 1842 from between
300 and 400 to fifty. Gun-shots or unusual noises in the night
convinced the residents that the attack had begun. Those who
remained in the town felt 'as men sentenced to death, or sheep
penned for slaughter'. Security only returned with the arrival
from Adelaide of a detachment of the 96th Regiment.

Cardwell lived with fears of Aboriginal attack for nearly twenty
years. In 1864 the resident police magistrate reported that he had
formed a volunteer force and a gun was to be fired to call it
together if the blacks approached at night. When the HMS *Basilisk*
called at the settlement in 1872 on a voyage along the Queensland
coast the magistrate asked Captain Moresby for assistance because
he was afraid the settlers in the hinterland, 'or even the town
itself, may be attacked by savages'. Even in 1879, fifteen years
after the first settlement, residents were frightened to let the
Aborigines come near the town.

Maryborough's early settlers suffered extreme anxiety for more
than a decade. The district was densely forested; it had a large
Aboriginal population and Frazer Island provided a secure sanc-
tuary to which the blacks could retreat after forays on the main-
land. Travel outside the settlement was considered dangerous for
years. In 1852 it was reported that labourers were fearful to go
any distance from the village because they were 'apprehensive of
certain destruction'. During the following year the Commissioner
of Crown Lands reported that it was hazardous to travel the four
miles from his camp into the township and his men were unwilling
to go to the garden, or to the creek for water or even into the

paddock for their horses, without their guns. Word went round in February 1854 'that the blacks were going to attack the town on a certain night because one of their number had been put in jail. The police warned all the inhabitants, and on the day previous to the night the raid was supposed to take place all the men were supplied with weapons of some sort, such as swords, cutlasses, old guns'. The attack failed to eventuate but insecurity remained. In 1855 timber was short because the sawyers refused to venture into the forest and surveyors could not get anyone to help them while working four miles from town. Women and children were even more circumscribed. The family of a local JP were afraid to move more than 100 yards from their house. In 1852 people were 'daily apprehensive of an attack upon our village' while a year later the Commissioner of Crown Lands reported that it was almost impossible for him to describe the 'constant state of alarm in which the townspeople are kept from a dread of the aggressions of the Blacks'. In 1856 the panic among the whites was 'greater than ever' and even in 1862 people were still apprehensive, the *North Australian* reporting that 'many persons' were daily expecting a 'wholesale massacre within half a dozen miles of the Court House'. At times the persistent insecurity appeared to threaten the future of the town itself. In 1855 migrant families left soon after arrival on learning of the prevailing anxiety and 30 settlers abandoned the town at the end of the year. The Commissioner of Crown Lands was uneasy about the future. In 1852 he feared that if the population fell 'some great catastrophe' would occur through the 'insufficiency of the population for mutual protection', and four years later he thought the panic would 'become insurmountable'. But the fate which merely threatened Cardwell, Port Lincoln and Maryborough actually befell Gilberton.

Gilberton was one of the ephemeral boom towns of the North Queensland gold rushes which was founded in 1869 and grew to a community of perhaps several thousand in 1871 and 1872. Gold was found over a wide area among the extremely rugged country where the Gilbert river cut back into western slopes of the Great Dividing Range before flowing out across the plains to the Gulf of Carpentaria. There had been minor skirmishes with the local

Aborigines on the outlying claims, but the first serious attack took place late in 1872 when the Chinese camp was rushed and five miners killed. It seems probable that the Aborigines were forced in towards the main river by the drying up of all other surface water at the end of the long northern dry season. With the coming of the wet, further attacks failed to materialise, but in Gilberton there was considerable foreboding. The *Queenslander*'s correspondent wrote: 'there is an idea that the blacks have got an inkling of our small population, and judging from the ease they had in putting the Chinese to flight...no doubt...they thought to have put the coup de grace on old Gilbert, and start a grand corroboree on the ruins of its empty habitations.' The most serious blow, however, came not from the blacks but from news of the rush to the Palmer Field which reached Gilberton in August 1873 and enticed away the bulk of the population. About 100 remained, mainly Chinese diggers, but including a few Europeans—the storekeeper, the publican, the owner of the stamping machinery, and their families. The crisis came at the end of the year. The police were withdrawn to the Palmer in November, leaving the town without protection. The Aborigines began to move in once again, presumably by an imperative need for water. In a couple of concerted attacks the Chinese were driven from their camps into the town, leaving behind their stores and large quantities of wash dirt which was being stockpiled in anticipation of the rains. With that the Chinese left the town. Contemporary accounts invariably impute their exodus to the fear of the Aborigines, although there is no evidence from the Chinese themselves. The few remaining Europeans were in a perilous position. The wet season was imminent with its certainty of flooded creeks and impassable tracks. Teamsters refused to come to the town through fear of attack and the greater profits to be made on the road to the Palmer. In December the remaining residents burnt many of their belongings in the main street and abandoned the town, leaving behind stores, equipment, the 15-head stamping machine and ripening crops in vegetable and fruit gardens. Though the evidence is not conclusive it seems probable that Gilberton was abandoned largely through fear of the blacks.

This was certainly the conclusion drawn by settlers elsewhere, and Gilberton entered the folklore of the North. The field was reopened at the end of the seventies. The sentiments expressed by the *Queenslander* in 1879 were no doubt echoed around a hundred camp fires. A promising district 'now maintaining more than 600 men' had been 'deserted at the instance of a few howling savages'.

Plunder and penury

Hundreds of individuals in all parts of the continent—pastoralists, small farmers, horse and bullock teamsters, pearl and beche-de-mer gatherers—were ruined as a result of Aboriginal attack. Sheep and cattle men on isolated stations were particularly vulnerable. Sheep and cattle were speared where they stood or were driven off into the bush. Huts were raided, burnt and looted. Shepherds were speared. When Aboriginal resistance intensified, extra hands had to be taken on to provide security, and labour costs spiralled. 'I have experienced much difficulty keeping our men,' a Port Phillip squatter wrote in 1840, 'They run away when a black makes his appearance, and I had to abandon three sheep stations to that account, and crowd the sheep together in anyway to prevent shepherds leaving the service altogether.' A generation later a central Queensland pioneer wrote to his bank manager explaining that it was 'hard under any circumstances to keep down the expenses up here, and it is absolutely more than we can afford to keep up the existing staff that the task of self protection imposes on us. At the present time I have four of my best hands out after Blacks—so much that ought to be done on the place in the way of work has to be neglected'.

Stations were abandoned all over the country, whole districts temporarily given up. The explorer Thomas Mitchell travelled through one such district in northern New South Wales during an expedition in the 1840s. 'We had,' he wrote in his journal, 'crossed the neutral ground between the savage and the squatter. The advanced posts of an army are not better kept, and humiliating proofs that the white man had given way were visible in the remains of dairies burnt down, stockyards in ruins, untrodden roads.' Farmers suffered too as crops were burnt or pillaged before

22

harvest; the problems first encountered on the Hawkesbury in the 1790s were repeated throughout the following century as selectors pioneered the moist fertile valleys notching the east coast. Europeans living at isolated bêche-de-mer stations were speared; pearling luggers were seized by their Aboriginal crews to be beached and looted. Miners on the north Australian fields came into bitter conflict with resident clans who robbed their tents and speared their horses. Horse and bullock teams servicing mine fields and pastoral stations were constantly harassed. A recent study of the Palmer River goldfield has underlined the economic impact of Aboriginal resistance. In ten years 500 horses and 100 bullocks were speared; 130 of the horses and 65 bullocks died. Many others were driven off into the bush. At the time horses were worth about £50 or £60, which represented about six months' wages for the average unskilled or semi-skilled worker. The professional teamsters were badly hit, one losing £1000 worth of horses between May 1874 and November 1875. The lament of a Western Australian settler, writing to the government in 1851, reflected the experience of pioneers all over the continent. He wrote:

> now I find that my endeavours to improve my condition is [sic] only hastening my downfall and if I do not receive protection by the natives being repressed from plundering me the little I have acquired by a colonial struggle of 20 years (which God knows has been a severe one) will soon be wrested from me and I shall in my old age when I am no longer fit for exertion be reduced to penury.

Counting the cost

The devastating effect on individual fortunes notwithstanding, the general impact of Aboriginal resistance can best be appreciated by examining it at the community level in three widely separated areas at specific periods of time—Tasmania in 1830–31, Port Fairy in the Victorian Western District in 1842 and Maryborough in Queensland in 1855. The Tasmanian Aborigines Committee prepared a 'list of atrocities committed by the natives', between March 1830 and October 1831:

> March 1830.—About 40 natives attacked the house of Mr Broadribb, Black Marsh. They were divided into small parties, and made their attacks simultaneously. One man speared. On being driven off, they proceeded to the

hut of Mr Thomson, which they robbed of every thing in it.

On the same day a man was speared in bed at E. Denovan's, Black Marsh.

1 April.—John Rayner, speared in several places, and dreadfully beaten by natives, at Spring Bay.

18 May.—Mr Lord's hut, at Eastern Marshes, attacked. Of two men in it, one was dangerously speared, and the other dreadfully beaten; the natives then plundered the hut, and retired.

1 June.—Mr Sherwin's hut, Weasel Plains, plundered by natives.

15 June.—The Aborigines plundered the Den Hut, on Lake River, of every thing in it, and murdered Mary Daniels and her two infants in cold blood.

7 August.—S. Stockman's hut, Green Ponds, plundered by natives.

9 August.—The tents of Mr Sharland (surveyor) and his men robbed of muskets, powder, and shot by the natives. On the same day the Government hut, between Bothwell and Blue Hill, robbed by natives; as well as the houses of Mr Wood and Mr Pitcairn; a man servant of Mr Burr's wounded.

About 40 natives met by Mr Howell's party; a woman wounded.

23 August.—The huts of J. Connell and Mr Robertson attacked; the latter plundered; Mr Sutherland's shepherd's attacked and their arms taken; one of them speared. Arms taken from Mr Taylor's hut.

24th August.—James Hooper killed, and his hut plundered of every thing in it. The huts of Lieutenants Bell and Watts attacked by natives, who were repulsed from both.

8 September.—Captain Clark's shepherd attacked, but escaped.

13 September.—One man killed and one man wounded by natives on the banks of the Tamar.

14 September.—A man employed by government at the lime kilns, near Bothwell, chased by natives, but escaped.

18 September.—A private, 63d regiment, killed by natives; two sawyers speared, one of whom died of his wounds.

27 September.—Three men at Major Gray's wounded by natives, and one dangerously wounded with stones.

Mr G. Scott's house attacked by a mob of natives; they speared one man and killed another, the body of whom they threw into the river; they ransacked the house of everything they could find, and even went up stairs and broke the doors open, a proceeding to which they never before resorted. They took away blankets, shirts, sheets, knives, 600 or 700 pounds of flour (which they tied up in blankets and sheets), half a basket of tobacco, 100 pounds of sugar, a box of tea, and a considerable quantity of slop clothing; so great ingenuity was displayed in this attack that it was for some time supposed that Europeans had conducted it.

On the same day the natives plundered a hut opposite to Mr Scott's of all the tea, sugar, flour and bedding that were in it.

16 October.—The settlement at Sorell attacked by natives; one man killed; one severely wounded; four houses plundered of blankets, flour, tea

and sugar, and clothes of every description.

18 October.—Captain Stewart's shepherd wounded by spears; and Mr Guilders, a settler, killed by two spear wounds.

19 October.—Natives showed themselves on the farms of Messieurs Gatehouse and Gordon, and attacked the house of Mr Gangel, whom they wounded severely.

16 November.—Two huts robbed on the Ouse.

Captain Wight's shepherd killed by natives; dreadfully mangled.

27 November.—A hut on South Esk attacked by natives; every thing portable sent off.

3 February 1831.—The natives attacked Mr Burrell's house on Tamar; speared Mr Wallace in several parts of the body, and inflicted several severe and dangerous wounds on his head; they likewise wounded a child. The hut of L. Night attacked by them; plundered of everything in it. The hut of Mr Sutherland, North Esk, robbed; three horses speared; three others wounded. A woman named McCaskell killed at Retreat, near Westbury; house robbed of 300 pounds of flour, knives and forks, blankets, chest of tea, 100 pounds of sugar, tobacco, two casks of butter, three muskets and powder.

Mr Stewart's house attacked by natives; severely wounded. Two huts near New Norfolk, plundered.

12 March.—Mrs Cunningham's hut, at East Arm, robbed by natives; she and her child wounded very dangerously.

Mr Lawrence's servant wounded, and three men dangerously wounded, by the natives, on Norfolk Plains.

5 April.—T. Ratton speared through the body whilst at work, splitting wood.

6 April.—N. Eitzgerald speared twice through the body, whilst sitting reading at the door of his cottage; the house plundered by the natives of guns, blankets and other articles.

7 April.—The same house again attacked.

10 May.—Hut on Patrick Plains, containing Government stores, burnt to the ground by natives. Mr Kemp's establishment at Lake Sorell, attacked by a considerable mob of natives; the fire-arms carried away; buildings totally consumed by fire; two men murdered, and one wounded.

6 June.—Several huts attacked near Hunter's Hill. J. Triffit's house plundered of every thing in it, and Mrs Triffit speared. Mr Marnetti's hut robbed; likewise Mr Bell's, of everything in it, and the wife of N. Long murdered. Mr Clarke's hut plundered.

5 September.—Thomas Smith, hut keeper at Tapsley, murdered; hut plundered; John Higginson speared, and hut robbed. A sawyer's hut robbed.

7 September.—B.B. Thomas, esq. and his overseer, Mr Parker, murdered, near Port Sorell, by a mob of natives, whilst (actuated by the most humane views) they were endeavouring to carry the conciliatory measures of Government into effect. Mr Thomas had received ten spear wounds, and Mr Parker eleven. The head of the latter was also fractured. Stocker's hut

desperately attacked; a child wounded; a man named Cupid speared.

22 September.—Mr Dawson's hut, on Bushy Plains, attacked, and his servant severely beaten with waddies.

23 September.—Mr Dawson's servant, Hughes, severely beaten by natives; nearly losing his life.

13 October.—The natives, having possession of fire-arms, attacked and robbed the premises of Constable Reid, and plundered the house of Mr Amos, junior.

Twelve years later the Port Fairy settlers petitioned the Superintendent of Port Phillip, listing attacks made by local Aborigines in the previous two months:

Man killed, 100 sheep taken, and hut robbed of everything it contained including a double-barrelled gun, with ammunition.

300 sheep and 100 tons of potatoes.

Five horses taken, and seven head of cattle killed; 56 calves; also 33 driven off; and two men wounded.

The station has been attacked four times.

600 sheep taken, of which 130 were recovered; hut robbed, and two double-barrelled guns taken; 10 cows and 40 calves killed; hut attacked several times, and man severely wounded.

Three flocks attacked simultaneously, one of which was taken away, and the shepherd desperately wounded. The major part was eventually recovered; one man taken, but recovered.

200 sheep taken, and man speared.

Shepherd fired at.

Two horses taken, station attacked, and flock of sheep carried off, and shepherd dreadfully wounded.

Two horses killed, hut robbed, and men driven off the station.

Shepherd killed; found with a spear through his heart.

One horse taken.

30 sheep.

50 sheep.

250 sheep, and man wounded.

50 sheep.

260 sheep, and man killed.

300 sheep.

700 sheep taken, but mostly recovered.

180 sheep, station attacked and robbed, and hut-keeper severely wounded.

A very valuable bull killed, and a number of calves.

Six cows, three bullocks, 20 calves, man killed, and cattle driven off.

200 ewes, and 150 lambs.

450 ewes and lambs.

In 1855 the Commissioner for Crown Lands at Maryborough

prepared a report listing Aboriginal forays in the town during a six-week period in November and December:

November	7	Mrs Whites's house robbed of a quantity of flour.
	9	Mr Palmers stores robbed of tobacco.
	12	Cahills dray robbed of 200 lbs of flour.
	13	Hughes dray robbed of 200 lbs of flour and a quantity of rations.
	18	Mr Melvilles house robbed 60 lbs sugar.
	19	Jas. Frectius house robbed of tea, sugar and flour. Thos. McCrudden robbed of 100 lbs of sugar and 48 lbs of Flour.
	22	J. Church robbed of wearing apparel and rations. Mrs Gadd—laundress robbed of linen, clothes etc.
	25	Mr Reid's dray robbed of 70 lbs of Flour.
	26	Two of Mr Reid's bullocks speared.
	27	Dowdle speared by the Blacks. Denny and [*illegible*] beaten and ill used by the Blacks and robbed of Blankets clothing 145 lbs of Flour, 45 lbs of Beef, 50 lbs of Sugar, 2 lbs tea and a quantity of cooking utensils.
	28	Jas Western robbed of 4 sovereigns and beaten.
December	2	Walsh's dray robbed.
	5	George Furber and Jos. Wilmshurst murdered and a large quantity of rations blankets clothing and Tomahawks stolen.
	6	Michael Joyce nearly murdered being left for dead and his hut robbed of rations, clothing etc.
	7	Dowzer and [*illegible*] store broken into and robbed.
	8	Mr Uhr's house and garden robbed.
	9	Comm. C. Lands garden robbed.
	10	Herberts drays robbed of 800 lbs of sugar and 600 lbs of Flour.
	11	Martins house entered.
	17	Mr Landrigans house entered and robbed at night.
	18	J. Arthurs carrier dray robbed of a quantity of sugar and flour.
	19	J. Leitchs house entered and robbed during the night.
	20	Mrs Bennet assaulted and head cut with a Tomahawk.
	21	Mr Uhrs store attempted to be broken into.
	22	Powers store entered and robbed.

Progress stalled

At times Aboriginal resistance appeared to threaten the general prosperity of colonial society. There was both the immediate fear that frontier settlers would abandon their farms and stations and the long-term threat that the flow of immigrants and capital would dry up. 'What is to be the end of this, God only knows,' wrote a settler in northern New South Wales at a time of heightened frontier conflict. 'I think it will stop the influx of capital into this colony.' A writer in Hobart's *Colonial Times* worried in 1830 that fear of the blacks would choke off immigration and so undermine island prosperity. 'We want capital and capitalists,' the editor of the *Port Denison Times* proclaimed a generation later, but he doubted if capitalists would invest in so unsettled a community. The *Western Australian* wrestled with the same problem in 1888. It was agreed that frontier settlers could not be given a free hand; the government could not 'allow our colonists to be massacrers' but neither could it 'allow insecurity to chase away investors'.

There was concern in Queensland in the late 1850s and early 1860s that Aboriginal resistance would stall the outward thrust of the frontier. In 1857 a writer in the *North Australian* argued that unless the blacks were crushed 'one of the finest grazing districts' would have 'to be vacated and left to the original inhabitants'. After the successful Aboriginal attack on Cullin la Ringoe Station in 1861 the problem loomed even larger. The *North Australian* commented:

> So injurious to the best interests of the colony do outrages by the blacks become, in deterring settlement and keeping out capital, that we look upon them as the worst evil of our position, and as the greatest barrier to the development of our resources. If there be in Queensland at the present moment one subject, which more than any other is of the highest importance ...that subject is the better protection of the frontier districts.

Peace was imposed on central Queensland, but the problem of security moved north with the frontier. Conflict was at its height during the 1870s as settlers surged into all parts of north Queensland. Reflecting on the problem of Aboriginal resistance, the *Queenslander* observed in 1879:

> During the last four or five years the human life and property destroyed by the aboriginals in the North totals up to a serious amount...[S]ettlement on the land, and the development of the mineral and other resources of the

country, have been in a great degree prohibited by the hostility of the blacks, which still continues with undiminished spirit.

Perhaps the deepest concern was felt in Tasmania in the late 1820s. Alarmed Clyde River settlers petitioned the government, fearing that the hostile clans would march in formidable bodies into the settled districts with their 'firebrands in one hand and their unerring and deadly weapons of war in the other'. They would move 'from one advance to another gathering boldness every time, until at last our very towns and inmost sanctuaries would be subject to invasion, property would become valueless, and the colony would no longer be worth continuing in.' A prominent citizen warned a public meeting in Hobart in September 1830 that if Aboriginal attacks were not prevented they would 'come and drive us from this very Court room and compel us to take refuge in the ships'.

Private panic was reflected in official circles. Members of the Aborigines Committee believed that 'a sentiment of alarm' pervaded the minds of settlers throughout the island; the 'total ruin of every establishment [was] but to certainly to be apprehended'. The Executive Council observed that 'great and well founded alarm generally prevails'. Governor Arthur, not given to extravagant emotion, told his superiors in Britain in 1831 that the state of the colony 'with reference to the Aborigines' had been the 'most anxious and important concern upon my hands' for the previous three years. Writing from his camp at Sorell to justify the famous Black Line, he argued that such was the insecurity of the settlers that he feared 'a general decline in the prosperity' and the 'eventual extirpation of the Colony'.

The death toll

How many settlers died on Australia's 'unrecorded battlefields'? It is a difficult question to answer with any certainty. The most detailed studies so far have been done in Queensland, Loos and Reynolds estimating that somewhere between 900 and 1000 Europeans and their 'allies'—mainly Chinese miners and Aboriginal stockmen—were killed between 1840 and 1897. Official figures suggest that Tasmanian Aborigines killed 160 settlers, but in her recent research Ryan has argued that 200 is a more realistic figure. Christie has estimated that a similar number of settlers died in Victoria. There are a few relevant regional studies. Green believes that 30 settlers were killed in Western Australia between 1826 and 1852 and Prentis suggested that twenty died in the settlement of the Northern Rivers District of New South Wales.

There have been few attempts to estimate the number of Europeans wounded. Only two regional studies have addressed the problem. Green calculated that while 30 settlers were killed in Western Australia 34 were wounded. Kirkman came up with a similar result for the Palmer River between 1874 and 1884 where 40 were killed and the same number wounded. If these regional figures were generally applied we could assume that about 3000 settlers died and another 3000 were wounded in Australia as a whole.

Total figures disguise the wide fluctuation over time and the differing impact of Aboriginal resistance in particular districts. Queensland, for instance, averaged fifteen to twenty deaths a year during the second half of the nineteenth century but the figure fluctuated widely from as few as one or two to as many as 30 or 40, reaching an all-time high of 46 in 1874 with the northern gold rushes at their height. There was a similar figure in Tasmania in 1830 when 43 Europeans were killed. In small districts the impact of frontier conflict was sometimes much greater. During the early 1840s 25 Europeans were killed on the McIntyre river, on the Burnett in 1857–58 30 settlers died; 24 were killed in the Tasmanian midlands between August and December 1830.

But the most striking feature of frontier conflict was not the loss of life or destruction of property, although both were considerable, but the duration of the species of warfare waged around the fringes of settlement. It continued for almost 150 years, spanning three-quarters of the time of European occupation. A direct line can be drawn from the events of October 1788 when Governor Phillip led an armed party to confront a group of blacks, firing on them to 'compel them to keep at a greater distance from the settlement' to the punitive expeditions which decimated the

Aboriginal community in central Australia in the late 1920s. In order to understand this violent tradition it is necessary to trace it back to its origins in those early months when the English were establishing their beachhead at Sydney Cove and then watch its development as the settlers spilled out across the vast and varied hinterland.

– 2 –

Deeds of Blood

On the evening of 9th December 1790 a small party—a marine sergeant and three convicts including McEntire, Governor Phillips' 'gamekeeper'—left the infant settlement and walked towards Botany Bay. They stopped at a bough hut recently built for 'the accommodation of sportsmen who wished to continue by night in the woods' and slept until 1.00 am, when they woke to find a group of Aborigines creeping towards them. McEntire stepped forward, saying to his fellow huntsmen: 'Don't worry I know them.' As he advanced the Aborigines retreated. When they had gone some distance one of the blacks—identified subsequently as Pemulwy—jumped on a fallen tree, spun around to face McEntire and speared him in the chest. The blacks fled into the darkness; the Europeans began a slow and difficult journey with the badly wounded McEntire back to the settlement.

Phillip was told of the incident when he returned from one of the outer settlements. He responded officially two days later by issuing a General Order which read:

> Several tribes of the natives still continuing to throw spears at any man they meet unarmed, by which several have been killed or dangerously wounded, the Governor, in order to deter the natives from such practices in future, has ordered out a party to search for the man who wounded the convict in so dangerous a manner...though no offence was offered on his part, and to make a severe example of that tribe.

The following day a detachment of 50 marines marched into the bush only to return empty-handed, having shot at some blacks seen at a distance, apparently without effect. A second party sent out a week later was equally ineffectual, returning on Christmas Day 'after a most tedious march as ever men went in the time'.

An universal terror

Tench, the leader of the two expeditions, provided the clearest account of Phillip's motives and objectives. Tench's original instructions were to capture two members of the clans around Botany Bay and kill ten others whose heads were to be chopped off and carried into the settlement. Axes and bags were provided for the purpose. At Tench's suggestion the aims were moderated. He was to capture six blacks and return them to the settlement. Two were to be hanged and four sent to Norfolk Island. If capture could not be effected the six were to be shot and decapitated.

Both Hunter and Tench commented on the two expeditions, Hunter noting that the Governor was convinced that 'nothing but a severe example, and the fear of having all the tribes who resided near the settlement destroyed would have the desired effect'. Tench wrote in his journal:

> His Excellency was now pleased to enter into the reasons which had induced him to adopt measures of such severity. He said that since our arrival in the country, no less than seventeen of our people had either been killed or wounded by the natives:—that he looked upon the tribe known by the name of Bid-ee-'gal, living on the beforementioned peninsula, and chiefly on the north arm of Botany Bay, to be the principal aggressors—that against this tribe he was determined to strike a decisive blow, in order, at once to convince them of our superiority, and to infuse an universal terror, which might operate to prevent further mischief.

In Tench's two fruitless excursions it is possible to see all the features of the punitive expeditions which were to be launched against the Aborigines during the following 140 years. The killing was to be both grossly disproportionate and indiscriminate, even though the Governor's gamekeeper was still alive and his assailant known. Violence was to be used not only to punish the guilty but to deter 'all of them' from future resistance. In that way it was thought conflict would be reduced and in the long run fewer would suffer. 'There was reason to fear,' Hunter wrote at the time, 'that the innocent might suffer', but the 'punishments inflicted on a few would, in the end, be an act of mercy to numbers.'

The likelihood of killing the innocent while seeking the guilty was already well appreciated by the settlers, Phillip himself writing a year earlier that it was impossible to punish the blacks 'without punishing the innocent with the guilty'. David Collins, Phillip's private secretary and chronicler of the colony, wrote that there was

> little probability that such a party would be able so unexpectedly to fall in with the people they were sent to punish, as to surprise them, without which chance, they might hunt them in the woods for ever; and as the different tribes (for we had thought fit to class them into tribes) were not to be distinguished from each other, but by inhabiting particular residences, there would be some difficulty in determining, if any natives should fall in their way, whether they were the objects of their expedition, or some unoffending family wholly unconnected with them.

Many writers have stressed the benign intentions of the English in 1788, referring to official instructions to treat the Aborigines with 'amity and kindness', and it appears that Phillip hoped to avoid unnecessary conflict with the clans resident around Sydney Harbour. While still in England he wrote that it would be 'a great point gained' if the settlers could proceed 'in this business without having any dispute with the natives'. When conflict began he blamed the convicts. He refused to take any action when speared in the shoulder. Convicts who attempted to take their own revenge on the Aborigines were severely flogged. Six months after the arrival of the Europeans Phillip re-emphasised his determination 'never to fire on the Natives, but in a case of absolute necessity'. Yet three months later when a group of Aborigines threw several spears at a convict, harmlessly as it turned out, Phillip immediately 'went to the spot with an armed party' and when blacks were heard in the bushes they were fired at, Collins explaining that it had become 'absolutely necessary to compel them to keep at a greater distance from the settlement'. There were other incidents as well. In January 1791 an armed party was sent to disperse a group of Aborigines who were trying to steal potatoes. When a club was thrown, the soldiers 'fired in among them'. Later in the year the blacks were reported to be assembling near the brickfields; an officer was 'ordered out with a strong party to disperse them, and to make a severe example of them, if any spears were thrown'. By the time the soldiers arrived the Aborigines had fled.

The kindest piece of violence

While assessing the development of official policy towards the Aborigines it is necessary to consider a decision of December 1788 to take several Aboriginal captives. Phillip told his superiors that he was taking the action for the purpose of learning the language and so 'reconciling them to us'; it would turn out to be 'the kindest piece of violence that could be used'. But Tench's account presented a much more complex picture. At the time 'unabated animosity continued to prevail' between the settlers and the Aborigines. A gathering of about 50 blacks near the brick kilns gave birth to rumours that hundreds, even thousands, were massing. Troops were dispatched but the tribesmen had gone before they appeared. Tench reported Phillip's reaction at length:

> Tired of this state of petty warfare and endless uncertainty, the governor at length determined to adopt a decisive measure, by capturing some of them, and retaining them by force; which we supposed would either inflame the rest to signal vengeance, in which case we should know the worst, and provide accordingly; or else it would induce an intercourse, by the report which our prisoners would make of the mildness and indulgence with which we used them.

Much depends on how we interpret the words 'provide accordingly', but it appears that one of the options considered was to provoke the Aborigines to an open confrontation where European firepower would prevail. They could then be decisively defeated, bringing all resistance to an end.

Phillip's record regarding the Aborigines is less impressive than traditional accounts suggest. There were at least two instances when military parties fired indiscriminately into groups of Aborigines and four other occasions when troops were sent out with the intention of 'making a severe example of them' but failed to catch their quarry. Had they been successful the history of race relations in the first years of settlement may have looked very different. Many more blacks would have been killed; Aboriginal anger and desire for revenge would have intensified and, as happened so often later, violence would have spiralled out of control. The extent of bloodshed was not determined solely by the sincerity of European goodwill but by the degree of resistance offered by the blacks. Talk of amity and kindness could not hide the fact that once the decision to settle had been made Aboriginal opposition was to be crushed regardless of the cost in lives. The marines were there to see to that. Their role was so obvious that it rarely needed comment, leading many later commentators to overlook it altogether. But Phillip discussed the direct relationship between military power and expectations of Aboriginal resistance in a letter to the Secretary of State for the Colonies in August 1789, arguing that 500 troops would be sufficient to meet any Aboriginal threat. 'It will appear to your Lordship', he wrote, 'after what has been said of the natives, that a less force will be wanted for the security of the settlement than what I considered as necessary soon after my arrival in this country, although that was not considerable...I presume that a battalion of 500 men will be sufficient, which will admit of one hundred being detached for the security of Norfolk Island.'

A tradition develops

Within a couple of years of the first settlement it had become clear to at least some of the Europeans that the occupation of Aboriginal land would inevitably lead to conflict, amity and kindness notwithstanding. The natives, observed Lieutenant William Bradley, were 'well pleased with our people until they began clearing the Ground at which they were displeased and wanted them to be gone'. Collins considered the situation after the soldiers had fired at Aborigines taking potatoes from the gardens. It was, he wrote,

> much to be regretted that any necessity existed for adopting these sanguinary punishments, and that we had not yet been able to reconcile the natives to the deprivation of those parts of this harbour which we occupied. While they entertained the idea of our having dispossessed them of their residences, they must always consider us as enemies; and upon this principle they made a point of attacking the white people whenever opportunity and safety concurred.

Collins' assessment of the situation, made when the great majority of Europeans still lived within sight of Sydney Harbour, did not augur well for Aboriginal clans scattered over the surface of a vast continent. It foreshadowed the conflict which broke out as the settlers moved into the Hawkesbury Valley—Australia's first frontier—and into practically every other district in the country. By 1800 the advance of settlement was marked by a 'line of blood', Governor King reporting to his superiors in England that in the fighting the Aborigines suffered disproportionately; indeed there was 'an astonishing difference in the numbers' killed.

Attitudes which pioneers carried with them on every frontier were already consolidating in the 1790s. Collins reflected this development. By 1797 he was reconsidering the attempt to assimilate the Aborigines, which had characterised the first years of settlement, advocating in its place a policy which came to be known as 'keeping them out'. While writing about Aboriginal attacks on settlers along the Lane Cove and Hawkesbury Rivers he observed:

> Could it have been foreseen, that this was their natural temper, it would have been wiser to have kept them at a distance, and in fear, which might have been effected without so much of the severity which their conduct had sometimes compelled us to exercise towards them. But the kindness which had been shown them and the familiar intercourse with the white people in which they had been indulged, tended only to make them acquainted with those concerns in which they were most vulnerable, and brought on all the evils which they have suffered from them.

Collins' colleague Tench had even earlier attributed the blame for deteriorating relations to the character of the Aborigines, 'to the fickle, jealous, wavering disposition of the people we have to deal with, who, like all other savages, are either too indolent, too indifferent, or too fearful to form an attachment on easy terms, with those who differ in habits and manners so widely from themselves.'

Punitive expeditions became the common response of governments threatened by Aboriginal resistance and the prospect of settlers abandoning their farms and stations. Military parties were dispatched to the Hawkesbury in the 1790s and the early years of the nineteenth century, they were deployed around the fringes of European settlement on the Cumberland Plain in 1814 and 1816, at Bathurst in 1824 and along the Hunter two years later. They were used in similar fashion in both Tasmania and Western Australia. Paramilitary forces—Roving Bands, Border Police, Native Police—took their place in the 1820s and 1830s. Justification for punitive expeditions was always ready to hand. In 1795 the soldiers were ordered to 'drive the natives to a distance' in order to protect Hawkesbury settlers. Thirty years later Governor Brisbane declared martial law around Bathurst because 'by experience it hath been found that mutual bloodshed may be stopped by the use of arms against the natives beyond the ordinary rule of law in time of peace'. Atkins, the chief legal officer in New South Wales, noted in 1805 that it was impossible to bring the blacks before the courts either as defendants or witnesses; the 'only mode at present', he explained, 'when they deserve it, is to pursue them and inflict such punishment as they may merit'.

Acts of decisive severity

Phillip's desire to 'infuse an universal terror' was echoed again and again by his successors. In 1795 when conflict broke out along the Hawkesbury the soldiers were dispatched with instructions to 'destroy as many as they could meet with of the wood tribe' and in the hope of 'striking terror to erect gibbits in different places, whereon the bodies of all they might kill were to be hung'. In 1816 Governor Macquarie wrote to his superiors in Britain announcing his intention to drive the blacks to a distance 'so as to Strike them with Terror against Committing Similar acts of violence in the future'. Two years later he discussed the consequences of a second punitive expedition; while innocent men, women and children might have died, the severity would 'eventually strike Terror amongst the surviving Tribes, and deter them from further Commission of such Sanguinary Outrages and Barbarities'. Macquarie's successor Brisbane adopted a system of keeping the clans around Bathurst 'in a constant state of alarm' in order to bring them 'to a sense of their duty'.

In Tasmania Governor Arthur discussed the necessity of treating the blacks as open enemies. 'Terror,' he explained to the Secretary of State for the Colonies, 'may have the effect which no proffered measures of conciliation have been capable of inducing.' Western

Australia's Governor Stirling considered that the only method of control was the early exhibition of force or 'if the evil [had] already gained strength, such acts of decisive severity as will appal them as a people'. While discussing the so-called Battle of Pinjarra, Irwin, the commandant of the military at the Swan River, said that while the loss of life was 'a very painful consideration, and deeply to be deplored, yet it seems manifest that without some severe defeat to convince this tribe of their inferiority in power to the whites, a petty and harassing warfare might have been indefinitely prolonged, with ultimately much heavier loss on both sides'.

Vigorous measures amongst yourselves

During the first years of settlement Phillip tried to prevent individuals from taking their own action against the blacks. In March 1789 seven convicts were each given 150 lashes for attempting to revenge themselves on the Aborigines following the spearing of a friend. But once settlement dispersed it was impossible to control the Europeans or to depend on the military for protection against the Aborigines. A settler noted in his journal in May 1792 that few people 'travel the woods' without a gun. Four years later the government ordered Hawkesbury settlers to 'mutually afford their assistance to each other by assembling without a moments delay when ever any numerous bodies of the natives are known to be lurking about the farms'. By 1801 government instructions were even more specific; the blacks were to 'be driven back from the settlers' habitations by firing at them'. In a proclamation of 1816 Governor Macquarie announced that if the Aborigines approached the European settlements with any weapons, or if they were unwilling to leave the settlers' properties when told to do so, they were 'to be driven away by force of arms by the settlers themselves'. While answering demands for military protection from Hunter Valley settlers in 1826 Governor Darling commented:

> Vigorous measures amongst yourselves would more effectually establish your ascendancy than the utmost power of the military, as, when the latter

is withdrawn, and circumstances do not permit their being despatched for any length of time, the chance is that, no longer fearing the Settlers, the natives will renew their depredations. I therefore, strongly recommend you to take measures for your own defence, and you may be satisfied that in any exertion you may make, you shall receive every necessary support.

Similar encouragement to settler action was given by both the Tasmanian and the Western Australian governments. Grappling with the problem of a turbulent frontier, the Tasmanian Aborigines Committee recommended in 1830 that every male of competent age 'should be well provided with arms'. Governor Stirling informed Swan River settlers in 1837 that he wished to 'impress on every white person the necessity there is for aiding in his own protection by keeping arms in order'.

With the explosive expansion of settlement in the 1830s and 1840s there was a commensurate growth in the scope for vigilante violence. The hanging of seven stockmen in 1838 for their part in the Myall Creek massacre was a dramatic assertion of the letter of the law, but it failed to undermine attitudes already deeply entrenched, and gradually the 'original and customary course of things was permitted to return', and the whole matter 'fell into its true and old form'. From his desk in Sydney Gipps lamented: 'all we can do now is to raise, in the name of Justice and humanity, a voice in favour of our poor savage fellow creatures, too feeble to be heard at such a distance.' There was pessimism in Whitehall as well. The powerful Under-Secretary of State for Colonies, James Stephen, noted in a minute to Lord Glenelg: 'there has been much bloodshed on either side. The causes and consequences of this state of things are alike clear and irremediable, nor do I suppose that it is possible to discover any method by which the impending catastrophe, namely, the elimination of the black race, can be averted.'

Phillip sought to suppress Aboriginal resistance by creating a universal terror. His successors encouraged settlers to carry guns in order to drive troublesome blacks away by 'force of arms'. In Whitehall concern with frontier violence was matched by pessimism about the possibility of halting the 'impending catastrophe'. At Government House in Sydney sympathy for 'our poor savage fellow creatures' was outweighed by the need to create conditions which would promote continued economic growth. When Governor Gipps first met G.A. Robinson, the recently appointed Chief Protector of Aborigines, he told his guest that notwithstanding the government's goodwill, 'nothing was to interfere with the improvement of the Colony'. All of these ideas and sentiments were interwoven in the settlement of inland Australia where in district after district pioneers came face to face with long-resident clans.

By fear alone

Frontiersmen eagerly took up the idea of a universal terror promoted by governors in the first 50 years of settlement. A Tasmanian settler argued that the only way to deal with the blacks was to 'dismay them so that revenge may be drowned in terror'. In discussion with G.A. Robinson a Victorian squatter asserted that it was his firm opinion that 'the only way to Govern the blacks was by fear'; nothing could be done with them until they were 'one half destroyed'. Similar attitudes flourished in north Australia in the second half of the nineteenth century, the editor of the *Hodgkinson Mining News* arguing in 1877 that regardless of cost a police force had to be maintained 'equal at least to terrifying the blacks to such an extent' that they would not 'venture to interfere with either the settlers or their property'. Commenting on the situation of squatters in remote areas of Western Australia, the explorer D.W. Carnegie argued that 'by inspiring fear alone is he able to hold his position'. At the end of the nineteenth century a north Queensland pioneer argued that experience had shown that 'no savage race can be safely dealt with without the exhibition of an awe-inspiring force'.

Many settlers came to believe that conflict with the Aborigines was inevitable, and increasingly the historical experience bore out their expectations. That being so it was widely accepted that it was prudent to use massive force at—or even before—the first sign of resistance. European lives and property, it was argued, would be more secure and even the blacks would benefit in the end by bringing conflict to an abrupt although bloody conclusion. A Tasmanian settler in the troubled Derwent Valley insisted that the most vigorous action was also the most merciful. 'Protracted and partial measures,' he explained, 'only tend to Excite the energies of these unfortunate Creatures to surmount them, without inspiring that feeling of terror and dismay, which, from their savage nature will alone be the means of inducing them to surrender and become peaceable.' The New South Wales Inspector-General of Police agreed, informing the Colonial Secretary in 1855 that 'real humanity dictates the meeting of aggression on their part, by prompt, decisive and even stern measures'. William Howitt, the prominent explorer and author, explained in a letter to his mother at home in England in 1859 that while it might seem 'very dreadful to you this hunting blackfellows', severe measures were 'in fact the kindest in the end'.

A wanton and savage spirit

The concept of savagery bolstered the belief that Aborigines, 'like savages all over the world', could only be subdued with violence, controlled by terror. The source of conflict could, therefore, be traced not to the actions of the Europeans, or to the general colonial situation, but to the nature of the Aborigines themselves. The official Tasmanian Aborigines Committee investigated the 'origin of the hostility displayed by the Black Natives of this Island against the Settlers'. While not underestimating the violence of the whites, the committee was 'most decided' that Aboriginal attacks were not the result of retaliation for 'any wrongs which they conceived themselves collectively or individually to have endured'. They proceeded instead from 'a wanton and savage spirit inherent in them, and impelling them to mischief and cruelty'. Backhouse, the Quaker missionary who toured the colonies in the 1830's, found that the whites were convinced that Aborigines 'must be made to fear you before they will love you'. Many a black, he concluded, had been 'shot under this persuasion'. The editor of Rockhampton's *Northern Argus* commented with the directness and the brutality of the frontier. There was, he asserted in 1864, 'but one law for them that they will ever respect—the bullet; the sole logic, the cock of the rifle'. After many years on the fringe of European settlement the New South Wales Crown Lands Commissioner W.H. Wiseman informed his superior in Sydney that

> conciliation so laudably enjoined and so agreeably adopted by the humane spirit of the age is when put in practice with Savages decidedly an erroneous principle of action. The Savage cannot understand the benevolence and humanity inculcated by the Christian religion. Intimidation is the only principle of dealing with them...They respect the man who rifle in hand demands an eye for an eye a tooth for a tooth. They despise the man whose humanity offers them presents and gives them blankets, such conduct they attribute to fear not to Justice and benevolence.

Although there were always settlers who grudgingly admired the courage and resourcefulness of Aboriginal resistance, the predominant view was that the blacks were unworthy of any respect even when they stood up to the Europeans. 'As cunning, treachery, and cowardice are the principal characteristics of savages,' a Tasmanian settler wrote, 'so universal report makes their whole art of war to consist of a concealed, silent and treacherous attack.' A Queensland squatter recalled how his party had only just settled on a station when the local clans made 'a cowardly attack' in the dark. This was, he wrote, normal behaviour for 'sneaky savages who never think of anything like fair play'. While assessing the impact of Aboriginal resistance on the bêche-de-mer industry the editor of the *Cooktown Independent* argued that Indians, Africans and Maoris were 'never guilty' of 'such acts of black ingratitude and hellish treachery'. There was, he argued, not a 'particle of manhood or even brute bravery about the Aboriginal, his weapons being treachery patiently nursed'. Blacks in the north, a writer in the *Queenslander* argued in 1899, were troublesome and dangerous but 'not for their courage and strength but for their treachery and cunning'.

Europeans were convinced that Aborigines had an uncontrollable urge to kill. West, the historian of early Tasmania, concluded in 1852 that the colonists in general 'believed them to delight in blood, by an innate cruelty of temper—to find pleasure in the terrors they excited, and the convulsive agonies of dying'. 'Do what you will for them,' a Moreton Bay squatter wrote in that same year, 'gratitude they have none, and it is only fear that prevents them doing their utmost to destroy us.' The editor of the *North Australian* insisted in 1857 that 'their appetite for blood seemed to increase in proportion to the number of victims'; they were consumed by a 'terrible passion for life' according to a colleague writing in the *Hodgkinson Mining News* twenty years later. In 1895 a writer in the Roebourne *Northern Public Opinion* referred to the 'absolute necessity of overmastering [the Aborigine's] tendencies to murder'; a Darwin colleague was convinced that the 'nature of the black is to kill and this nature breaks forth on every opportunity'. A Westen Australian explorer noted in his journal in 1865 after clashing with a group of Aborigines:

> as in the nature of all savages they attribute kindness and forebearance to fear and as long as there are such savages in the world this state of things must last; knowing no future they live only for the present—strategy, cunning, lying, and an insatiable thirst for blood, are the first creeds taught them, upon which, as they grow up, each day teaches them to look as the crowning virtues of their race.

Convinced of their opponents' innate savagery, it was easy for the settlers to conclude that it was the whites who wanted peace and the blacks who sought conflict. A pioneer Darling Downs squatter observed in the 1840s that the great majority of his fellow settlers were 'prepossessed with the idea that the natives are the aggressors'. Aboriginal resistance drew forth gusts of self-righteous anger. 'If it could be shown that the whites have hitherto been the aggressors,' the editor of the *Sydney Herald* wrote in 1839, 'then the question would assume a totally different appearance. But such is *not* the fact. The whites have not been the aggressors.' In fact in nineteen out of twenty cases the whites had been 'the assailed, not the assailants'. The editor of the *Hodgkinson Mining News* argued in 1877: 'It is not the rule that the white men are the aggressors. The first settlers came peaceably on to the land which they had got by right from the Crown, and no sooner have they done so than the hostilities of the natives compel them to adopt not merely defensive but offensive measures.'

An intensity of hatred

Officials who witnessed the growth of frontier violence often realised that fear was a major determinant of European behaviour, driving humane men on to acts of barbarity, enticing the tough-minded ever deeper into atrocity. Governor King considered the reasons for the conflict which had marked his governorship while preparing a memo for Bligh, his successor. He concluded that if it were possible to investigate 'how the quarrels arose', much of the blame would 'attach to the White Man in the first instance', not so much due to 'wickedness as from fear and mistrust'. Much the same view was expressed by James Stephen of the Colonial Office who, although a long way from the Australian frontier, probably read more reports on conflict between whites and Aborigines than any one else in either Britain or the colonies. The heart of the matter, he explained to the Secretary of State for the Colonies, was the hatred with which 'the white man regards the black'. That feeling, he wrote, 'results from fear'. The Government Resident at Roebourne made the same observation a generation later. 'The fears of the whites,' he believed, were 'more the cause of disorder than the aggressions of the blacks.' A *Sydney Morning Herald* correspondent, who wrote a series of articles on the north Queensland Aborigines in the 1880s, considered the question of whether killing was 'ever done wantonly...in an unprovoked manner and for the pure satisfaction of killing'. After travelling all over the north he concluded that 'mere wanton slaughter would be unknown if the natives were not feared so much'.

Racial hatred grew rapidly in the frontier environment. A settler on Victoria's Ovens River was disturbed to find in the 1840s that among most of his neighbours there existed 'an inveterate and deadly hatred of the Aborigines'. In 1857 a visitor to central Queensland noted 'an intensity of hatred' among local settlers. 'None but those who have witnessed it,' wrote a pioneer of north Australian settlement, in 1846, 'can understand the bitter hatred that is engendered, even in the most humane disposition, by a constant dread of attack.' In his book *Settlers and Convicts*, published in 1847, Alexander Harris referred to the bitter enmity which took possession of the person who lived 'in hourly fear of his life from them'. A Swan River pioneer wrote in 1832 from the troubled Guildford district that he was prepared 'to watch and attack the natives, and kill, burn, blow up and otherwise destroy the enemy'. On the other side of the continent G.A. Robinson recorded in his journal in 1839 the sentiments of a party of stockmen overlanding sheep to Port Phillip, with whom he had camped overnight. It was, he wrote, 'the most cruel that could be—they wished them to be burnt—hung—drowned or speared —by any means they wished them got rid of'.

An animal craving for revenge

Violent hatreds, always surging close to the surface, boiled over with volcanic fury whenever Europeans were killed, particularly if women or well-known settlers suffered. On such occasions the desire for revenge became overwhelming, as numerous surviving accounts graphically illustrate. In a book published in 1854 F. Eldershaw, a New England pioneer, described the aftermath of an Aboriginal attack on a station resulting in the death of three shepherds and the loss of their flocks. When the revenge expedition was being planned the stockmen were 'savagely anxious to be chosen for this painfully imperative task'. The thought of their dead friends made them 'pant for an opportunity of vengeance' and when the party cornered a group of blacks 'shot after shot, with curses wild and deep, the excited fellows launched at their hated foes'. Writing ten years later, the prominent squatter G.S. Lang related how a friend had come across the bodies of two young men whom he had only recently induced to emigrate. As a result 'he could have eaten the blacks, and from that time killed ruthlessly, yet was a most benevolent man'. In May 1831 a large group of settlers gathered from surrounding properties in the small Tasmanian town of Bothwell for the inquest of two young men killed by the blacks. As they viewed the bodies, 'a glance of indescribable emotion passed over the features of every person present. A feeling of indignation, mingled with horror, was visible in every countenance...The most hard hearted could not behold the mournful spectacle without inwardly cursing the perpetrators of murders so foul and barbarous'.

Perhaps the most interesting account of the growing passion

for revenge comes from the writing of J.B. Jukes, a scientist on board the Royal Navy survey ship HMS *Fly*, which worked in Australian waters in the 1840s. Jukes was far from being a rough frontiersman. He was inclined to humanitarianism, was well educated and went on to become one of Britain's most prominent scientists. During the *Fly*'s slow voyage along the Queensland coast Jukes had numerous contacts with the Aborigines. Most of them were friendly, but eventually a party from the ship came into conflict with a group of blacks and Jukes saw one of the crew speared. It was, he wrote, 'the first time in my life in which I had seen wounds (and, as it turned out, death) inflicted in open field, or in any kind of strife, and the sensations were as new to me as they were unpleasant. A burning feeling of mixed rage and grief, and a kind of animal craving for revenge, seemed to take possession of the heart, and a reluctance to leave the spot till some kind of amends had been obtained'. When back on board Jukes was able to analyse the development of his own feelings. He wrote:

> I have always joined in reprobating the causeless injuries sometimes inflicted by civilized, or quasi-civilized man, upon the wild tribes of savage life; and many atrocities have doubtless been committed in mere wantonness, and from brutality or indifference. I have always looked, too, with a favourable eye on what are called savages, and held a kind of preconceived sentimental affection for them, that I believe is not uncommon. I had been inclined to suppose that they were rarely the aggressors, and were always more sinned against than sinning. One such practical example as this, however, wrought a great change in my feelings on these points; and though far, I hope from abetting cruelty, I could make great allowances for any one who, under such circumstances as I have detailed, took a larger revenge than the strict justice of the case demanded. I felt that the life of one of my own shipmates, whatever his rank might be, was far dearer to me than that of a wilderness of savages, and that to preserve his life or avenge his death I could willingly shoot a dozen of these black fellows; and I could read the same feelings in the eyes of those around me. Nor was this feeling very transient; for many days or weeks after, it would have been felt as a relief by all those who saw Bayley's fall, to have come into collision with any party of black fellows they could have been justified in firing on.

Perhaps the strongest community response to Aboriginal resistance arose in Queensland between 1857 and 1861. During that time eleven Europeans were killed at Hornet Bank station in 1857 and nineteen at Cullin La Ringoe four years later. Women and children were among the victims on both occasions. In 1860 Fanny Briggs was raped and murdered near Rockhampton by Native Police troopers. When news of Hornet Bank reached Ipswich even those 'habitually calm and merciful' were heard to advocate 'vengeance and extermination'. W.H. Wiseman, an official who after years on the frontier was pleased that he had never killed a black, was overwhelmed 'with feelings of grief, horror and indignation such as I hoped could never affect me'. Three years later he reported that following the rape and murder of Fanny Briggs popular feeling was 'running tempestuously against all Blacks'. But there was an even more violent reaction to the events at Cullin la Ringoe. At Taroom the 'greatest horror and indignation was felt by all classes'; in Rockhampton 'a universal cry of indignation burst forth'; in the Burnett district it was reported that while the fate of the Wills family dominated every conversation, 'mercy and quarter appear to be the last things thought of'. In a letter to the *Queensland Guardian* 'Australian' said that he found the news 'so sudden and horrible as almost to take away all power of language or even thought'. The tribe, he insisted, must be punished 'whether it number scores or hundreds...the deadly bullet must do the work of the more legitimate executioners—justice must triumph over law'. Writing in the *Moreton Bay Courier*, a frontier squatter argued that the death of Wills family had 'armed our hands for revenge'. It was time, he argued, 'to abolish that absurd and false law which made it murder to kill a wild beast...when peace and tranquility must be enjoyed through this beautiful land, and when all traces of an hostile, barbarous and useless set of beings must be swept away by the torrent of Christian civilization.'

Doing the needful

The Europeans exacted revenge out of all proportion to the number of settlers killed. In his recent study of Hornet Bank, Reid concluded that in punitive expeditions mounted by both squatters and Native Police, at least 150 and possibly 300 Aborigines were killed. Even more may have died in the bloody aftermath of the Aboriginal attack on Cullin La Ringoe. But central Queensland was not unique in this respect. Similar massive reprisals were seen in many parts of Australia. They typically followed the killing of a prominent settler or a group of Europeans when frontier communities decided that it was time to teach the blacks a lesson 'once and for all'. Such action followed the Aboriginal attack on Faithful's droving party in 1838, the death of Alistair McAlister in Gippsland five years later, the killing of Mary Watson, the Strau and Conn families in north Queensland in the 1870s and 1880s, the attack on a mining camp on the Daly River in 1884 and on several groups of settlers in the Kimberleys between 1892 and 1894. The sites of such massacres were given names like 'Fighting Hills', 'Slaughterhouse Creek', 'Gravesend', 'Murdering Island', 'Skull Camp', 'Skull Creek'.

Discussion of racial conflict became more open, if not necessarily more common, in the second half of the nineteenth century. Comment in frontier newspapers was often brutally frank, the editor of the *Rockhampton Bulletin* remarking in 1865 that it was 'well known that the frequent use of firearms is indispensable to the outside settlers. Hundreds of blacks are shot down in the Colony every year'. The Charters Towers *Northern Miner* was even more to the point, observing that shooting blacks was 'one of the commonest accessories of bush life all over Queensland'. Settlers developed a collection of euphemisms to facilitate discussion of frontier brutality. The most common was the term to 'disperse' which the Queensland Attorney-General admitted in 1861 'meant nothing but firing into them for that purpose'. Newspapers reported Native Police 'dispersals' in a variety of ways—the force 'duly and efficiently pounded' the blacks, gave them the 'customary chastisement', dispersed them 'in the usual time honoured fashion', gave them 'a dressing down', a 'thumping', 'a shaking up'. A critic of Queensland frontier traditions observed in 1874 that 'private persons go out to kill blacks, and call it "snipe shooting". Awkward words are always avoided, you will notice "shooting a snipe" sounds better than "murdering a man". But the blacks are never called men and women and children; "myalls" and "niggers" and "gins" and "piccanninies" seem further removed from humanity.'

Private punitive expeditions were reported in the papers in the same oblique way, readers being informed of a squatter who 'did the needful himself', and others who variously 'got a brace or two of black game', gave the blacks 'a warm time', a 'baptism by fire', dealt with them in 'the energetic way', had a 'brush' or a 'battue', who '*withdrew* some sixty blacks down the Coen River', who was 'adverse to civilizing them by anything but one certain method', who provided 'a little persuasion from a Colt's appetiser'. A correspondent calling himself 'Dry Tiddler' wrote to the *Queenslander* in 1876 reporting breathlessly: 'the hatchet is raked up; our best shots are after them; I am off too; there will be weeping and wailing somewhere shortly after I have started, you bet.'

Ten years later another correspondent wrote to the *Cairns Post* in similar vein: 'A little "black birding" appears to be necessary, and if the limbs of the law do not look sharp and have some fun themselves, the selectors will be out skirmishing when "long pig" will probably be plentiful.'

Boasting about exploits among the blacks—real and imaginary —became a characteristic of frontier society from the early years of the nineteenth century. In the 1840s Edward Eyre noted the prevalence of 'a recklessness that leads them to think as little of firing at a black, as at a bird, and which makes the number they have killed, or the atrocities they have attended...a matter for a tale, a jest or a boast at their pot house revelries'.

Fiery young gentlemen

But such attitudes were not confined to the pot house, sly-grog shanty or shepherd's hut. They were probably heard as often, though phrased a little more carefully, around the dining tables of the colonial gentry. Colonel Mundy, who toured the Australian colonies in the early 1850s, was 'no less shocked than surprised at hearing men of station and cultivation' advocating sweeping and indiscriminate retaliation against the blacks. A friend who had 'sojourned among the border settlers' told Mundy that he had heard 'plans for the destruction of the Aborigines constantly and openly discussed'. Mundy was entertained by a squatter who casually told him over dinner of a 'brush' with the blacks in which eleven were killed and many wounded, 'as great a loss of life', Mundy calculated, as in 'many a well fought frigate action'. On another social occasion 'a fiery young gentleman of the interior' boasted to Mundy that he would 'shoot a blackfellow wherever he met him as he would a mad dog'. Mundy was so shocked that he reported the conversation to the Governor. Other observers of colonial society reported similar experiences. Bishop Polding informed a Legislative Council Select Committee that a well-educated squatter had told him there was 'no more harm in shooting a native than in shooting a wild dog'. Aboriginal Protector James Dredge talked with a man 'calling himself a gentleman' who did not hesitate to affirm that the blacks were 'mere brutes'. A visitor to New South Wales in the 1840s noted that there were people in what were considered 'respectable stations in society' who had the hardihood to defend 'the savage butcheries that have been committed by the whites on the natives, by asserting that they resemble so many wild beasts, and that it is proper to destroy them accordingly'. Fifty years later a West Australian clergyman met two gentlemen in Fremantle, 'both of them communicants', who asserted that the Aborigines should be treated 'only as horses or dogs'. In 1901 an old Queensland settler recalled the behaviour of a fellow pioneer 'bearing one of the most honoured of names', who used to entertain his companions with humorous sketches of the results of individual poisoning, diversified by equally amusing stories of the effect produced with a rifle. One could fill pages with pleasant stories of this sort'. The distinguished British colonial official Sir Arthur Gordon wrote to his friend W.E. Gladstone in 1883 at the end of his six-year term as Western Pacific High Commissioner. While denouncing Queensland's plans to annex New Guinea he explained that in the northern colony he had

> heard men of culture and refinement, of the greatest humanity and kindness
> to their fellow whites, and who when you meet them at home you would

pronounce to be incapable of such deeds, talk, not only of the *wholesale* butchery...but of the *individual* murder of natives, exactly as they would talk of a days sport, or of having had to kill some troublesome animal.

A pleasurable excitement

Though some frontiersmen carried guns grudgingly, and used them reluctantly, many found pleasure in the pursuit of the Aborigines. 'There were men,' observed the historian West in 1852, 'distinguished for the malicious vigour with which they tracked and murdered the native people'. There was 'a species of excitement in it', Mundy concluded, and it became 'by practice a pleasurable excitement'. A north Queensland pioneer recalled that he and his fellow squatters 'thoroughly enjoyed those days of wild and romantic life' when as well as physical hardship there was 'always the danger of being speared by some blackfellow'. Amidst all the dullness and monotony of frontier squatting, there were seasons of 'excitement and danger' including the constant skirmishes with the blacks. It was a life of wild and varied excitement, a New South Wales squatter recalled. There was the feeling of 'perfect independence by the full development and constant exercise of a man's own resources together with the stimulus of frequent and bloody conflicts with the Aborigines...'.

On the frontier immigrants often gained a sense of freedom from many of the constraints of life in Britain. In their relations with the Aborigines they were released from the normal moral restraints and felt they could do as they pleased without any worry about the law or public opinion. During his expeditions through the frontier districts of Port Phillip in the 1840s G.A. Robinson talked to many squatters and stockmen. When he taxed them about their behaviour towards the Aborigines they commonly retorted: 'we are on the border and can do as we like.' Forty years later the editor of a Brisbane paper remarked that the shooting of blacks was justified 'so long as such killing is confined to the Border-line, or the country abutting on the outskirts of civilization'.

Counting the bodies

How many blacks died in the 'species of warfare' fought out along the frontiers of settlement? For many reasons this is not an easy question to answer. Colonial governments showed little desire to count the bodies, and the occasional official estimates of mortality were quite inadequate. Police parties were expected to account for every death they caused, but they often ignored their instructions or deliberately falsified the returns. Most governments seemed satisfied with reports which baldly stated that the blacks had been 'punished', or 'chastised' or 'dispersed'. In Queensland during much of the time that the Native Police Force was patrolling the outer fringe of settlement its victims were 'incinerated rather than enumerated'. The actions of private parties are even more difficult to assess.

Australian historians have often been as evasive about frontier conflict as were colonial officials. However the upsurge of interest in Aboriginal history in the last fifteen years has led to a flowering of research and writing about the frontier, enabling scholars to develop a broad overview of conditions during the nineteenth and early twentieth centuries. Making use of recent work I attempted in *The Other Side of the Frontier* to assess the general impact of frontier skirmishing. The resulting figure of 20 000 Aboriginal deaths from violence was, and remains, little better than an informed guess. If anything subsequent research suggests that 20 000 is too low. The death toll may have been much higher.

Was it genocide?

But was it a case of genocide? In a literal sense clearly no. The Aborigines survived the invasion. The population has been increasing for a generation, although it has still not reached that of 1788. Many of those who died did so from disease; others were killed in an upsurge of conflict within Aboriginal communities. A rapidly falling birth rate may have been of greater demographic significance than a spiralling death rate. Yet even when those qualifications have been made the central question remains.

Did significant numbers of settlers seek the total destruction of Aboriginal Australia? It is an important and a complex question, and must be carefully answered.

It is clear that from at least the 1820s many colonists expected the Aborigines to 'die out' or 'pass away'. The belief grew stronger as the century progressed and was still widely held in the 1940s. Australians often talked of extinction and extermination, but their reaction to the prospect varied widely. Some were horrified, others thought the outcome inevitable while not necessarily welcoming it, and then there were those who were pleased with the thought and sought to hasten the predetermined result. This range of opinion was apparent in the 1820s and 1830s. A humanitarian colonist wrote from New South Wales in the 1820s to the Methodist Missionary Society in London, horrified at the bloodshed on the frontier. Tribe after tribe, he argued, 'must successively endure the same measure of suffering until the total annihilation of the natives of New Holland winds up the sad catastrophe'. West Australia's Governor Stirling assured the Colonial Office in 1835 that the Aborigines 'must gradually disappear' as the country was occupied; neither the humane intentions of the British authorities 'nor the most anxious and judicious measures of the local government [could] prevent the ulterior Extinction of that Race'. The *Sydney Herald* was blunter. Any attempt to civilise the blacks was futile; 'they will and must become extinct'; it was in the order of nature that savage nations 'must be exterminated'. Pessimism about the future was expressed in the Colonial Office itself. In a memo to his minister James Stephen said that little could be done to avoid the total destruction of the Australian Aborigines despite the Imperial Governments' public stance that they were subjects who might expect the full protection of the law. It was, he argued, really a military problem. It was not the will of God but the ill-will of the settlers that was pushing the blacks towards impending catastrophe. He wrote in a memo to Lord Glenelg: 'The only chance of saving them from annihilation would consist in teaching them the art of war and supplying them with weapons and munitions—an act of suicidal generosity which of course cannot be practised.'

It is impossible to determine what percentage of the colonists advocated the deliberate extermination of the blacks, but the 'extirpationists', as G.A. Robinson called them, were at least a substantial minority. A South Australian clergyman wrote home to England in 1840 explaining: 'Kill and exterminate is the general doctrine.' Jesuit missionaries, arriving in the Northern Territory in the 1880s, sensed that the settlers could 'hardly conceal the wish of their hearts that all the blacks should be exterminated'. A correspondent signing himself 'Philanthropist' wrote to the *Rockhampton Bulletin* in 1865 advocating a protectorate for the Aborigines. He observed: 'With many, I grieve to say it, the extermination of the blacks by any means is a consummation devoutly to be wished, and they act accordingly.' Two years later the editor of the same paper returned to the subject, deploring violence but expecting ultimate extinction of the Aborigines. He wrote:

> Whilst we regard the disappearance of the black race before the face of the white man as an inevitable fact to which we must of necessity submit as one of the conditions of successful colonization, we must protest in the name of humanity and justice against seeking to attain this end by a ruthless and indiscriminate extermination of the doomed race. Their extinction is only a question of time, and no unnecessary cruelty should be used to effect a result which the operation of natural causes will certainly accomplish.

Sharpened frontier conflict called forth increased demands for extermination. They became common, for perhaps the first time, in Tasmania between 1828 and 1830. Edward Curr, the manager of the Van Diemen's Land Company, argued that Aboriginal hostility was so serious that the colonists would either have to abandon the island 'or they must undertake a war of extermination'. A contemporary remarked that if conflict with the Tasmanian clans could not be brought to an end then 'the dreadful alternative only remains of a general extermination by some means or other'. A Port Phillip settler told Aboriginal Protector William Thomas in 1839 that 'there will be no peace till the Blacks are extirpated'. If a tribe offend, a second squatter said to G.A. Robinson, 'destroy the whole...they must be exterminated'. In 1858 an editorial in the *Moreton Bay Courier* argued that either the Europeans would have to abandon their outstations to the blacks or conduct 'an exterminating war against them'. Three years later a leading Queensland politician told parliament that extermination 'appeared to be all that could be done'. After several shepherds had been speared on nearby stations the editor of the Clermont paper the *Peak Downs Telegram* argued in 1867 that 'a war of extermination is the only policy to pursue, the alternative being an abandonment of the country which no sane man will advocate for an instant.' A humane police officer found in 1885 that the people of the Cooktown area strongly opposed his plans to ameliorate the conditions of local blacks. Their creed was 'extermination of the natives'.

Even when the fighting ceased and anxiety ebbed there were settlers who believed that colonisation was incomplete while any blacks were alive. Filled with a vast and terrible passion, they longed for the day when the Europeans would be 'placed alone in the midst of the earth'. The fallen Aborigine, 'like the uprooted forest, was thought of as an encumbrance removed'. In his early-twentieth-century history of the pastoral industry Collier concluded that 'this great obstacle to the complete colonisation of Australia had necessarily to be removed'. Norwegian scientist Karl Lumholtz, in Australia for several years during the 1880s, 'often heard it openly avowed that the country will never be what it might until the blacks are exterminated'. A senior Queensland official told a visiting clergyman in 1874 that it was all very well to have sympathy for the blacks but that the colony 'could not get on until they were exterminated'. A member of the Queensland Legislative Council informed the Roman Catholic missionary Duncan McNab early in 1881 that while he was attending the Governor's Christmas banquet conversation turned to the blacks and 'the conclusion arrived at...was that there was nothing for the Aborigines but extermination'.

The story was officially denied. We will probably never know what was actually said over the turkey and plum pudding at Government House in Brisbane in 1880. But it is clear that when Governor Phillip decided to produce 'an universal terror' around the site of the first settlement, he gave birth to a tradition of violence that outlived not only everyone of Phillip's generation but also all of the dignitaries who sat down to dinner with the Queensland Governor 90 years later.

– 3 –

Generations Hardened Against the Natives

In 1894 the West Kimberley correspondent of the Roebourne paper *The North West Times* suggested that if the West Australian government wished to solve the problem of Aboriginal resistance it should 'shut its eyes for three short months' and let the settlers deal with 'the niggers'. It would only have to be done once and 'once done could easily be forgotten'. But nothing could have been wider of the mark. The legacy of frontier violence lived on; spilt blood was not easily forgotten either by the Aborigines or the Europeans. Attitudes and patterns of behaviour learnt during the period of open conflict continued to influence relations between whites and Aborigines long after the shooting stopped.

A tradition of brutality

Many people had been directly or indirectly involved in conflict with the blacks; the insecurity of the frontier had touched them all at one time or another. Fear had not been confined to those most exposed to attack; it often ran like fire, far from the point of conflagration. The fighting lasted a long time in the larger colonies; three or four generations of Queenslanders and West Australians knew, if only by report, that somewhere in the outback whites were being speared and blacks shot for revenge in grossly disproportionate numbers. Most accepted it as a necessary corollary of progress. On the frontier awareness of conflict was more immediate. Anxiety and hatred were communal. Punitive action dominated conversations and when the blacks were 'punished' everyone knew and many exulted. Evidence of conflict was never far away. Black bodies were often left where they had fallen or were thrown together in poorly concealed hiding places which attracted crows and flies and inquisitive travellers. Exploits among the blacks were a staple of camp-fire swagger and many frontiersmen kept a tally of their kill, those not wanting to forget notching the handles of their rifles or revolvers. The Queensland historian W.H. Traill observed in 1880 that attacks on the Aborigines 'formed the text of yarns around the camp fire and in the shearer's hut, just as, within the recollection of men not now past middle age, in north Queensland, exciting accounts of battles of blackfellows were as common as sporting narratives'. There were atrocities too of one sort or another. Poisoning, rape, mutilation, torture, savaging with hunting dogs—all had accompanied frontier skirmishing. How frequently we will never know, but heads were cut off and skulls were put on open display on some stations; even ears and fingers were sometimes kept as mementos of murder.

In small towns or districts all the local 'incidents' were known, the killers secure behind the shield of overwhelming community approval and rigid codes of silence when outsiders were about. In New South Wales in the 1840s incidents of poisoning were known by 'the rumour of the whole countryside'; they were 'made no secret, but openly spoken and even boasted of'. In Queensland a decade or so later 'heinous cold blooded slaughters' were committed 'in the midst and to the knowledge of inhabitants' of the frontier districts. The killers 'wrapped themselves in the security of what they have termed public opinion'. It was well known in the 1860s that Queensland settlers who had 'repeatedly slain the natives in cold blood' were not only allowed to escape with impunity but did 'not even lose caste with their associates'. 'Everybody knew all about it,' W.H. Traill observed, 'but a certain reserve was maintained in general conversation. Names were omitted and localities merely shadowed.' A New South Wales Crown Lands Commissioner explained the situation in a

letter to his superiors in Sydney. He had tried to take action
against settlers who had killed blacks. He knew who they were,
in fact in all cases they were 'known to everyone by the common
fame of the country'. Yet no evidence was available, nor any
witnesses, such was 'the state of combination and system of
terrorism existing in [the] locality'. The opposing viewpoint
of the frontier settler was outlined in a letter published in the
Moreton Bay Courier in 1861 which read in part: 'If a squatter
was to be found guilty of murder for shooting a black the whole
bush would rise against the town and blood would be shed. This
is well known by the Government and the law remains ineffectual.'

The duration and intensity of conflict, the prolonged insecurity,
the widespread complicity in bloodshed—all fostered the growth
of a tradition of violence which was already apparent in the early
years of the nineteenth century. Recently arrived visitors from
Britain quickly noticed the ubiquitous firearms, the casual brutality of speech and action. Missionary Threlkeld recalled that
when he landed in New South Wales in the 1820s he was 'as-
tonished to hear a man boasting how many blacks he had killed
on his land'. A South Australian clergyman wrote home to friends
in England in 1840 about a co-religionist who since arriving in
the colonies had 'adopted the opinions of the other Overland
Desperadoes who glorify in shooting the blacks'. G.A. Robinson
believed it to be a fact, 'and deeply to be regretted', that when
settlers went into the wilds of Australia they 'at length become
cruel'. In 1843 an Adelaide newspaper editor asked his readers to
consider 'how callous have we grown since we left home?'.
Backhouse, the Quaker missionary, noted that people who before
they emigrated 'would have shuddered at the idea of murdering
their fellow creatures', had, in many instances, 'wantonly taken
the lives of the Aborigines'. Even those who originally desired to
cultivate a good feeling towards the blacks found their 'benevolent intentions superseded by a desire to have these hapless
people removed out of the way'. A Gippsland pioneer, similarly
concerned, wrote in the 1840s: 'I remember the time when my
blood would have run cold at the mention of these things, but
now I am become so familiarized with scenes of horror from

having murder made a topic of every day conversation. I have heard tales told and some things I have seen that would form as dark a page as ever you read in the book of history.'

The tradition of violence became more deeply rooted during the second half of the nineteenth century with conflict continuing all around the fringes of the expanding frontier. An old New South Wales colonist, concerned with Aboriginal welfare for 50 years, concluded in 1883 that the 'business of dispersing black fellows' had resulted in 'dispersing the conscience of white fellows'. A Queensland squatter noted that the most brutal killings were hidden from view, forcing him to believe 'that the whole community was becoming awfully debased'. A contemporary wrote to the *Moreton Bay Free Press* in 1859 to persuade the editor to use his influence 'to prevent that abominable feeling becoming a principle in the minds of the men of Queensland, that, to kill a blackfellow in cold blood is not murder'. Such views, he noted, were 'frequently promulgated'. Seventeen years later the editor of the *Rockhampton Bulletin* wrote with concern about 'the reckless disregard of the common rights of humanity so often exhibited by men whose moral sensibilities have been blunted by too great familiarity with deeds of blood in skirmishes which take place on our frontier settlements'.

Humanitarians fretted about the impact of frontier violence on colonial children. 'The stories told, and the acts that have passed without reproof,' a visitor to Queensland warned in 1885, 'tend to bring up a generation hardened against the natives.' A Rockhampton man, deeply concerned about the problem, remarked in 1865 that it was 'easy to see that familiarity with murder, as against the blacks', would eventually induce a 'recklessness of bloodshed in the rising generation, fraught with the most fearful consequences'. In 1867 a fellow townsman wrote to the local paper about the recent massacre of Aborigines by Native Police troopers at the nearby mining community of Morinish. He thought it a national calamity that such outrages could be enacted in a British colony 'without exciting that universal indignation which the mere report of them would undoubtedly elicit in any part of the United Kingdom'. One inevitable effect of the massacres remaining unpunished would be 'that the youth of the colony will grow up with a reckless disregard of human life, which, in due time will yield congenial fruit. Already the evil leaven has begun to work. I have frequently felt grieved and indignant at the levity, with which many of the colonial youth speak of those outrages on the blacks'.

The letter was prophetic. Just six months later a group of Maryborough boys acted out a grisly parody of a punitive expedition. They went out one evening with their guns. They surrounded the camp of the 'town blacks' in the accustomed manner. A 12-year-old presented his gun at an old woman and ordered her to get up and dance. She refused. He pulled the trigger and blew her brains out.

Some colonists were troubled by their conscience once the fighting was finished and the immediate danger had passed. G.A. Robinson met a soldier of the 40th Regiment in the Tasmanian bush whose advice was 'never to kill the poor natives', for ever since he had done so he had been unhappy. A Victorian pioneer who went out on four fruitless punitive expeditions was glad in retrospect that he 'never fell in with them' otherwise he would have felt 'that sting' always experienced by those who had blood on their hands. There were, he remarked, 'now but two settlers in the Portland district that I know who have been severe on the natives, and they are doing little good. It seems strange none have done any good who were murderers of these poor creatures— either man or master'. An old Queensland stockman with a reputation for 'shooting the Aborigines whenever he pleased' was dogged in his old age by fear of retribution; even in country 'where none were left he went about in fear of being speared in the night'. Rosa Campbell Praed, who grew up on a station in central Queensland in the troubled 1850s, confided 30 years later that she had 'not ceased to dream that I am on an out-station besieged by blacks; and during many a night do I fly through the endless forests and stony gullies' pursued by the Aborigines. A Northern Territory pioneer who had 'killed plenty of Aborigines' in his time died screaming in the Darwin hospital because 'he reckoned the ghosts of all the blackfellows he had killed were sitting round his bed, waiting for him'.

Letting the blacks in

Conflict came to an uncertain end everywhere sooner or later. There were no peace treaties, no formal negotiations. The only event which marked the termination of hostilities was when the blacks 'came in' to pastoral stations or fringe camps. With that development a whole new range of problems arose for both Aborigines and settlers as they learned to live in proximity and the blacks were taught to conform to the demands of the conquerors. These events have rarely been studied by Australian scholars although they must have been repeated a hundred times over during the nineteenth century and early twentieth century. Perhaps the best-documented case of the process of letting the blacks in took place in the small Queensland town of Bowen in 1869. By then spirited local resistance had been ruthlessly crushed after eight years of conflict. Neighbouring squatters were beginning to let the blacks in on their stations and were already profitably using their labour. Remnants of the local clans appeared around the outskirts of the town. The *Port Denison Times* carried letters and editorials arguing the cases for and against the development under the heading 'Shall We Admit the Blacks'. The editor contributed a comprehensive summary of European fears and expectations at that crucial point of time when Aborigines were about to be incorporated into settler society. He wrote:

> The Aboriginal question is again asserting its claim to our attention on all hands and in louder tones than ever.
>
> First and foremost we see daily in the midst of us numbers of the former lords and ladies of the soil in almost their native costume marching about with that lordly air that so distinguishes them and apparently taking stock diligently spying out the nakedness of the land and the weak points, maybe, of its holders. So far no one can have any objection. Indeed it is far better to see them coming thus fearlessly amongst us than to know they are skulking in the scrubs cowering from fear of the white man's bullet, their hand against every [white] man and every [white] man's hand against them. But on the other hand it becomes us as invaders to enforce submission to our laws on the part of the conquered. We have hitherto done this by the strong hand, that is to say, to unhesitating recourse to powder and ball. Against this system all right feeling men have thoroughly revolted and it has lately been hoped that the time had come when, with regard to our own safety, a milder system might be inaugurated and more friendly relations established between us and those whom we have supplanted. How to effect this is the problem now before us and it is needless to say that it is by no means

an easy one. In the first place of course it would be absurd under any circumstances to expect any kindly feeling to exist towards us in the breasts of the blackfellows especially so shortly after the reign of terror by which they have hitherto been kept in subjection. In whatever plan we may adopt with respect to them we shall do well to bear in mind that their feelings towards us are and must be those of resentment and hostility and that however the exhibition of those feelings may be restrained by motives of policy on their part they do exist and probably will continue to do while the race lasts, and that this smouldering fire will be ready to burst into flame when favourable conditions offer.

Whilst therefore it is one of our foremost duties to escape as soon as possible from the terrible necessities which our position has forced upon us, we must not cease to be firm and must take especial care to show our black neighbours that whilst we are willing, nay anxious, to hold our hands from slaughter, we are at the same time determined to enforce at all hazards and by any means submission to our laws and that any infraction of them will be met by retribution prompt and severe. If we do not we will be failing in our duty alike to them and to ourselves. For we shall not only endanger the safety of our own citizens, which after all should be our first care, but we shall render inevitable a return to the bloody system, the possible termination of which we have all regarded with so much hope and pleasure. Upon the attitude we now assume depends in very great degree the amount of success we may hope to achieve in the solution of this problem. Times of change from one system to another, that is of revolution, have in all cases their peculiar elements of danger. One of the first maxims of such periods is principius obsta—that is, check anything that appears likely to disturb the working of the new system at the outset. It is by far the wisest and most merciful plan. For this reason we hold that the action taken by the sergeant of police as described in our last issue, we mean that the flogging of the gin who had stolen the child's petticoat, was, though perhaps not strictly legal, quite the right thing to do under the circumstances. We should not perhaps have alluded to this but that during the past week there have come under our notice several instances of offences committed by the blackfellow which though not in themselves of a very heinous nature are just such as if allowed to pass unchecked will embolden the savages and lead to more serious outrages and eventually to the undoing of whatever progress has been made in the direction of placing our blackfellow policy on a better footing than heretofore. One of the instances to which we refer occurred at Muller's garden the other day, when one of them cut down a valuable peach tree, we suppose from the fancy that it would make a good waddy, and perhaps being unaware that it was good for anything else; and another broke, we do not know exactly under what circumstances, a grindstone belonging to Mr Muller; but assuming that both deeds were committed without malice, we maintain that in both cases they ought to have been punished, if only to teach them better for the future, but chiefly to teach those principles of submission which our position renders it so necessary for us to enforce...

We would however, before leaving this part of our subject, utter one word of warning to our white fellow citizens, and that is not to forget, as we said above, that the blackfellows are by force of circumstances our enemies and that their feelings towards us, however much fear or policy may smooth the behaviour, are those of undying hostility. In fact they hate a white man and the very sight of him and we do not see how they could do otherwise. Gratitude, except as 'a lively sense of favours to come', or perhaps a fear of future punishments, they have none, and it would be very odd if they had...The moral of all this is that we should not allow ourselves to be thrown off our guard in our dealings with them.

It is a fascinating document, a frank and comprehensive summary of attitudes inherited from nearly a decade of conflict and destined to play a fundamentally important role in the development of relations between white and black in the post-frontier period. Consider the major arguments presented: The Aborigines were by force of circumstances enemies; they hated white people, indeed they were consumed by an undying hostility which would never go away and which smouldered like a fire ready at any moment to burst into flame. Up till the time of writing the blacks had been kept in subjection by a reign of terror, by unhesitating recourse to ball and powder. In order to incorporate the blacks into the town and bring the reign of terror to an end it was necessary to teach those principles of submission which the vulnerability of the whites rendered so necessary to enforce. The conquered blacks must be shown that the settlers were determined to enforce submission to their laws at all costs and by any means including such illegal proceedings as flogging a woman accused of a very minor offence. The significance of this portfolio of ideas can be illustrated by reference to events in all parts of Australia.

Like the editor of the Bowen paper, many frontier settlers were aware of the legacy of 'universal terror' born of the species of warfare fought with the Aborigines. They appreciated the power it gave them, its value 'in keeping the blacks in their place' and in enabling employers to obtain cheap or unpaid labour. They were, then, both the conscious and the willing inheritors of a tradition of violence. 'The rule,' wrote Rusden the historian in 1883, 'was to inspire terror by slaughter, and then to treat with contemptuous sufferance or marked ill usage the remnant of the tribe.' Observers who saw the blacks 'coming in' witnessed their fear as they approached European settlements. In 1888 the local clans were 'let in' on the Palmer goldfield after fourteen years of conflict. When the first party of 25 walked, with acute anxiety, down Maytown's dusty main street, 'fear was depicted in every movement'. An official who met groups of Cape York Aborigines in the 1890s reported that they were like 'hunted wild beasts, afraid to go to sleep in their own country...having lived for years in a state of absolute terrorism'. Two policemen, in contact with Aborigines on the frontier, but on opposite sides of the continent, commented on the intensity of fear they inspired. A West Australian officer informed his commissioner in 1894 that the blacks 'run now like dogs the excrement dropping from them whenever my party surprises them'. Three years later Cooktown's inspector wrote to his superior in Brisbane describing reactions to his presence from a group of 400 Cape York Aborigines: 'The Inspector of Police with them is a "big" man—the Commissioner is still very much greater—but the Government is that unknowable, all powerful something in their opinion which can do anything and everything and which they revere and fear with their whole being.' One of the leading men stepped forward to speak with the white man. He was, the inspector believed, 'brave in coming to meet me. When I was getting and putting his name in my pocket book, his voice, great thighs and hairy chest were quaking with timidity'.

Such extraordinary terrorism

Aboriginal fear both stimulated European assertiveness and entrenched black submission. The frontier was a finishing school for white arrogance and brutality. For their part the Aborigines had 'learnt in their terror to submit to anything the conquering race' chose to do. In 1891 a South Australian police constable provided the Government Resident of the Northern Territory with a detailed inventory of brutalities suffered by outback Aborigines. 'No matter what it is these poor creatures have to submit to,' he explained, 'it is simply through fear...it is the one word fear all through.' At the turn of the century Archibald

Meston conducted a survey of the Aborigines in south-west Queensland, an area first settled 50 years before. There were 'scores of unfortunate blacks' on the stations where they were worked like slaves for 'a reward of coarse food and mean clothing'. They were retained in such uncongenial service by 'a terrorism only possible among blacks' who had 'no knowledge of any alternative to submission'. Never before, he recalled, 'had I seen aboriginal men living under such extraordinary terrorism, many of them fine athletic fellows who could in case of a row have settled with their terrorisers in a very summary fashion. But many of them had long been treated as the dogs are treated and were scared into a belief that their employers wielded the power of life or death'.

Large-scale killing of Aborignes came to an end when they moved onto pastoral stations and into fringe camps. Yet life remained hazardous. There was little protection from the law, from public opinion, established custom or even from settler self-interest. An unknown number of Aborigines died from injuries received while being 'disciplined' with whip and fist and boot. Such cases were occasionally reported in the papers and infrequently taken before the courts. Every now and then the violence of the frontier washed back into the pioneer towns. In Queensland the Native Police occasionally arrested 'town backs', marched them a mile or two down the road and shot them. In 1876, for instance, an Aborigine known as Jimmy was taken out of the township of Marlborough and executed. The incident came to public notice because the fire kindled to dispose of the evidence only smouldered and local children found the half-roasted corpse a few days later. In April 1861 Sub-Lieutenant Bligh led his troopers into Maryborough to disperse the town blacks. A couple were shot in the street, others were picked off while swimming in the river. By then a crowd had gathered to witness the spectacle. In Rockhampton a drunken police officer 'too beastly to sit upon his horse' rode out of town with the 'avowed and inflamed intention of shooting down the wretches'. Townspeople undertook their own vigilante action to capture presumed offenders or to drive the local blacks out of town. In

1863 a Rockhampton Aborigine escaped from the police and plunged into the nearby Eitzroy river. He was 'actively pursued by the European mob in boats, who struck his head with their oars every time it appeared above water'. Another mob chased a black through Townsville streets in 1884, cornering him in a quarry where he was shot in the shoulder, inflicting a wound which subsequently caused his death. But despite sporadic violence, the towns were safer for blacks than the bush. Even small settlements had residents opposed to the use of indiscriminate violence and who afforded protection to local Aborigines. In the larger towns newspapers and police forces restrained the more brutal members of the community. In the bush many squatters developed a tradition of stern paternalism which stopped short of murder. Yet in the absence of restraint it is likely that Aborigines were often killed, their fate passing unnoticed outside the immediate district. One such incident was reported in passing in Curr's book *The Australian Race* published in 1886–87. One of Curr's informants, while describing the funeral customs of clans living along the Belyando River, instanced the case 'of a girl of 15 years of age, who with several others were *dispersed* for unwittingly allowing the grass to take fire on the bank of a river on which they were fishing. This was on the territory of the tribe. She was brought here, and died the day after she received the shot'.

Keeping them in their place

Government policy from the 1790s, and conditions on the Australian frontier, had conspired to arm the settlers and encouraged them to engage in innumerable petty, private wars with the Aborigines. When the guns were put aside settlers continued to act on their own initiative, turning instead to whips and fists and boots. Defeat and dispossession of the blacks was not enough; white supremacy had to be constantly asserted district by district, even person by person. Many Europeans felt the need to reaffirm that supremacy over every black who came their way. For their part Aborigines were forced to run an endless gauntlet, subject on the way to arbitrary, capricious, personal violence against which they had no redress. 'Every man seems to consider himself,' a writer in the *Queenslander* observed in 1884, 'as quite justified in carrying out the utmost vigour of the law towards an Aboriginal, often for some very trivial and insignificant crime.' A correspondent in the *Moreton Bay Courier* twenty years earlier argued that it was time that the police were authorised to do 'what every private individual takes the liberty of doing when the occasion demands— administer a sound thrashing for offences against the decency or peace of the neighbourhood'. The problem had been perceived as early as the 1820s by a visitor who investigated the position of the Aborigines in New South Wales for the Methodist Missionary Society. He realised that the blacks were in a 'state of exposure to caprices and wanton punishment'. Their present condition, he noted, 'is, that they are exposed to the caprice, interests and whim of everybody, they are cast on the mercy of all and find protection from none. They are exposed without any fair means of redress to the ill treatment of all...The White assumes within himself the power of punishment, and inflicts it upon the black just as the feeling of the moment impels'.

Aborigines were expected—and usually compelled—to conform to a role created for them in advance of their entry into European society. The name changed over time and from place to place— nigger, coon, boong, abo, Jacky—but the role remained much the same. It was compounded of racial ideas shipped in from Europe, the experience of frontier conflict, the economic interests and psychological needs of the settlers. It was a demanding, constricting role to play. And it had to be played all the time, at least whenever Europeans were watching or listening. There was no room for initiative or independence or self-assertion. Speaking out of turn, looking a white man straight in the eye, assuming a facial expression considered inappropriate for a 'nigger'—each one could merit a fist in the face, a boot in the balls or a stockwhip around the shoulders. Above all else Europeans were united in their determination to keep the blacks in their place. There was no room for 'cheeky niggers' in the world the settlers were making—'cheeky niggers' usually had short and unhappy lives or they rotted slowly in penal institutions. An old drover, recalling his career in the outback in the early years of the twentieth century, remarked:

> Whether you were a manager or a yard-builder, if you employed a black-fellow and he ran away, you had to get him back...
>
> When you caught him you were expected to give him a bashing. If you did not, then the boss was likely to sack you for 'spoiling natives'. A reputation for being 'hard on blacks' was worth a dollar a week extra to a stockman—and that was big money on the wages of those days.
>
> We did not know what the Aborigines thought about it all. We would never have dreamed of asking them. They were tolerated on the face of the earth only to do what we told them and if any of them turned 'cheeky', well, we knew just how to deal with that.

'Keep them under', 'keep them down', 'keep them in their place'. These and similar expressions ran like a litany through the history of colonial Australia and can still be heard in some parts of the country. People who have grown up in metropolitan Australia since the Second World War often fail to appreciate how recently such ideas held sway unchallenged. The novelist Jean Devanny toured the Gulf country in the late 1940s. One of her hostesses told her seriously, 'You've got to keep them down...otherwise they become as cheeky as they are stupid'. She found that the belief that blacks were ruined if whites actually talked to them was 'subscribed to by almost the entire white population of the Gulf'. She was told, 'Apart from giving them orders we don't acknowledge their existence. If you talk to them they will walk over you in no time. Cheeky b——s'. A Queensland politician outlined the problem as he saw it in the local parliament in 1945. He had 'seen the treatment that policemen had given them not because they desired to be cruel, but because they wished to demonstrate to the native that they, the policemen, were their masters. If they had not done that, then the native would have assumed an air of equality or superiority, he would cast off his inferiority complex'.

When the settlers wanted the land they used guns; when they needed cheap labour they put them down and picked up their whips, brandishing them just as freely and with a little interference from the law. 'The only and best way to keep the blacks from annoying you,' a Gippsland settler argued in the 1850s' is to pitch into some of them with a whip and let them know you are the master and not them.' Outback settlers 'did not look upon the flogging of a black girl or the ill treatment of a black boy as anything wrong', a West Australian politician explained in 1905. 'These things to them are only discipline, only means of improving the race.' A Queensland government official touring the south-west of the State in 1902 reported that 'people out here make as light of knocking down a blackfellow with a slip-rail or flogging him with a stock-whip as though it was having a drink'. A West Australian squatter reminded a meeting of colleagues in 1893 that 'a native had a hide, and not an ordinary skin like a human being'. Whips used for official flogging only 'wiped the dust off a native'. A correspondent in the *North West Times* the following year agreed. 'Flogging is all very well in its way,' he observed, 'but a nigger can take a power of it to convince him.' A New South Wales clergyman, with a long history of involvement with the Aborigines, recalled in 1889 that there used to be common maxim among bushmen:'"It is no use to hit a blackfellow with your fist, he won't feel it", and the corollary was that a heavy boot or a stout stick, or an iron bolt or a stock whip, were legitimate and suitable instruments for hortatory or punitive purposes.'

Wild animals or impulsive children

Europeans saw their role as stern parent, racial aristocrat or animal trainer; all three had eager advocates and active practitioners. The belief that the Aborigines were similar to animals and had to be tamed was widespread in nineteenth-century Australia. 'Experience has proved,' a central Queensland settler argued in 1865, 'that as a rule, the Aborigines cannot be civilized, he can [*sic*] only be tamed like wild beasts.' The view found support farther north, a frontier squatter asserting in 1880 that 'if you take a black or a wild animal, young, each is capable of being domesticated and made useful'. Similar ideas were favoured among the educated elite, a writer in the *Melbourne Review* explaining in 1878 that, like animals, the blacks were 'in many respects tameable' but as with animals a taint of savagery remained even when the taming was complete. The prominent West Australian pioneer and explorer D.W. Carnegie discussed the best way of training blacks in his book *Spinifex and Sand*, published in 1898. His experience with blacks had convinced him that

> great tact is necessary in the education of the aboriginals. Neglect turns them into lazy, besotted brutes who are of no use to anybody; too kind treatment makes them insolent and cunning; too harsh treatment makes them treacherous; and yet without a certain amount of bullying they lose all respect for their master, and when they deserve a beating and do not get it, misconstrue tenderheartedness into fear. The 'happy medium' is the great thing; the most useful, contented and best behaved boys that I have seen are those that receive treatment similar to that a highly valued sporting dog gets from a just master...

For every settler who thought the blacks were akin to animals there was at least one who regarded them as children—impulsive, emotional, wilful—who needed stern guidance and prompt correction. 'We call 'em boys,' a Gulf squatter told Jean Devanny in the 1940s, 'even if they are ninety, because they never grow up. They remain boys till they die.' The West Australian Attorney-General told the local parliament in 1892 that he had come to the conclusion that the only way of dealing with Aborigines and other coloured races was to treat them like children. 'You can,' he argued, 'only deal with them effectually, like you deal with naughty children—whip them.' A writer in Roebourne's *North West Times* argued in 1892 that 'the aboriginals of this part of the world are nothing more than children, and require to be treated as such. As a parent has a perfect right to chastise his child, or a schoolmaster his pupil...of couse within due bounds, so the native must be treated if he is to be made a useful servant'.

Another Kimberley pioneer addressed himself to the question of how the small number of white men could maintain themselves among numerically superior Aboriginal tribes. He concluded that moral superiority was the key to success. 'In some such conscious mood,' he wrote, 'we look around on these savages so greatly superior in number, and at once, almost as an instinct, assume the superior tone of command and the attitude of superiority. They are told to minister to the wants and requirements of the numerically insignificant company, to fetch water, light fires, carry wood *etc.*'

Black velvet

Moral superiority was all very well, but most frontiersmen were much more interested in the physical advantages of being in a position of absolute power over the Aborigines. Ready access to black women was one of the attractions of outback life and there is abundant evidence that women were forcibly abducted in all parts of Australia from the early years of settlement until the 1930s and 1940s. The nature of the abduction varied widely. There were casual episodes when women, seen by chance in the bush, were run down and raped in brief, brutal encounters. On other occasions parties of stockmen went out on 'gin hunts' deliberately seeking women for sex. The Normanton Protector of Aborigines explained in 1904 that it was a common practice for Europeans, accompanied by the Aboriginal 'stock boys', to round up 'small mobs of wild natives' and despoil their women. White men frequently took black women away from their kin for long periods and often removed them from their own country. It is likely that many women never found their way back home. To prevent escape women were kept under lock and key, chained, tied up, terrorised. An experienced station manager explained that after they had been taken by force the women were 'even kept in irons until they are too terrified to make any attempt to return to their own tribe'. A Northern Territory policeman reported in 1898 that he felt sure

> that if half the young lubras now being detained (I won't call it kept, for I know most of them would clear away if they could) were approached on the subject, they would say that they were run down by station blackguards on horseback, and taken to the stations for licentious purposes, and there kept more like slaves than anything else. I have heard it said that these same lubras have been locked up for weeks at a time—anyway whilst their heartless persecutors have been mustering cattle on their respective runs. Some, I have heard, take these lubras with them, but take the precaution to tie them up securely for the night to prevent them escaping. Of course, sirs, these allegations are, as you know, very difficult to prove against any individual persons, still I am positive these acts of cruelty are being performed, and I think still worse.

W.E. Parry Okeden, the Queensland Police Commissioner, was concerned with the same problems after touring the north of the colony in 1897, describing the absolute vulnerability of the blacks and the brutality and sadism of their oppressors. On outback stations were to be found 'some of the blackest scoundrels alive—wretches who have wrought deeds of appalling wickedness and cruelty', who thought it 'equal good fun to shoot a nigger at sight or to ravish a gin'.

Catch 'em young

Aboriginal children were kidnapped in all parts of Australia. Boys as young as five and six were taken to be 'bred up to stock work'; girls only a little older were abducted to work as servants and to double as sexual partners. The trade in children probably began in the first half of the nineteenth century and developed rapidly during the settlement of north Australia between 1860 and 1920. Concerned Queensland colonists complained to the government about the practice for 30 or 40 years before anything was done. By then the state had taken the place of private individuals in the wresting of Aboriginal children from their families. A prominent Bowen squatter wrote to the Attorney-General soon after the settlement of the district protesting about the practice of kidnapping children, explaining that six weeks before two Europeans had stolen two boys, locked them in a hut and then taken them to the gold diggings to sell. He feared the practice would continue 'because it pays so well'. Three years later the problem engaged the attention of the Police Commissioner. In his annual report for 1871 he explained that many Aboriginal attacks took place 'on account of settlers carrying off gins and small boys to be made servants'. The police magistrate at Normanton had no hesitation in telling his superiors in Brisbane in 1874 that the stealing of women and children was 'a matter of frequent occurrence here'. Twenty years later a retired northern JP wrote to the *Queenslander* arguing that kidnapping was 'done every day both in the interior and on the coast, and one of the greatest offenders are the police'. Three weeks earlier a German selector on the Daintree River summoned up his inadequate English to write to the government complaining about the local constable who 'on his last parole to Cristol Springs...catched an carried a little gin from Mary River.' The Normanton Protector of Aborigines told his superiors that a large number of settlers had 'an idea that they can trade an aboriginal as they would a horse or bullock...One lady informed me an aboriginal had been left to her by will'. He explained:

> Settlers in outside districts who have plenty of myalls about their country are often importuned by town residents and others to bring them in a boy or a girl. In due time the child arrives. How the children are separated from their parents is a subject of conjecture and surmise. Most people will tell you that the child is better off with Europeans: in my opinion the contention is absurd. Most of the children will bolt (if old enough, and the distance not too great), and then they are termed ungrateful by *their owners*. This practice has been going on for years, and, with the exception of one or two cases personally known to me, without good results to the children: they change masters and mistresses, prostitution and disease follow, they can only speak pidgin English, and finally become pariahs amongst both whites and blacks.

Their hidden nature

While assessing the problems associated with 'letting the blacks in', the editor of *Port Denison Times* warned his readers that the Aborigines would continue to regard the Europeans with deep hostility which would smoulder like a fire ready at any moment to burst into flame. It was a powerful image, combining the anxiety and hatred of frontier warfare, fear that the blacks would ultimately have their revenge, and the conviction that savages were by nature violent and unpredictable. It continued to haunt colonial society long after the fighting ended and among people who had never experienced it. But for the Aborigines it merely added to their difficulties in European society. Whatever they did they couldn't win. If assertive they were cheeky and dangerous and suffered accordingly; if submissive they were merely hiding their true feelings. 'Cringing servility' was the guise assumed to 'conceal inveterate animosity'. Few blacks could ever be fully trusted. 'You can never win their affections to you so as to trust them like any other individual', a Queensland pioneer told a parliamentary committee in 1861. The only reason for their being 'in a state of subordination' was to be found in their dread of the white man; it was not 'respect or love but fear'. The influence of such ideas on European behaviour was illustrated by the experience of a Cape York squatter who spent six years working a remote cattle station with a group of Aboriginal stockmen. Despite the long and close association and sharing of hardship the white man never relaxed his guard. 'So closely did I observe their hidden nature', he later recalled, 'that a revolver generally loaded, was, like my stock whip, my constant companion'. It was, he believed, 'the only way to keep in check their latent evil passions'.

Occasionally Europeans tried to understand the historical reasons for difficulties experienced with Aboriginal workers. Reflecting on his years in the outback, an old squatter wrote in 1901:

> All those who have had an intimate acquaintance and knowledge of the blacks of North Queensland in the pursuit of stockkeeping etc., have been impressed with the total absence of genuine gratitude in the blacks. It is a lamentable truth that kindness produces a diminished respect for the white, and that strict and even harsh treatment will gain for the white man the best services of which they are capable. We therefore find them a striking contrast with the other black races of the world.
>
> It seems a fair means of deduction and elucidation to review the first generation of the white man's occupation of the country and the history relating to it and from it to gather the facts that unmerciful and unnecessary butchery and punishment were often inflicted upon them to bring them into subjection. In other words, the dawn of their civilization presents a picture to the blacks, handed down from their forefathers till now, of a hunted beast of the field whose very existence was only at the white man's will.
>
> In spite of the improved civilization to the present day, the better welfare and conditions of the blacks, and the now most generally humane treatment by the whites, there stands this hereditary barrier of inappreciation and ingratitude—the remembrance of the blood-red dawn of their civilization. The 'contempt' of the white man in the early days of their occupation is now reflected in the 'contempt' of the blacks for every benefit he receives, so that whatever a white man may do to gain fidelity in his black employees, by kind and just reward, he is baulked and baffled in all his endeavours by the traditions of the past—the hereditary hatred of the whites through the butchery of their ancestors.
>
> It is therefore a question of speculation whether the Queensland blacks are the lowest type of blacks in the world, or whether the hereditary biased

prejudice they have against ourselves is the result of inhumanity to man handed down by their forefathers, which may account for the ingratitude of the present generation.

Frontier folklore was replete with the settlers' experiences, prejudices and fears. One of the most commonly told stories was of a squatter and his faithful blackboy who had been together for many years. One day the squatter was walking in front of the Aborigine—some versions have him bending down to drink from a stream and seeing his 'boy's' reflection in the water—when he suddenly turned and found the black about to strike him with an axe. When disarmed and appropriately chastised the 'boy' explained that when he walked behind a white man he was overwhelmed by an uncontrollable urge to kill; it was even more compulsive if the European bent down. The actual words attributed to the 'boy' vary somewhat. One version has him saying: 'Boss never do so again. Close up I have to kill you. What makes me want I no savvy.'

The story appeared in print at least as early as the 1880s and was repeated many times. It is still with us. Invariably the events— or variations of them—were experienced by the narrator or a close friend or relative. The story brought together many white beliefs: blacks were impulsive, instinctive; they could not control their lust for blood; they were never to be trusted; they might at any moment lash out in a frenzy of revenge and long-hidden, long-nursed hatred. There is no doubt that people believed the story and absorbed the lessons it taught. They really did make Aborigines walk or ride in front of them. An interesting example was the behaviour of a Mrs Maunsell, a young English woman who went to live with her husband on a remote north Queensland station. In her reminiscences she explained that on most afternoons she was in the habit of going down to the nearby river with the 'station gins' where they swam, fished and washed clothes. The station blacks had never 'given any trouble' and indeed they were most protective of the 'white missus'. She recalled that 'someone [was] always keeping an eye on me to see I came to no harm'. Yet an old hand had told her when she first arrived in the district: 'Never let a blackfellow get behind you, even a gin; you don't know when he'll take in into his head to belt you over the skull.' Despite what she objectively knew to be true the folk wisdom was too powerful and on her daily walks to the river she always brought up the rear of the procession.

The black bandits

The half-hidden fears running through rural Australia in the post-frontier era came to the surface with fierce intensity if there appeared to be any challenge to white supremacy. This was seen most clearly in the community response to the black bandits or bushrangers who emerged in many parts of the country in the second half of the nineteenth century. Men like Pigeon, Captain and Major in Western Australia, Jimmy and Joe Governor in northern New South Wales and Johnny Campbell and the so called Dora Dora brothers in southern Queensland are fairly well known, but there many other lesser-known figures who at one time or another opened the wounds of white insecurity. The bandits had a good deal in common. They were young men who had grown up since the arrival of the Europeans and were sometimes of mixed parentage. They had some contact with traditional life although the amount varied—Pigeon had a lot, the Governors very little. Most had lived with Europeans and had worked as trackers, troopers or stockmen. They spoke at least some English, were often proficient horsemen and good shots while still retaining much traditional bushcraft.

The European reaction was often out of all proportion to the actual danger presented by the black bandits. But 'savages' who could ride and shoot sent a thrill of horror through many rural communities. Black revenge, long feared, had suddenly arrived—on horseback and with a repeating rifle. All the folk wisdom of the frontier was confirmed. Even apparently civilised blacks could not be trusted. Given half a chance they would revert to a savagery rendered more dangerous by a veneer of sophistication. Writing of the Dora Dora brothers the editor of the *Mackay Mercury* argued in 1894:

These highly civilized blacks, with all their native cunning, and with the knowledge of police service acquired in Victoria, have done as many other aboriginals have done and some assert all such civilized natives will do. Without warning or apparent reason they threw off the garments of civilization, and with that took upon themselves once again the nature of the aboriginal.

The *Mudgee Guardian* noted in 1900 that Joe Governor was well known in town and had never been regarded as a 'blood thirsty character by any means', but the same could be said of most blacks, 'who seem harmless and innocent beings under ordinary circumstances, but when the inbred passions of the savage nature assert themselves and greed and lust is uppermost in their minds, few if any Australian Aborigines will shrink from committing murder.'

Europeans often feared that black bandits would provoke a general rising among the Aborigines. Kimberley settlers were deeply concerned that Pigeon's gang would lead an all-out assault on the stations and small towns. The editor of the *Northern Public Opinion* was convinced that if the police had not carried out a series of ruthless punitive expeditions the blacks 'would have commenced an open war' because the whole of the natives were beginning to take up arms. A writer in the *Pilbara Goldfields News* believed that Pigeon was 'trying to incite the natives to either murder all the whites or endeavour to drive the latter out of the country'. The fear of Kimberley settlers was not surprising given their small numbers and their tenuous hold on the country. Harder to understand was the terror provoked by the Governor brothers over large areas of northern New South Wales in 1900 where settlement was long established and where Aborigines had long been a small and peaceful minority.

While the Governors were on the run many people relived the anxieties of the frontier era 50 or 60 years earlier. Few of those swamped in the wave of terror would have had any experience of racial conflict. Yet in farmhouses across hundreds of square miles of country the guns were taken down, cleaned and anxiously loaded. Those who did not own guns stormed the gun shops. In Mudgee alone £300 worth of firearms were sold in a few days. Families abandoned isolated selections and moved into nearby towns where armed vigilantes patrolled the streets. The editor of the *Dubbo Liberal* detected a 'thorough feeling of alarm', a 'reign of terror' in the community; anxiety had 'even crept into larger towns' and the nerves of men and women were shattered. Fear of insurrection was abroad. People from all over New South Wales wrote to the chairman of the Aborigines Protection Board seeking the removal of local blacks' camps. All the Aboriginal families at Wollar where the Governor relatives lived were taken into custody and then deported to Brewarrina. The *Gulgong Advertiser* reported that great fears were 'entertained locally that there will be a rising among the half-castes in this district, of which, unfortunately there is a large number'.

How long fears of an Aboriginal rising persisted is difficult to say. That they remained so powerful for so long is remarkable in itself. But 40 years after Jimmy Governor died on the gallows an anthropologist was working in the north-west of New South Wales. Investigating an increase in police convictions among the 'half-caste' community she came across the activities of 'a group of head strong white youths who continually provoked the Aborigines to fight'. These youths, she discovered,

> conscious that the white male population has decreased considerably during the war, are obsessed with the idea that they must protect the white women of the town from the aborigines and prevent the aborigines from over-running the town. They are convinced that the incident (an assault on a woman four years before 'at a distance') was the beginning of an Aboriginal campaign to take back the country by murdering the male whites and raping the females.

But while violence, hatred and fear were common characteristics of frontier society there were always Europeans who defended the blacks and fought for their rights. This alternative tradition will now be considered.

—PART II—
Ideology

— 4 —

Black Brothers

A perceptive visitor to New South Wales in the 1840s concluded that there were 'two opinions, diametrically opposite to each other, respecting the character of the Aboriginal population'. One group of settlers, which, he felt obliged to confess, was a 'numerous one', maintained that the blacks were 'not entitled to be looked on as fellow creatures' and adopted the 'harshest and most severe measures towards them'. The second group was composed of 'philanthropic individuals', who were 'deeply impressed with a sense of the sufferings', which had 'accrued to the Aboriginal inhabitants in consequence of the pressure of the European' and viewed 'with horror the inroads made into their possessions'.

Philanthropic individuals

Humanitarian opposition to the destruction of Aboriginal society has yet to receive the attention it deserves. Throughout the nineteenth century there were 'philanthropic individuals' who struggled against the relentless economic, political and intellectual currents which engulfed Aboriginal society. They were often lonely figures, attracting derision as they stood out against the great weight of colonial opinion. Their careers have intrinsic interest but should also be studied to avoid the twin temptations of thinking that there was only one view about the blacks abroad in nineteenth-century Australia or that the debate concerning Aboriginal rights was the invention of the present generation.

Part II: Ideology

Moral outrage

The missionaries and Aboriginal protectors who came to the colonies between 1820 and 1850 were shocked by the bloodshed and outraged by the easy acceptance of racial violence. Writing in 1826 of blacks killed in frontier skirmishes, L.E. Threlkeld wondered 'what must be the aggregate throughout the Colony and what must be the feelings of the Aborigines'? Missionary Tuckfield described himself as one who 'feels keenly and bewails bitterly, the oppressions and abuses to which these poor creatures are subject'. He wrote home to his mission society in 1840, lamenting: 'we still behold the blood of the blackman pouring forth and reeking up to heaven.' Protector Dredge did not know how to 'repress the struggling fire in my bones—while a witness of the awful tragedy in course of performance around me...the widespread devastation, heartless cruelties, wholesale robberies, and endless murder'. After finding the body of an Aborigine shot by Port Phillip settlers, G.A. Robinson thought of the 'helpless wives and offspring, of their deep lamentation...of their bitter indignation against the white and unrelenting persecutors and oppressors'. While travelling with Tasmanian Aborigines he learnt of their fear of the Europeans. 'O God,' he wrote in his journal, 'what has filled these poor unoffending people with such dire apprehension! Can I imagine for a moment that a white man, my fellow man, has murdered their countrymen, their kindred and their friends, has violated their daughters, and has forcibly taken their children...Yes, it is only too true. Regardless of all laws, human or divine, they have imbued their hands in the blood of these poor unoffending people.'

Divine vengeance

Scorned by contemporaries, impotent to halt the ongoing tragedy, the 'philanthropists' warned their fellow colonists that their behaviour was 'raising up a vast treasure of divine vengeance'. 'Can [our] heavenly father look down with any degree of pleasure upon a country located on such terms?' asked William Thomas in 1844. His colleagues had no doubts as to the answer; Dredge expected God to thunder forth with 'righteous retribution of insulted heaven upon the European innovators and oppressors'. Tuckfield urged the settlers to 'avert the wrath of that righteous God who most assuredly heareth the voice of our Brothers blood'; a Victorian settler wrote to an English missionary magazine in 1860 warning the world that when the blacks 'become plaintiffs and we defendants, in Heaven's court of judicature, we have reason to apprehend that the decision will be in their favour'. Late in the century the Jesuit missionary D. McKillop had similar premonitions of ultimate vengeance. While God seemed more distant than 50 years before, a resurgent Asia appeared closer and he looked over the Timor Sea for the source of retribution. The Australians, he wrote in 1893, would 'remember the lessons of history only when an invading people shall have meted out to it the justice which it has shown to the helpless blackman. A hundred years, perhaps hundreds may pass; but with the teeming millions of Asia at our door, who shall say no day of retribution will come upon Australia?'

Emotional commitment

The 'philanthropists' often displayed deep emotional commitment to the blacks even though they were frequently highly paternalistic and more concerned with salvation than physical suffering, more interested in Aboriginal chances on the fields of heaven than their fate on the sunlit plains of Australia. Joseph Orton was moved by 'mingled feelings of pitiful commiseration'; his soul 'truly went out after their welfare'. J.B. Gribble remembered in later life the kindness he received as a child when visiting an Aboriginal camp, and his concern for the blacks, he wrote in 1884, had increased since then as he had been 'confronted with the terrible wrongs to which they have been subjected'. Three years later he told the secretary of the Aborigines Protection Society that 'as I think of the injustice which still continues my heart yearns for the victims. I would fain go to the North at once and settle amongst the poor people...'. On the other side of the continent New South Wales missionary Daniel Matthews penned an appeal on behalf of the Aborigines in 1873, explaining that for seven years 'I have raised my voice, and wielded my pen in endeavour to waken the sympathies of the public on their behalf'. Few identified with the blacks as closely as G.A. Robinson. On one occasion while out in the Tasmanian bush he was with a group of blacks who received news of relatives killed by the settlers. This information, he wrote, 'was the occasion of general lamentation and there was not one aborigine but wept bitterly. My feelings was [*sic*] overcome. I could not suppress them, the involuntary lachryme [=tears] burst forth and I sorrowed for them. Poor unbefriended and hapless people. I imagined myself an Aborigine.'

The great tide of opposition

Missionaries and protectors who took up the Aboriginal cause were always unpopular and their 'Exeter Hall sentimentality' became progressively more unfashionable as the nineteenth century advanced. On the frontier 'nigger lovers' were hated; even in the cities they were regarded as trouble-makers. The first missionaries to arrive in New South Wales met a hostile reception, L.E. Threkeld receiving a warning from the Attorney-General in 1826 that many people would banish him from the colony if they could in order to 'prevent every attempt of a missionary nature among the Blacks'. J.C. Handt reported to the Church Missionary Society a few years later that the popular view was that missionary activity was both useless and a waste of colonial money, but as they could not 'defeat it in that way they make it an object of ridicule'. G.A. Robinson faced strenuous opposition when he began his 'friendly mission' to the Tasmanian blacks in 1829, although with his success in bringing them in from the bush he was able to report that he had 'overcome the great tide of opposition rolling against me with irresistible fury threatening to overwhelm me in its mighty torrent'. Louis Giustiniani, sent to Australia by the London Missionary Society, had less success in Perth. In 1837 he took his defence of the Aborigines into court, but the case was dismissed and after this humiliation 'his few parishioners deserted his church and he became a figure of ridicule'. He left the colony early in 1838. When in the following year William Thomas, the first of the Port Phillip protectors, arrived in Sydney, his appointment was 'assailed in the public journals'; all 'the scurrilous language that could be made use of was employed' in attacking the Imperial Government and the Protectorate, while the 'poor Aborigines were designated as Brutes, Beasts and denied the lineage of humanity'.

A variety of people endeavoured to defend the blacks during the second half of the nineteenth century as the settlers shot their way deeper into Aboriginal Australia and policy passed from the imperial to the local governments in every colony except Western Australia. If anything the humanitarian critics of colonial policies and attitudes were even more unpopular than the first generation of missionaries. In Queensland the Rev. Duncan McNab found in the 1870s that there was a prevailing disposition 'to regard and treat as a fanatic, anyone who shows an inclination to advocate the cause of the Aborigines or to benefit them'. Journalist A.J. Vogan, who wrote a book in 1890 attacking the Native Police Force, found that his profession was closed to him, 'marked man as I now am', he added ruefully. He did little enough for the blacks, he confessed, but it was, he wrote, 'all I could dare to do'. Robert Short, who took up the cause of both the Kanakas and the Aborigines in the 1870s, incurred an 'amount of obloquy, hatred and ill will...inconceivable to any man living in England'. He wrote to a friend in Melbourne: 'I made a thousand enemies, active and unscrupulous but scarcely half a dozen friends...it closed against me in Queensland every avenue for advancement and every channel for employment.' In Western Australia in the 1880s J.B. Gribble attacked the settlers of the north-west, exposing their brutality towards the blacks. As with Giustiniani 50 years before he drew down upon himself the concentrated wrath of the whole colonial establishment. He was shot at in the bush, nearly lynched while sailing to Perth, ostracised and reviled when he arrived there. Attacked in the colony's leading paper, the *West Australian* in 1886, he sued for libel but lost the case and was driven from the colony. 'Anyone,' he wrote in hindsight, 'who disturbs the relationship existing between the settler and his bond servant is a marked man.'

Perhaps the most persistent campaigner in the Aboriginal cause was the West Australian ex-convict David Carly. Having lived for more than a decade in the small towns of the north-west, he was fully aware of, and deeply shocked by, the persistent brutality, the rape, kidnapping, forced labour and murder which characterised the relations between blacks and whites. He began by protesting to the local authorities, took his case to Perth and ended up directing his appeals to the Aboriginal Protection Society in London and the Secretary of State for the Colonies. With all that he got nowhere. He was bashed by the police and jailed in the north, treated with disdain in Perth and ignored or patronised by the polished people in London who may not even have read his less than literate letters. He gave up his livelihood to take his cause to Perth and spent his savings in the process. In 1886 he wrote to the secretary of the Aborigines Protection Society, 'I have defended these murdered Slaves to the best of my ability for 13 years and to my Complete Ruin so I will defend them to the last as I have long since given up all hope of aid from any quarter'. He was still trying five years later to shake the authorities out of their complacency—and their complicity— eventually attacking Lord Knutsford, Secretary of State for the Colonies, with a directness that would have shocked polite society in the colonies. 'Again I write to you,' he thundered in 1891 '...from this land of murder and slavery and fraud. You have upheld and protected those in this colony that have committed far worse crimes than any done in Russia. You have done this with the full knowledge of the terrible acts done to the Native slaves of Western Australia...The same atrocities are still sanctioned by you Lord Knutsford and your Governors of this infamous Colony West Australia.'

The eyes of England

Colonial humanitarians placed great faith in the power of English public opinion and from the 1820s until the 1930s looked to

Britain for support in their campaigns to help the Aborigines. Missionaries kept in constant touch with the metropolitan missionary organisations—Church Missionary, London Missionary and Methodist Missionary Societies; concerned colonists wrote to the London-based Aborigines Protection Society and Anti-Slavery Society, to the English papers or the Colonial Office pressing for action to suppress racial violence. Missionary Orton hoped in 1841 that English opinion would 'respond to the piteous cry of their Australian brethren's blood'. A correspondent wrote to the *Port Phillip Gazette* in 1840 informing fellow colonists that the 'tale of Aboriginal wrongs' was well known abroad. 'The eyes of England are upon us,' he warned. A South Australian clergyman wrote home in 1840 explaining, 'depend upon it if there were not the dread of things being enquired into in England the Natives would be far worse treated than they are'. A Queensland clergyman wrote to the Anti-Slavery Society in 1882 calling for what he called 'British action'—a party of bluejackets put ashore, court martial for the government, flogging for the magistrates. His colleague J.B. Gribble wrote from Perth in 1887, while locked in conflict with the most powerful people in the colony, informing the secretary of the Aborigines Protection Society that he depended 'very much in my efforts in this Colony on the support of your society if that should be relaxed I must give up my endeavours'. Almost 50 years later the Aboriginal rights campaigner M.M. Bennett wrote a similar letter to the same organisation. 'The only help for our poor natives that there is,' she insisted, 'comes from knowledge and public opinion in England—Australians are sensitive about that.'

Scruples on the frontier

Frontier settlers and their urban allies believed that 'nigger lovers' were sentimental idealists, far removed from danger and with no economic interests to defend. Give them a taste of outback life, it was said, and their tune would change. There was some truth in this argument, certainly enough to sustain it for many years. There must have been many settlers, who like the scientist Jukes, began with goodwill and ended up with blood on their hands. Yet there were individuals in many parts of the country who defied frontier opinion and protected the blacks against the police and fellow settlers—a course of action that could never have been easy. The problem was outlined by Daniel Cameron of Planet Downs in central Queensland. He had pioneered the district, developing good relations with the local clans. But pristine racial harmony did not survive the arrival of other squatters and the Native Police. Things went from bad to worse, revenge and counter-revenge culminating in the Aboriginal attack on Cullin La Ringoe Station in 1861. Cameron was placed in an impossible position. He realised that following the killing of the Wills family 'the advocates of treating them little better than inferior animals [would] exult in their extermination', while those like him 'holding different views will be anomalously placed . . . [I]ndividuals of both sexes in their exasperation at this calamitous catastrophe will not scruple to condemn those who afford the natives an asylum or any tolerance as fosterers and abettors of crime'.

Frontier squatters took up a number of different positions between the extremes of protection and indiscriminate destruction. A South Australian pioneer, riding out reluctantly on a punitive expedition, 'drew a loaded pistol at a human breast' for the first time in his life but was pleased that he was 'saved firing'. He was concerned that 'these poor beings' were 'much shot at' but could not see 'how to avoid it'. The Gippsland squatter Meyrick decided in the 1840s that while he would shoot any black he found stealing his sheep 'with as little remorse as he would a wild dog', he drew the line at massacre. 'No consideration on earth,' he wrote, 'would induce me to ride into a camp and fire on them indiscriminately, as is the custom whenever smoke is seen.' Though disgusted by the slaughter, Meyrick did not think he could do anything about it. 'If I could remedy these things,' he explained, 'I would speak loudly though it cost me all I am worth in the world, but as I cannot, I will keep aloof and know nothing and say nothing.'

A different answer to the moral dilemma of the squatter with scruples was provided by G.S. Lang, who became a strong critic of frontier violence after having ridden out with revenge parties in South Australia. Reflecting on the morality of one such punitive expedition in 1846 he wrote: 'No mischief was done, but my conclusion afterwards was that if anyone had been killed I would have been a murderer, and came to the determination to which I have adhered, never to shoot a black unless in circumstances which would justify me in shooting a white.' It took even more moral courage to actually resist the murderous intentions of one's neighbours and colleagues. Ernest Thorn, an old Queensland pioneer, recalled in 1901 how he had been ostracised for opposing the indiscriminate violence of fellow settlers. 'I once got myself a bad name,' he wrote,

> which followed me for many years, and rose up in judgement against me in unexpected places, as a dangerous man, because of an objection to allow a neighbouring squatter and his men the use of my boat to cross a wide river for the purpose of making a night attack on a tribe of blacks, who, it was supposed—I found there was no evidence at all—had visited the run, and killed and partially eaten a bullock. Amongst the tribe were men who had done me many acts of kindness, merely from a natural good-heartedness. One of them was as fine a sample of a man as I have seen on three continents. He was a poet, an orator, and a philosopher. He had saved my life on an occasion. We had been travelling companions in places where never a white man had previously trod; we had exchanged blood, which gave me all the privileges of his tribe; and, in short, there was a friendship between us such as one only chances on at rare intervals. And because I would not allow this man and his relatives to be assassinated in cold blood, my name was covered with opprobrium, and I was branded as a dangerous man, who was false to his race, and unworthy of the confidence of decent white men.

Humble protectors

Defenders of the Aborigines were not all well-educated middle-class gentlemen although the accessibility of their views in books and newspapers might suggest a correlation between moral sensibility and polite manners. In more obscure historical documents there are numerous references to humble colonists who defended, and even befriended, the blacks. A selector living on the Daintree River in north Queensland wrote to the government in 1893 protesting at the treatment handed out to the local blacks, for in his '43 years experiense among the Australien Abiriganols i never saw friendly blacks treated lik some have treated them here' (sic). A miner on the remote Coen field sent a telegram to the Brisbane Aborigines Protection Society in 1894, with the brief but alarming message: 'Aborigines are being hunted here like dingoes what shall or can I do to protect them.' John Cook, another miner, was 'not a bumtious sort of an individual' but he had taken the blacks' part for fifteen years and had, as he explained in a letter to the Queensland Colonial Secretary in 1891, 'stood a good deal of abuse from people on account of defending the black people or rightful owners of Australia'. J.C. Hogflesch was another person who wanted to help the north Queensland blacks. He described himself in a letter to the Colonial Secretary in 1889: 'I Am Australian not born Moderate Egucation a thorough Bushman and last not least can understand the Blacks language and Yabber to them' (sic). He had written to the government: 'on the behalf of the Cruell Uuse and Abused Race on Face of the Earth this day If A Book was Written on Uusiage thease Unfortunate Peopol and the way they have been treated it Form one of the Blackest Pages in the History of Queensland' (sic). Hogflesch had lived for 25 years north of Rockhampton and had carried the mail in some of the most remote parts of north Queensland. He had discovered the bodies of a couple killed by the blacks and as a result: 'happened unfortunately to be Swarn In as an Espichial Constabel and was Pressent at the Scull Camp Massicere it was nothing else. I was not a Participator I could not do it' (sic). William Thomas, the Port Phillip Protector of Aborigines, noted a similar story in his journal in 1845 about a Sergeant Bennett, who was dismissed from the Native Police Force by the Superintendent Mr Dana, who severely censured him:

> for not killing the blacks...he remark you have no idea how I have been treated because I have endeavoured to pacify the blacks and not kill and slay all I met with yes, sir I do believe had I slaughtered the bodies of Natives as I occasionally met them that I should never have been dismissed from the Police and in my present state would have had some pay from Govt.—But it is now a great consolation to me that I have never shed the blood of a black, I have been in great danger often, but always managed by

parlying with them to accomplish the object I had in view. But you know not Sir what I have had to contend with from Mr Dana. (sic)

Of one blood

Underlying much of the activity and attitudes of clergymen and missionaries was their belief in the traditional Christian view of the creation, that all human beings, regardless of colour or culture, were descended from Adam and Eve. They were all created in the image of God, all alike candidates for salvation and proper subjects for evangelisation. The 'philanthropists' took as their central theme the biblical text 'God hath made of one blood all the nations of the world'. It was quoted, and misquoted, over and over again, and was the single most important buttress to racial equality in colonial Australia, used in agitation against frontier violence and in favour of humanitarian and missionary activity. E.S. Parker, the Port Phillip Protector, explained in 1854 that man 'whatever be the varieties of his colour, his social grade, or civil condition, stands forth as the CREATURE OF GOD, the offspring of a common parent, the inheritor of a nature identical with his own, in its origins, its capabilities and its destination.'

Much had happened since the Creation. The conventional view was that the Aborigines, and other similar people, had suffered a slow process of deterioration in the centuries of wandering the face of the earth. By transgression, the Rev. Atkins wrote in 1869, 'the Divine image was marred: the human spirit became a ruin'. Yet for all their debasement, a West Australian clergyman insisted in 1867, they were 'brethren according to the flesh'; though 'fearfully sunk' they were 'partakers of the same human nature as that which the Son of God took upon him'. While different in complexion, features and language 'one and all are to be regarded and treated as brethren'. G.A. Robinson looked upon the Tasmanians 'as brethren not, as they have been maligned, savages'. He expanded on the point in his journal in 1830: 'No, they are my brethren by creation. God has made of one blood all nations of people, and I am not ashamed to call them brothers. They have been represented as only a link between the human and brute species, and nothing more false could proceed from the lips of men—they are equal if not superior to ourselves.'

Such ideas were dangerous in a society engaged in dispossession and destruction. If they were taken to heart the frontiersman who shot blacks was both sinner and murderer, guilty in this life, damned in the next. The 'philanthropist's' attack on frontier morality was well illustrated in a powerful sermon delivered by a Rev. John Saunders in Sydney just before the Myall Creek trials in 1838. His text, Isaiah 26:21, was carefully chosen: 'For behold the Lord cometh out of his place to punish the inhabitants of the earth for their iniquity: the earth also shall disclose her blood, and shall no more cover her slain.' The central message was clear—the black was man and brother. 'Does it seem strange,' he asked his congregation, 'to speak of the majesty of the New Hollanders, wilt thou despise the Saviour of the world, then despise not him who sprang out of the same stock, despise not him for whom Christ died, the Saviour died as much for him as he did for you, and he now reigns in Glory as much for him as he does for you, now by every sentiment of humanity and love you are bound to love him, to admit him into your fraternity and to treat him as a fellow man.'

Thunder from the pulpit, pleading in the press, did little to ameliorate the black's long agony. But the assertion of racial equality—even with qualifications—set up a powerful poll of opposition to the folk wisdom of the frontier, producing debate in the community, division in the family, tension within the individual. The conflict of opinion was illustrated in the letters exchanged between the engaged couple Alexander Crawford and Lillie Matthews in the 1880's. He was running a remote sheep station in the Murchison District of Western Australia; she was on the family farm in Victoria. In his letters he explained a situation common to many frontier districts. Conflict with the blacks was endemic. The whites 'were in arms' throughout Crawford's sojourn. There were numerous 'nigger hunts', much anxiety. Lillie Matthews was deeply disturbed both by the immediate dangers and the brutalising effect of the frontier environment. 'I do wish you had not so much to do with the blacks', she wrote:

It is a dreadful thing to be continually hunting down ones fellow creatures, for they are our fellow creatures, and have precious and immortal souls. Oh my darling keep your hands free from your fellow creature's blood. For you to need to fire on them makes me feel miserable...Be very careful in your use of firearms my darling, poor degraded wretches though they are, yet in God's sight they are precious, Christ died for them as well as us, and for this reason we should protect them as far as lies in our power.

We are, I know, apt to look down on them as something little better than beasts, but remember...they have souls as well as we, and don't let them rise up in judgement against us in the last great day. Keep your hands free from human creatures' blood, or how can we expect God's blessing to rest on us...We will not prosper if we disregard his commandments.

Enlightenment philosophy

Other tributaries—of lesser importance than holy scripture—fed the belief in racial equality in early colonial Australia. Enlightenment philosophers stressed the universality of reason and attributed racial and cultural differences to the influence of physical environment and social customs. The Scottish moral philosophers Adam Ferguson, Hugh Murray and James Dunbar advocated such ideas in the British Isles during the first generation of Australian settlement, Murray arguing in 1808 that it could be laid down as a fundamental principle 'that between any two great portions of the human species...there exists no radical distinction, that the total amount of moral and intellectual endowments originally conferred by nature, is altogether or very nearly the same; and that the wide differences which we observe arise wholly from the influence of external circumstances'. The influence of such ideas can be discerned in books written about the Australian colonies. The English translator of Labillardiere's *Voyage in Search of La Perouse* published in 1802 provided a classic summary of the enlightenment view of the indigenous people of the Pacific. The moral philosopher, he wrote in his preface, sees 'savage life everywhere diversified with a variety, which, if he reason fairly, must lead him to conclude that what is called the state of nature, is, in truth, the state of a rational being placed in various physical circumstances which have contracted or expanded his faculties in various degrees'. Watkin Tench, the marine captain at the first settlement, reminded his readers that only by the 'fortuitous advantage of birth alone' did the Europeans possess superiority over the Aborigines, that 'untaught unaccommodated man, is the same in Pall Mall as in the wilderness of New South Wales'. Dawson, the director of the Australian Agricultural Company, emphasised in 1830 that it was essential when making an assessment of the Aborigines to 'distinguish between the force of habit and what they call the nature of the people'. Local situation and climate, he explained, 'have more to do with the civilization of savage tribes than has generally been imagined'. Cunningham agreed; writing four years later in his book *Two Years in New South Wales* he noted that civilisation depends more upon 'the circumstances under which man is placed than upon any innate impulse of his own'. We may, he asserted, 'in a great measure impute their present low state of civilization, and deficiency in the mechanical arts, to the nature of the country they inhabit, the kind of life they lead, and the mode of government they live under'.

The noble savage

The noble savage was a fashionable figure in Europe when Australia was first settled. Cook's final assessment of the Aborigines was fully in the mode. Writing at the end of his voyage along the east coast he observed:

> From what I have seen of the Natives of New Holland they may appear to some to be the most wretched People upon Earth; but in reality they are far more happier than we Europeans, being wholly unacquainted not only with the superfluous, but with the necessary Conveniences so much sought after in Europe, they are happy in not knowing the use of them...The Earth and Sea of their own accord furnishes them with all things necessary for life. They covet not Magnificent Houses; Household stuff etc; they live in a Warm and fine Climate, and enjoy every Wholesome Air...in short they seemed to set no Value upon anything of their own nor any one Article we could offer them. This in my opinion Argues, that they think themselves provided with all the necessarys of Life, and that they have no Superfluities.

But frontier life was not conducive to idealisation of indigenous lifestyles, and in Europe itself the noble savage slipped from fashion between 1810 and 1830. But traces remained even in the colonies. It was common until the 1840s to regard traditional life as one of freedom and liberty. The failure to adopt European ways—to settle—was seen as springing from a positive choice in favour of a freer way of life in the forest. Oliver Fry, the Commissioner of Crown Lands at the Clarence River, explained in 1848 that their decision to stay in the bush was not due to any 'supposed natural intellectual inferiority'. 'Their present barbarism,' Bishop Broughton argued in 1836, was not the result of 'any unconquerable dullness of intellect, but merely to their love of erratic liberty', to their 'wish to be entirely unshackled in their movement', as W.H. Breton explained in his book *Excursions in New South Wales, Western Australia and Van Diemens Land* published in 1833. The problem for those seeking to assimilate the blacks was that there was, according to the surgeon Peter Cunningham in 1834, 'something so irresistably captivating in a wild, roaming life'. In 1850 the Commissioner of Crown Lands on the Darling Downs reported that their 'roving life still has charms for them far too powerful for any inducement that the habits and customs of civilization can offer to overcome'. Robert Dawson, of the Australian Agricultural Company, explained in 1830 that it was understandable that the blacks around the fringes of European settlement manifested 'an unwillingness to yield up a life of liberty in such a climate, and in the forest which supports them without labour and toil, quietly placing their necks in the yoke of servitude, at the bidding of men whose bodies differ from them only in colour'.

Personal experience

Belief in racial equality dwindled in colonial Australia. Persistent conflict on the frontier, Aboriginal destitution and depopulation, shifting intellectual currents—all played their part. But many individuals defied the growth of communal contempt partly through continuing adherence to the ideas already discussed, though they became increasingly unfashionable, but also as a result of direct experience of Aboriginal society as explorers, overlanders, employers, missionaries, inquisitive neighbours. They accepted the evidence of their eyes and ears in preference to popular racial theories. 'We who saw them with our own eyes,' wrote the Jesuit missionary Strele at the end of the century, 'were astounded at what we saw the blacks were capable of.' At much the same time the veteran Protestant missionary Daniel Matthews was telling a meeting of Adelaide's Royal Geographical Society about his long experience with the Aborigines of the upper Murray River, in a speech where experience and dogma clashed head on. The blacks, he explained, displayed 'a degree of intelligence that would scarcely be expected in a people so inferior'.

Developing appreciation of the Aborigines often took place in the teeth of contemporary opinion and even the individual's own preconceptions. After meeting Aborigines around Port Essington in the Northern Territory, T.B. Wilson concluded that far from being 'untameable savages as originally represented', the blacks were in reality 'a mild and merciful race of people'. In a paper prepared for Britain's Anthropological Institute in 1884 Fred Bonney, an old Darling River pioneer, protested that the Aborigines were 'often spoken of as the lowest type of humanity'. It was, he said, 'a libel on the whole of them and I am positive it is so as regards the tribes I know best'. He provided information about the Darling River clans in the hope that

> others who have had like opportunities, will do the same, so that sufficient information may be brought forward to prove their race to be better, nobler, and more intellectual than is generally believed to be by those who have not lived among any of the tribes. All who have done so, and taken the trouble to learn something of their language, so as to better understand them, must have formed a good opinion of them.

While reflecting on his experiences during the early years of settlement at Port Phillip, Edward Cur. remarked that 'notwithstanding many differences' between whites and Aborigines, their 'sympathies, likes and dislikes were very much what ours would have been if similarly situated'. This fact, he explained, 'only gradually dawned on me, as I had somehow started with the idea that I should find the Blacks as different from the whitemen in mind as they are in colour'.

Aboriginal Protector William Thomas attacked the 'ridiculous accounts' and 'humiliating ideas' of the blacks which were abroad in the community. 'I can bear testimony,' he explained, 'to their being a rational, reflective and observant race, minutely upon earthly movements and well conversant with the starry heavens, acquainted with all the notions of the civilized' (*sic*).

During the 1820s a representative of the Methodist Missionary Society investigated the condition of the Aborigines in New South Wales. In a report to the society he explained that, from every source he could collect information, he was led to believe 'that of all human beings, the New Hollander was the most truly wretched, pitiable and ignorant neither having mental energy nor natural resources'. It took him a long time to give up these ideas, 'so prejudiced was I', he confessed, 'and bigotted to this opinion'. However, contact with the Aborigines brought a dramatic change of heart. He explained to the society, 'But now that I have lived with them, and have had some opportunity of observing their character my opinions have undergone, on the best possible grounds, an entire change. I consider them intelligent and acute, grateful and affectionate'.

Brilliant intellects

A number of settlers in contact with the Aborigines rejected the widespread view that they were mentally inferior to Europeans. George Grey, explorer and Governor of South Australia, thought the blacks 'as apt and intelligent as any other race of men I am acquainted with'. Bishop Polding considered that they 'possessed a very considerable degree of natural intellect and no person could possess finer feeling of sensibility'. Missionary William Watson 'never found any deficiency' of intellect 'in reference to things with which they are acquainted'. He looked forward, in 1832, to the time when they would 'equal if not outvie some of the now civilized and polished nations of Europe'. Writing of his experience in South Australia in 1846, Dutton observed that he had come across 'examples of great intelligence' among the local Aborigines. The editor of the Adelaide *Examiner* remarked, in 1843, that several of the local blacks were 'as intelligent samples of the human race as are usually met with' and one could take 'a thousand individuals of the lower orders either in England or Ireland' without being able to find 'one in ten their equal in common sense'. A clergyman living near the mouth of the Murray asserted in 1840 that he would 'boldly affirm anywhere any time that finer formed men and more brilliant intellects are not to be found than some among the Natives around us—some there are of an opposite class and so there are in England and elsewhere.'

A real commonwealth

Aspects of Aboriginal society called forth admiration—often involuntary—from the settlers who came to understand how it worked. 'There [*sic*] kindness to each other surpasses all commendation,' wrote William Thomas in 1840, 'they look only for the day and what the day brings forth is divided—Oh if whitemen were so how many tears would be wiped from the widows and orphans eyes.' After witnessing a formal exchange of loaves of bread between Yarra and Goulburn blacks in 1844, he noted in the margin of his journal, 'real commonwealth'. Following a large ceremonial fight Thomas noticed that the wounded on each side cared for former opponents. 'To see opposite tribes sucking each others wounds,' he remarked 'is an affection not equalled in civilized sympathy.' The German missionary H. Meyer was impressed with the way in which the Aborigines treated their children, who were 'brought up with great care, more than generally falls to the lot of children of the poor class of Europeans'. He observed in 1846 that when a child cried 'it is passed from one person to another and caressed and soothed, and the father will frequently nurse it for several hours together'.

Other observers admired the way in which the Aborigines cared for the elderly. In 1821 the Methodist missionry S. Leigh remarked that 'their treatment of aged and infirm should be emulated by Christians'. The central Queensland squatter Robert Christisson recalled an incident in the 1860s soon after he had established himself on his Lammermoor run. He rode out one day looking for Aborigines whom he believed had been stealing his sheep. Seeing two men carrying a suspicious-looking bundle tied to two saplings he galloped towards them. They put the bundle down and fled in terror. Christisson dismounted and examined the bundle, finding to his amazement 'a very old crippled woman lying among kangaroo skins; her hair was quite white and her teeth were worn to the gums, but she looked well nourished and well cared for...[She] had been born deformed and had been carried about in a litter and cared for all her life, members of the tribe taking it in turn to carry her'. Christisson was surprised and moved, feeling that 'never could he think ill of a race that tended a fragile, useless old cripple with such loving care'.

Craft and cunning

Occasionally settlers were forced to admire the skill and determination which underpinned Aboriginal resistance. Tasmanian blacks displayed 'a cunning and superiority of tactics which would not disgrace some of the greatest military characters'. Forty years later a miner on north Queensland's Hodgkinson field complained that the local blacks were 'so thoroughly cunning they seem to have studied strategy in the school of a sable Von Moltke'. Appreciation of the intelligence of black resistance forced some Europeans to reassess their general view of Aboriginal ability. The editor of Hobart's *Colonial Times*, reporting details of an Aboriginal foray in 1831, observed that in this instance 'as in many others' they had 'evinced a degree of craft and cunning', indicating that they were not that 'inferior order of beings which we have so often been told'. His colleague, writing in the *Hobart Town Courier* a few months earlier, observed that when taking action against the settlers the black was using the 'natural weapons of his condition':

and it must be acknowledged that he does use them, and that with wonderful dexterity. Sir Joseph Banks and the other philosophers who first visited this island to make comments on its Aboriginal people, called them an inferior and degraded race merely through ignorance. The being who appeared a naked, rude, comfortless savage to them, had nevertheless intellectual powers perhaps commensurate with those of his learned visitors but which being directed in a different channel could not be discerned. The judgement of each party on the other was no doubt reciprocal and because the habits and enjoyments of each were entirely opposite, they were prejudiced accordingly.

Part II: Ideology

Linguistic lessons

Settlers who made a serious study of Aboriginal languages were often deeply impressed by what they discovered. Tuckfield, the Methodist missionary at Port Phillip, totally rejected the idea 'so frequently pronounced' that Aboriginal languages were deficient in structure and vocabulary. He had never heard the blacks 'at a loss to express their thoughts or emotions, or to describe any of the qualities of matter with which they are acquainted'. Indeed the language he studied was, he observed, in 1840, 'copious and I might add very significant combining great power with simplicity'. Half a century later the Jesuit missionaries on the Daly River reached a similar conclusion. It was, wrote McKillop, 'a beautiful language' abounding in 'highly metaphysical distinctions unknown' to English. His colleagues agreed. It was a 'very perfection' in the view of Strele. It had, according to Corath, 'distinctions between concepts which our classical languages do not make, and a richness of verb form which surpasses even the Greek'. James Dawson, who spent a long time recording the dialects of Victoria's Western District, was deeply impressed by his Aboriginal informants and their dedication to the task. They showed 'the utmost anxiety to impart information' and the 'most scrupulous honesty in conveying a correct version of their own language as well as the languages of neighbouring tribes'. During the tedious process of recording, occupying several years, in the 1870s, Dawson found that

> my previous good opinion of the natives fell far short of their merits. Their general information and knowledge of several dialects—in some instances four, besides fair English—gratified as well as surprised me, and naturally suggested a comparison between them and the lower classes of white men. Indeed it is very questionable if even those who belong to what is called the middle class, notwithstanding their advantages of education, know as much of their own laws, of natural history, and of the nomenclature of the heavenly bodies, as the Aborigines do of their laws and of natural objects . . . [T]heir moral character and modesty . . . compare favourably with those of the most highly cultivated communities of Europe. People seeing only the miserable remnants to be met with about the white man's grog-shop may be inclined to doubt this; but if these doubters were to be brought into close communication with the Aborigines away from the means of intoxication, and were to listen to their guileless conversation, their humour and wit,

and their expressions of humour and affection for one another, those who are disposed to look upon them as scarcely human would be compelled to admit that in general intelligence, common sense, integrity, and the absence of anything repulsive in their conduct, they are at least equal, if not superior, to the general run of white men.

Bushcraft

From the earliest years of settlement the Europeans took Aborigines with them on journeys into the bush and were often totally dependent on their black guides to find water, to find food, even to find the way. The brilliance of black bushcraft was commonly attributed to instinct and therefore not worthy of particular admiration. But the more perceptive travellers appreciated that they were the beneficiaries of an ancient and intellectual heritage, one black in a party being worth 'half a dozen white men, for their sagacity, and capacity in finding and tracking cattle, and general knowledge of locality'. While recounting his expedition into central Queensland in 1846 T.L. Mitchell remarked that although the blacks had been described as the 'lowest in the scale of humanity' he found those who accompanied him 'superior in penetration and judgement to the white men composing my party'. An early Port Phillip settler, appreciating the value of Aboriginal guides, remarked that they 'not only guided us accurately, but taught us many lessons in bush craft...which we should never have picked up otherwise'. 'In my own experience of work in the bush,' a West Australian pioneer observed, 'progress would not have been half what it was if we had not the natives with us.'

Adaptability

Generous-minded settlers appreciated the speed with which Aborigines picked up those aspects of European civilization which interested or had value to them. Edward Curr noted that the blacks who normally spoke a handful of dialects had much greater linguistic skills than the majority of Europeans and picked up a working knowledge of English in a matter of weeks. William Thomas found in the 1840s that all the 'men and women under 25 could speak, pronounce and understand English better than half the Scotch and Irish emigrants'. The speed with which blacks picked up the skills needed in rural industry was noted by a magistrate living in West Australia's York district. 'They are a most intelligent race,' he wrote in the 1860s. 'It is wonderful to see how readily the bush natives can comprehend and adapt themselves to our habits and pursuits. He soon comes to ride, to shoot, to reap, even to plough and to take care of sheep, and keep them free from scab.'

The impact of ideology

The 'philanthropic individuals' who took up the Aboriginal cause were well aware that they were swimming against the tide and that fellow colonists held them in contempt. They appreciated too that the conflict over ideas grew out of and was shaped by the struggle over land, that racism was as functional for the frontier squatter as the Colt revolver. One cleared the land, the other cleared the conscience. Bishop Polding was convinced that the blacks were killed 'under the influence of principles and ideas which parties to soothe remorse or conscience...are willing to adopt'. A Royal Navy captain, who visited Australia in the 1840s, believed that the settlers 'started with an erroneous theory which they found to tally with their interests' and to relieve them from 'the burden of benevolence and charity. That the Aborigines were not men, but brutes, was their avowed opinion, and what cruelties followed from such a doctrine'. The first step in oppression, a correspondent in the Sydney paper *The Colonist* observed in 1838, 'is to degrade the objects of our hate, and, if it be possible, to convince ourselves, or others, that the beings we have to do with, are not entitled to the full rights and privileges of humanity; and the oppressors will be still more successful if he can assert that his proposed victims are not men'. Protector William Thomas remarked that the 'vile truth' propagated about the blacks during the 1840s had 'no doubt been the cause of the Sang froidness in the civilized breast to treat them as brutes' having obliterated the ties of humanity and 'so seard [*sic*] the conscience as to encourage their extinction by actual violence...'. The missionary Threlkeld was similarly convinced of the crucial role of racist ideology. 'If sophistry and worldly philosophy could but succeed,' he wrote in 1838, in persuading people that the Aborigines were 'merely brutes, without reasoning faculties and incapable of instruction', the natural consequences would be that 'to shoot them dead would be no more a moral evil, than the destroying of rats by poison'. James Dredge thought that the racism of the Port Phillip pioneers was calculated

> to mislead the thoughtless, gratify the vicious, and push on the reckless to the perpetration of deeds alike disgraceful to civilized men and pregnant with the most fearful consequences to the Aborigines. For if it could be satisfactorily shown that the native blacks are anything but men, then they who may have been instruments of their extinction, would be exonerated from the hideous stain of blood; and those who may be tempted to resort to exterminating means, will find nothing in their character which can claim for them the exercise of tender and sparing mercy.

The claims of capital

The philanthropists who came up against powerful opponents realised that they faced both the influence of capital and the ideas favourable to its appreciation. 'Remember Greed is at the bottom of it all,' a clergyman explained in a letter to the Anti-Slavery Society in 1883, 'greed is Queensland's God.' David Carly wrote to England from Western Australia the following year expressing similar sentiments about his colony. 'The whole system of Horrors as is done to the Natives,' he asserted, would continue until the 'Home Government send someone here that has got a mind that will not be ruled by a few Settlers whose whole Heart is set on getting Gold by any means.' J.B. Gribble explained that public opinion was against him in his battle with the northern settlers because people 'dare not go against the men of money and political influence'. Alfred Davidson, who campaigned tirelessly on behalf of both Queensland Aborigines and Kanakas, explained in a letter to the Aborigines Protection Society in 1870 that 'a few of us have endeavoured to do our best under many disadvantages: public opinion has not the power here that it has in England: the Employers have a clear hold on newspapers: the claims of capital are felt'. But perhaps the bluntest assessment of the situation was made by L.E. Threlkeld in 1826. 'No man,' he observed, 'who comes to this Colony and has ground and cattle and corn can dispassionately view the subject of the blacks, their interest says annihilate the race.'

The pastoral industry was the single most important agent in the destruction of Aboriginal society and the squatters were often the most persistent advocates of racist theories. 'It is from the Squatter then,' wrote a Gladstone resident in his diary in the 1850s, 'that opinion has arisen respecting the Australian Natives and I am not singular in this statement.' Stupidity and want of intelligence were 'the characteristics given unjustly and pray may I ask who gives these characteristics, who in his opinion stamps the Native at once as a brute and denies him all human intelligence...[who,] to the contrary, will not consider him in the light of human being, and shoots him like an ox, who but the Squatter, whose advantage it is to clear his territory of Natives.

There, were, then, 'two opinions, diametrically opposed to each other', respecting the characters of the Aborigines. One was held by 'philanthropic individuals' who regarded the Aborigines as equals although disadvantaged by social customs and environmental constraints; the other was accepted by a majority of settlers who viewed the blacks as less than human and adopted harsh and severe measures towards them. As the nineteenth century progressed and settlement expanded, belief in racial equality diminished because of developments both in Australia and overseas. Not that there was more objective evidence to support the second opinion; seen from today's perspective both reason and reality resided with the philanthropists. But the concept of racial equality was inconvenient in a society bent on dispossession and a threat to all those individuals and institutions with capital invested in Australia. 'Interest,' observed a writer in the *Sydney Gazette* in 1824, 'is a powerful machine to regulate opinions.' Governor Gipps put his finger on the central issue when he assured G.A. Robinson that while the government favoured humanitarian measures nothing was to hinder the improvement of the colony. That improvement was highly dependent on the easy and continuing acquisition of Aboriginal land. The ideas, relating both to the Aborigines and the nature of European settlement, which assisted that process must now be examined.

– 5 –

Savages

The British were convinced that the Aborigines were savages even before the settlement of Australia, and they knew all about savages. For centuries a composite picture of the savage had been building up in the European imagination. When in the middle of the seventeenth century the English philosopher Thomas Hobbes described the primitive condition of man as 'solitary, poore, nasty, brutish and short' he was summarising both 'a large body of literature and the existing state of informed opinion'. Even when the educated elite were toying with visions of noble savages 'the same infavourable conception of the brutal and debased savage was still afloat in the parish ethnology of Britain'. The image was impervious to experience; it was much the same in 1888, after a century of settlement, as it had been in the first few weeks at Sydney Cove. In their writing the settlers gave vent to their feelings of contempt, disgust and horror. The Aborigines around Sydney were, a First Fleet surgeon wrote, 'altogether a most stupid insensible set of beings'. They were, another early settler argued, 'the most irrational and ill-formed Human beings on the Face of the Earth'. 'In a word they compose altogether the most loathsome and disgusting tribe on the surface of the globe,' asserted a visitor to the colony in the first years of the nineteenth century, 'indeed they appeared altogether the most stupid and insensible race of men I have ever seen.' A writer in the *Hobart Town Gazette* in 1825 referred to the 'wild and gothic minded savages cradled in wilderness, amidst the horrors of houseless and garnerless vagrancy'. In 1841 one of the German missionaries at Moreton Bay expressed his personal disgust at the people he hoped to 'save'. Whether the physical or moral condition of 'these children of the forest' was considered, the picture presented was 'one of gross darkness and misery. Their God is their belly; their will, or rather their passions, are their law, as long as they are able through violence and cruelty to maintain their point, and the testimony of the Scripture, that "The dark places of the earth, are full of habitations of cruelty", finds in their case an awful vindication'. Fellow missionary William Ridley was scarcely more complimentary, observing in 1856 that 'it had been remarked that they were the most degraded and lowest race in the world. It must be admitted, as far as he knew, that in some points they were singularly, and also uniquely defective, as if some features of human nature were wanting, or else they were much demented'. Queensland's Select Committee on the Native Police Force, reporting in 1861, noted that 'credible witnesses show that they are addicted to cannibalism; that they have no idea of a future state, and are sunk in the lowest depths of barbarism'. In a lecture to the Rockhampton School of Arts in 1865, a Mr White told his audience that whatever the origins of the blacks, 'all travellers and historians agree that a more abject race never dwelt upon the face of the earth'. W.H. Willshire, in charge of the police in central Australia during the 1880s, explained in 1891 that 'from a very long experience of the blacks, and careful observation of their character and habits [I] cannot speak much in their favour. They are ungrateful, deceitful wily and treacherous. They are indolent in the extreme, squalid and filthy in their surroundings, as well as disgustingly impure among themselves'.

The great chain of being

The great chain of being was an influential concept at the time of Australian settlement and helped shape attitudes towards the Aborigines throughout the first half of the nineteenth century. It was a means of arranging all living matter in an ordered, hierarchical pattern beginning with the simplest creatures, ascending through the primates to man who was in turn overawed by beings of the spirit world. The great chain was referred to by the celebrated anatomist Charles White in an address to Manchester's

Literary and Philosophical Society in 1795 during which he observed:

> everyone who has made Natural History an object of study must have been
> led occasionally to contemplate the beautiful gradation that subsists amongst
> created beings, from the highest to the lowest. From man down to the
> smallest reptile, whose existence can only be discovered by the microscope,
> Nature exhibits to our view an immense chain of beings, endued with
> various degrees of intelligence and active powers, suited to their stations in
> the general system.

During the eighteenth century it became common to distinguish
different types—or races—of men and to arrange them in hierarchical sequence. The Europeans were invariably placed on the
top, with non-Europeans strung out down the chain till savages
merged with the more advanced monkeys. Black people were
always placed at the bottom of the chain, White arguing that, 'in
whatever respect the African differs from the European, the parti-
cularity brings him nearer to the ape'. It was as if a place had been
reserved on the great chain for the Aborigines in advance of the
settlement of the continent.

Such ideas of racial hierarchy were carried to the Australian
colonies and were widely disseminated. Many of the colonists
who commented on the Aborigines in the 1830s and 1840s were
clearly influenced by the concept of the great chain of being. In
1832 Henderson argued that the blacks fully deserved their reputation 'of ranking the lowest of the nations in the order of civilization'; two years later Cunningham placed tham 'at the very zero
of civilization, constituting in a measure, the connecting link
between man and the monkey tribe'. In 1841 Arden insisted that
they could 'only be placed in the great animal family as one
degree above brute creation'; later in the forties Byrne described
them as the 'lowest race in the scale of humanity'.

Settlers and officials who did not necessarily accept these ideas
were fully aware of their popularity. George Grey, explorer and
Governor of South Australia, observed that the blacks were commonly 'represented as a very inferior race, in fact as one occupying
a scale in creation which nearly places them on the level with the
brutes'; Tasmania's Governor Arthur noted that they had 'been
designated the lowest order of human beings, removed but one

shade from brutality'. A New South Wales settler who prepared a report on the Aborigines for the Methodist Missionary Society in 1826 was struck by the 'absurd opinions so frequently urged that the Aborigines are a nondescript race, a new production, forming a link in the grand chain between the human and brute creation; Human indeed outwardly but without mind, Soul or intellectual powers'. Twenty years later the Port Phillip Protector James Dredge similarly found that

> in almost every reference to the moral condition of the Aborigines of Australia which has obtained publicity, they are represented as a race of beings either entirely destitute of rational mind, and thus ranging only at the head of the order of inferior animals; or, if allowed to be men at all, are described as possessing such diminished mental capabilities, as exhibit such a humiliating specimen of the degradation of which human nature is susceptible, as to indicate their position at the very lowest point in the scale of rationality.

Comparisons between blacks and monkeys were commonplace especially with orang-outangs, who were thought to be closest to mankind on the great chain. James Dawson, the manager of the Australian Agricultural Company, noted in 1830 that fellow colonists thought that the blacks were 'only a third, fourth or fifth link in the same creation, and nearest of all to the monkey or ourang-outang, and therefore incapable of enjoying the same state of intellectual existence as themselves'. A Darling Downs pioneer observed in 1846 that many Europeans viewed the Aborigines as 'a species of...tail-less monkeys'; the Presbyterian clergyman J.D. Land claimed that it was 'A damnable doctrine of some, at least, of the Australian squatters—that the black man of the forests of Australia is originally no better than the ourang-outang or monkey'. While arguing in 1844 against a proposal to allow Aborigines to give evidence in courts the prominent New South Wales politician W.C. Wentworth said that it would be 'quite as defensible to receive as evidence in a Court of Justice the chatterings of the ourang-outang as of this savage race'.

The smallest brains

Many attempts were made, in the late eighteenth and early nineteenth centuries, to find an objective way of classifying racial groups, to discover measurable differences in order to place them with more certainty in their correct place on the great chain. Anatomists measured the size, shape, weight and capacity of the skull and every other supposed physical characteristic of racial groups, but while the methods changed the relative positions in the hierarchy never varied. The Dutch scientist Peter Camper measured the angle formed when the slope of the forehead was compared with the vertical in order to illustrate 'the difference betwixt the faces of different nations and likewise the resemblance between the head of a negro and that of a monkey'. The English anatomist William Lawrence concluded, in his *Lectures on Comparative Anatomy*, published in 1819, that the differences between racial groups 'both in bodily formation and in the faculties of the mind, are so striking, that they must have attracted the notice even of superficial observers'. One only had to compare 'the highly civilized nations of Europe...to a troop of naked, shivering and starved New Hollanders, a horde of filthy Hottentots, or the whole of the more or less barbarous tribes that cover the entire continent of Africa'. The American scientist S.G. Morton, who classified racial groups by measuring the volume of skulls, placed the Aborigines at the bottom of the hierarchy. He considered his few Aboriginal skulls as 'the nearest approach to the ourang type' he had seen. J.C. Nott, who popularised Morton's work in his book *Types of Mankind*, argued that the Aborigines 'represented the lowest grade in the human family. Their anatomical characteristics are certainly very remarkable. While, in countenance, they present an extreme of the prognathous type hardly above that of the ourang-outang they possess at the same time the smallest brains of the whole of mankind'.

European anatomists developed competing systems for measuring skulls, but their conclusions differed little from those of Morton and Nott. In his influential book *Lectures on Man* Carl Vogt concluded, in 1864, that there was 'an almost regular series in the cranial capacity of such nations and races, as since historical times, have taken little or no part in civilization. Australians, Hottentots and Polynesians, nations in the lowest state of barbarism, commence the series, and no-one can deny that the place they occupy in relation to cranial capacity and cerebral weight corresponds with the degree of their intellectual capacity and civilization'.

Phrenology

Phrenology was the most influential offshoot of early scientific racism. It was founded by the German doctor F.J. Gall and popularised in the English-speaking world by George Combe's books *Elements of Phrenology* of 1824 and *The Constitution of Men* published four years later. Phrenology was based on the twin assumptions that specific areas of the brain were responsible for particular moral and intellectual characteristics and that the shape of the skull reflected the inner structure of the brain. The trained phrenologist could, therefore, feel the skull and assess the characteristics of individuals or even of whole racial groups. Combe and his followers had no doubt about the nature of the Aborigines; every practitioner knew that they were 'distinguished by great deficiencies in moral and intellectual organs', a fact 'demonstrated by specimens in most Phrenological collections'. With their 'present brains', Combe asserted in 1828, it was impossible for them to be civilised because the 'organs of reflecting, intellect, Ideality, Conscientiousness and Benevolence' were 'greatly inferior in size'.

Phrenology was popular in colonial society during the generation 1825–50. Professional phrenologists set up practice in the major cities and went on lecture tours into the country. The 'science' was discussed in newspapers and magazines and its distinctive terminology found its way into everyday speech. How widely accepted its basic ideas were is impossible to say, but there is no doubt that they were commonly applied to the Aborigines. A correspondent argued in the *Colonial Literary Journal* in 1844 that the great 'pre-ponderance of brain in the New Hollander, as in all savage Nations' was found at the back of the head which was the 'seat of the passions and inferior sentiments'. A phrenologist informed a Brisbane audience in 1851 that he had 'examined the skulls of many blackfellows in different parts of the colony and invariably found that these were about double the thickness of a whitefellow' so that even if black heads appeared to be the same size as European ones they would not have the same 'thinking power'. In fact, he concluded, 'the smallness of the aboriginal brain is the cause of all his miserable manifestations of mind'. In 1859 the Victorian Select Committee on the Aborigines called before it Mr Sohier, a practising phrenologist, who informed the members that with their small brain and inferior temperament the blacks could never be 'permanently improved'.

Mental poison

Defenders of the Aborigines were concerned about the influence of phrenology. A New South Wales settler explained in a letter to the Methodist Missionary Society in 1826 that their 'want of mental capacity' was being 'triumphantly urged', supported by 'Phrenological Speculations' which in turn were based 'on the weak evidence of external elevations or depressions of the skull'. In 1838 the missionary Threlkeld argued that

> the fashionable philosophy of the day, speculating on the intellectual powers of the Aborigines, as manifested in the Bumps of the Brain, is a splendid specious fallacy leading away the mind from the hope of the influence of God's holy spirit...and instead of depending as christians, on the promised divine secret influence of the Holy Spirit, this specious science, contemplates only the quantity of accumulation of matter in the formation of the brain, the depositions of bone in various corresponding concavities and convexities of the skull...to assume an hypothesis, amusing in theory, but dangerous in practice. The miserable attempt to deduce from such a science, falsely so called, that these Black human beings, 'have an innate deficiency of intellect rendering them incapable of instruction', would arrive at the natural conclusion that it would be useless to attempt it, and consequently the Blacks being but part and parcel of brute creation, being deficient of intellect, there can be no responsibility attached to their destruction, more than there is to the extirpation of any other animal whose presence is obnoxious to the possessor of the soil.
>
> It is to be lamented that such sentiments have most likely had their influence on men of corrupt minds who gladly avail themselves of any specious argument to enable them to gratify their love of cruelty, which has ended in blood...Nor, have some, it is to be feared, who are termed well educated minds, escaped the contagion of the mental poison, which insidiously perverts the judgement, and has led to the adoption of means and arguments alike discreditable to Christian honor.

The 'contagion' can be illustrated in the remarks of settlers who were basically in sympathy with the Aborigines but were, to varying degress, influenced by the new 'scientific' theories. The Attorney-General of New South Wales Saxe-Bannister had strong humanitarian views and was one of the few defenders of Threlkeld when he first arrived in the colony. Yet in September 1825 he made a point of writing to the missionary to tell him that a visiting 'French medical gentleman has confirmed his opinion of the *innate* deficiency of these poor people by a careful examination of many heads'. In his *Excursions and Adventures in New South Wales* John Henderson observed that the Aborigines displayed considerable intelligence and wonderful ingenuity even though they were 'classed by physiologists, on account of the facial angle and form and capacity of the skull, in the lowest order of human beings'. The explorer Charles Sturt, who was an experienced and sympathetic observer of Aboriginal society, remarked in 1849 that 'if there is any truth in phrenology they must have their share of brutal passions. The whole appearance of the cranium indeed would lead to the conclusion that they possess few of the intellectual faculties'. Similar comments were made by Captain J.C. Stokes, an intelligent and perceptive visitor, who wrote about the Aborigines with considerable insight. He too argued that 'if the principles of that science are admitted to be true, these savages are woefully deficient in all the qualities which contribute to man's moral supremacy'. But the influence of phrenology and other related theories was nowhere near as great as that of social darwinism in the second half of the nineteenth century.

Evolutionary philosophy

The ideas of Charles Darwin had a major influence on racial thought, both directly through his major works, *The Origin of the Species*, 1859, and *The Descent of Man*, 1872, and indirectly through his many disciples who applied his ideas to society in the form of social darwinism. The importance of Darwin for late Victorian and Edwardian intellectual life, both in Britain and the colonies, was emphasised by C.G. Henderson, professor of history at Adelaide University, in a lecture to the 1911 Australian Association for the Advancement of Science Congress. Henderson argued that

> the publication of Charles Darwin's 'Origin of Species' in 1859 was the greatest event in the reign of Queen Victoria. The idea of evolution, known to the ancient Greeks, was rediscovered and put so plainly and convincingly that in less than a decade principles of the doctrine of evolution were known even to people who were without systematic scientific training. Not only in the strictly more scientific world, but also throughout the realm of learning generally that book exercised an influence which can only be described as stupendous. From 1870 onwards evolutionary philosophy has pervaded all departments of intellectual activity, and it has stimulated patient and painstaking research in all directions.

Darwin's evolutionary synthesis overturned some aspects of early-nineteenth-century racism but confirmed others, giving them the backing of the greatest scientific achievement of the age. Social darwinism incorporated the concept of race itself, the idea of a racial hierarchy and the commonly accepted grading of the world's people. But whereas the great chain of being had been static the darwinian hierarchy was in flux, constantly evolving; the great chain was a spatial concept, a staircase of living matter; the darwinians saw the hierarchy as a temporal sequence. 'The various living races of Man,' a leading social darwinist explained, 'seem almost to form a kind of living genealogical tree.' Early-nineteenth-century racists believed that savages were physically below Europeans; their successors thought they were less evolved. In the one scheme they were like monkeys because they were next to them on the great chain; in the other they were akin to monkeys because they had evolved from them.

Living fossils

Darwinian scholars were convinced that the Aborigines were among the oldest surviving races; they were relics of the early history of mankind, living fossils to be studied, discussed, argued about, patronised and persistently and grossly defamed as a people. 'The Australian native,' observed Drummond in his *Ascent of Man*, 1894, 'has been repeatedly, almost exclusively, chosen to illustrate the lowest stage of human development.' 'The lowest stage...of all the human species,' argued Haekel in his *The His-*

tory of Creation, 1892, 'is occupied by the Australian or Austral negro.' Such ideas were abroad in Australian scientific circles until the 1930s, Pulleine and Woolard observing in a paper delivered to the Royal Society of South Australia in 1930 that it had been 'repeated again and again that the aborigines of Australia represent the most primitive variety of man still existing'. Even activists who worked for the Aboriginal cause were caught in the same intellectual net. M.M. Bennett, who spent much of her life agitating for the blacks, referred in 1930 to 'the fresh artless lovableness of the latest surviving children of the primitive earth'.

Ape-like characters

The darwinians accepted without question much of the anatomical research of the early nineteenth century and swept it up uncritically into their new synthesis. Like their predecessors they collected and measured skulls and brains, proving to their satisfaction that Aborigines had smaller, less developed brains, than did Europeans. The way things were to move was apparent soon after the publication of *The Origin of the Species*. T.H. Huxley, one of Darwin's closest associates, published his *Evidence as to Man's Place in Nature* in 1863. He made particular reference to Aboriginal skulls to prove the process of evolution and echoed the work of an earlier generation of anatomists in his contention that 'the difference in the volume of the cranial cavity of different races of mankind is far greater, absolutely, than that between the lowest Man and the highest Ape...'. Where the luminaries of the age led colonial scholars were bound to follow. At a conference on the Aborigines in 1886 the historian James Bonwick observed that those who 'accept the evolution doctrine as applied to the physical origins of man, regard the Australians as, in some respects, nearer than most existing peoples to the anthropoid apes'. He concluded that 'many atavic reminiscences, or ancestral marks are distinguishable', and having listed them all noted that they were all 'relics of transitional humanity'. At the Australian Association for the Advancement of Science Congress at Adelaide in 1907, the leading medical scientist W. Ramsay-Smith delivered a paper entitled, 'The Place of the Australian Aboriginal in Recent Anthropological Research'. It was, he argued, fairly certain that man had evolved from the anthropoid apes and that he possessed 'about three hundred structural features in common with the gorilla and chimpanzee. While the similar features were not all concentrated in any single race it had been established that the Aborigines had 'furnished the largest number of ape-like characters'. He concluded that the more 'one investigates the truer does his statement prove to be'. Such ideas were still in vogue in Australian scientific circles until the 1930s.

The childhood of the race

The frontiersman's belief that Aborigines were either animals or children was given credence by science during the late nineteenth century. Eminent British scholars proved to their satisfaction what racist settlers had always known. In a paper delivered to London's Anthropological Institute in 1872 entitled 'The Mental Characteristics of Primitive Man, as Exemplified by the Australian Aborigines', C.S. Wake concluded that 'in all questions of morality and in all matters connected with the emotional nature', the blacks were 'mere children'. In fact, he asserted, 'they represent the childhood of humanity itself, revealing to us the original condition of mankind'. In his book *Pre-Historic Times* the scholar Sir John Lubbock argued in 1865 that 'savages have the character of children with the passions and strength of men'. They had often been likened to children, 'but so far as intelligence is concerned, a child of four years old is far superior'. The darwinians believed that the adult European passed through the stages of human evolution while growing up. Thus primitive races had the emotional and mental make-up of young children and could never grow out of them. They were child races locked in perpetual infancy. In his *Principles of Sociology* Herbert Spencer asserted that 'on the hypothesis of evolution, the civilized man, passing through the phases representing phases passed through by the race, will, early in life, betray this impulsiveness which the early race had. The saying that the savage has the mind of a child with the passions of a man...thus possesses a deeper meaning than appears'. Australian scientists followed their imperial mentors.

The celebrated anthropologist Baldwin Spencer believed that mentally the Aborigines was 'about the level of a child who has little control over his feelings'. A fellow medical scientist Dr H. Gregory argued in 1917 that 'mentally he is a weak child, with uncontrolled feelings, without initiative or sense of responsibility'.

Survival of the fittest

One more sinister aspect of social darwinism was the sanction it gave to racial violence. The various races were regarded as similar to the different species in the natural world. They were therefore in ceaseless struggle. This was not only inevitable but desirable because all progress came from an ever-present struggle for survival, out of which the fittest and the best emerged. 'The struggle means suffering,' wrote social darwinist Karl Pearson in 1901, 'intense suffering, while it is in progress; but that struggle and that suffering have been the stages by which the white man has reached his present stage of development... This dependence of progress on the survival of the fittest race, terribly black as it may seem to some of you, gives the struggle for existence its redeeming features, it is the fiery crucible out of which comes the finer metal.'

In colonial discussions about the Aborigines references to racial struggle and the survival of the fittest became commonplace from the 1860s onwards. The South Australian politician J.H. Barron told the local parliament in 1866 that he believed that 'all inferior races must disappear before the superior nation'. Humanity was progressing 'and he did not think it was undesirable that the lowest types should be supplanted by the highest. It was so with animals, and no one regretted it, and so it would be with men. Progress was the law of the world, and in obedience to that law the inferior must give place to the superior'. In a paper on the Tasmanian Aborigines James Barnard, a member of the island's Royal Society, told the second Australian Association for the Advancement of Science Congress in 1890 that it had 'become an axiom that, following the law of evolution and survival of the fittest, the inferior races of mankind must give place to the highest type of man...'. A year earlier the prominent Queenslander

Archibald Meston, later to become the colony's Southern Protector of Aborigines, had discussed the same question in a report to the government on a recent exploring expedition. In all cases, he wrote,

> the strong colonising race has treated harshly and contemptuously the weak race which it displaced. This is the history of all new countries, and the slaughter of the aboriginals by the invader is the one monotonously conspicuous fact in all records of colonisation. No euphemism of expression or sentimentalism of thought can conceal that from the historian or the student of ethnology. In all human progress and the transition and rise and fall of nations we see the all ruling influence of the law of the survival of the strongest...The Australian blacks are moving rapidly on into the eternal darkness in which all savage and inferior races are surely destined to disappear. All effort to preserve them, though creditable to our humanity, is a poor complement to our knowledge of those inexorable laws whose operations are as apparent as our own existence.

Pitiless nature

Inexorable laws left no room for right or wrong. The destruction of Aboriginal society was, James Collier argued in *The Pastoral Age in Australia*, 'simply a question of superiority of race and the greater inherent capability on the part of the whites'. The Victorian historian A.G. Sutherland argued in 1888 that Australian colonisation represented 'a distinct step in human progress, involving the sacrifice of a few thousand of an inferior race'. The fact was 'that mankind, as a race, cannot choose to act solely as moral beings. They are governed by animal laws which urge them blindly forward upon tracks they scarce can choose for themselves'; they acted in obedience to 'natural laws over which they had no control'. 'It seems a law of nature,' the editor of the *Age* observed in 1888, 'that where two races whose stages of progression differ greatly are brought into contact, the inferior race is doomed to wither and disappear...The process seems to be in accordance with a natural law which, however it may clash with human benevolence, is clearly beneficial to mankind at large by providing for the survival of the fittest. Human progress has all been achieved by the spread of the progressive races and the squeezing out of inferior ones.' If natural laws explained and justified the extinction of whole races it could scarcely be doubted that they also justified the actions of individual frontiersmen; personal vendettas against the blacks could be raised to the status of biological crusades. In the outback the white man 'began to consider...that it was a duty he owed to himself and his colour to shoot down every blackfellow that came within range of his rifle'. A correspondent in the *Queenslander* in 1876 observed that cases were 'constantly brought under notice which tend to show that many a white man thinks it a duty he owes to his colour and civilization to shoot down every nigger he encounters in the bush'. Personal brutality might still be condemned, but nature itself was cruel. It was in the words of the *Age* 'absolutely and wisely pitiless'. In the new harsh darwinian world a Queensland settler could declare publicly: 'and being a useless race what does it matter what they suffer'. Even the bushman's belief that the blacks felt pain less than Europeans was confirmed by the scientists, anatomists arguing that primitive races had underdeveloped nervous systems. A Dr R.W. Felkin informed the 1889 meeting of the British Association that it was 'very generally supposed that negroes feel pain to a less degree than Europeans'. The 1913 Congress of the Australian Association for the Advancement of Science was told by a Natalie Robarts in a paper on the Victorian Aborigines that they didn't suffer pain as do higher races: 'their skin seems not so sensitive.' In a book entitled *The Australian Aborigines and the Christian Church*, published in 1914 by the Society for the Propagation of Christian Knowledge, the author, H. Pitts, declared that the Aborigines 'having a much less highly developed nervous system, feel pain to a much less extent than we do'.

A dying race

Settlers thought that the Aborigines were a dying race from at least as early as the 1820s, and the rapid decline of the indigenous people appeared to bear out their belief. They referred to similar developments in other parts of the world and assumed that it was 'the design of Providence that inferior races should pass away before the superior races'. Captain J.L. Stokes observed in the 1840s that most colonists were willing to 'content themselves with the belief' that it was in 'accordance with some mysterious dispensation of Providence'. The Pole Strzelecki remarked that inquiry into such matters had, like an 'inquest of the one race upon the corpse of another', usually ended with the verdict: 'Dead by visitation of God.' Metaphors abounded—the blacks were variously fading away, fading out, decaying, slipping from life's platform, melting away like the snow from the mountains at the approach of spring, perishing 'as does the autumnal grass before a bush fire'. But metaphors were not enough for the inquiring mind. In his lectures on colonisation delivered at Oxford in 1839–1841 Herman Merivale argued that the decline of the Aboriginal population was not due to such causes as warfare, the introduction of spirits and new epidemics or the destruction of game. There were 'deeper and more mysterious causes at work; the mere contact of Europeans is fatal to him in some unknown manner'. The young Charles Darwin, visiting Australia on the *Beagle* in 1837, concluded similarly that there appeared 'to be some mysterious agency at work'.

Evolution provided the answer to the mystery. In a paper on 'Natural Selection Applied to Anthropology' Alfred Russell Wallace argued in 1867 that 'the native Americans, the New Zealanders, the Australians and the Polynesian races are all doomed. It is a mere question of time as to when these will become extinct'. It was, he argued six years later, 'the same great law of the preservation of favored races in the struggle of life which leads to the inevitable extinction of all those low and mentally underdeveloped populations with which the Europeans come in contact...not from any one special cause, but from the inevitable effects of an unequal mental and physical struggle'. The conviction that extinction was inevitable, backed by the most prominent scientists of the age, dogged all discussion about the Aborigines until the 1940s. Every assessment of their situation, every evaluation of policy, took place in the shadow of that certainty. J.B. Cleland, professor of pathology at Adelaide University, argued in 1928 that 'the pure blooded Australian aborigine is fast dying out. Already over very large areas in the settled parts he has entirely disappeared. With the march of civilization only a few years will see, in all probability, the complete disappearance of pure-blooded natives'. Two years later

J.W. Bleakley, Queensland's Chief Protector of Aborigines, wrote an article for the *Australian Quarterly* entitled 'Can Our Aborigines be Preserved?' Although interesting to many people, he observed, 'the subject of this paper can hardly be said to be a keenly debated question, for it seems to be the generally accepted view that the extinction of the Australian Aborigines is inevitable'.

A malign influence

Under the influence of social darwinism hope of Aboriginal advancement died. They were too primitive, too archaic, to adapt to modern society and nothing could stay the scientific sentence of death. 'That the race is doomed is admitted by all who have studied the subject', wrote A.C.G. in the *Queenslander* in 1880, 'and those who know the nigger best feel most the impossibility of doing much to ameliorate his condition or protract the existence of his race. This callousness as a rule arises from no lack of sympathy with the blacks, but from a firm conviction that their stage of civilization is too many hundred or perhaps thousand years behind our own to allow their race to thrive side by side with our own'. The Norwegian scientist Karl Lumholtz, who spent several years in Queensland in the 1880s, related how a settler, who had done much to protect the blacks, had written to him explaining: 'If I thought that anything I might say on the treatment of the Aborigines would in any way tend to ameliorate their present wretched condition I would not for one moment grudge my lost health and would plead their cause to my last breath. But alas! It were vain to hope for any improvement in their condition; for it is an immutable law of nature that the strong will prey upon the weak.'

It is well!

The unchanging savage was the benchmark which could be used to measure the reality of colonial progress. 'In no other land has evolution been so noticeable,' J.S. Dunnett argued in an article the *Empire Review* in 1907, 'and no other land promises so much in that direction during the currency of the present century.'

Evolution was sending the blacks 'hopelessly onward towards the gulf of extinction' and with them went the indigenous flora and fauna which were disappearing in the path of progress. The great majority of settlers were pleased with colonial development; the 'passing of the Aborigine' was 'a small drawback to a vast good'. 'The black man has all but passed away,' Ida Lee wrote in her book *The Coming of the British to Australia*, published in 1906,

> his voice is never heard...The land acknowledges a new master; the change is inevitable. But as we press forward let us turn to the few that remain and watch their vanishing figures—let us ask, we who scattered them and who now possess the country which they so dearly loved 'Is it well with the land'? The white townships growing where once all was dark with forest; the axes ringing through the backwood; the network of masts fringing the busy port; the golden corn colouring the grassy plains; the wealth of mine drawn from the barren waste, all unite in full, clear answer 'It is well'.

But evolution held promise of more than material progress. Man himself was ascendant. 'I feel elated,' confessed Richard Semon in his book *In the Australian Bush*, published in 1899, 'by the certainty that the development of humanity has not come to its end either in a physical or a moral sense'. At the first meeting of the Australian Association for the Advancement of Science in 1888, the distinguished scholar J.J. Wild delivered a paper entitled 'Outlines of Anthropology' which traced the 'gradual progress of man towards a higher civilization'. Human history showed evidence of a 'steady advance', and in spite of many vicissitudes 'the higher type of man, like the phoenix of the fable, has always sprung from its ashes in order to continue its course towards a still higher destiny'. Victory over the Aborigines illustrated the fitness of the white race to survive and progress. 'We may use... the unvarying savage,' argued the distinguished British scholar Walter Bagehot in 1872, 'as a metre to gauge the vigour of the constitutions to whose contact he is exposed.' 'Let us consider,' he wrote, 'in what a village of English colonists is superior to a tribe of Australian natives who roam about them. Indisputably in one, and that a main sense, they are superior. They can beat the Australians in war when they like; they can take from them anything they like, and kill any of them they choose...' 'The path of progress,' Karl Pearson asserted in 1901, 'is strewn with the wreck of nations; traces are everywhere to be seen of the hecatombs of inferior races; and of victims who found not the narrow way to the great perfection. Yet these dead people are, in very truth, the stepping stones on which mankind has arisen to the higher intellectual and deeper emotional life of today.'

Few regretted the 'passing of the Aborigines'. Nature itself had issued the death sentence; inexorable laws were carrying them away. The Victorian historian A.G. Sutherland observed in 1888 that there would 'ever cling a pathos round the story of a vanishing race; and when we think of the agile forms that once held dominion over these widely forested lands; when we see them vanishing with terrible speed to be but a memory of the past, the contrast affects our feelings, even though our intellects refuse to be moved, recognizing the workings of a law above that which man makes himself'. Many saw the fate of the Aborigines as a powerful symbol of colonial progress. The land was being cleared, distance tamed and the blacks were dying. Edward Curr, the Victorian pioneer, looked back in the 1880s over 30 years of colonial development. Of the Aborigines he wrote: 'scarce one remains. His cooey is heard no more in these parts, whilst the old forest itself is fast being converted by steam saw mills into railway sleepers. In our go ahead days people of course are jubilant about such things, and I suppose I ought to be so too.'

Victory over the blacks represented victory over the past itself, not just in a local and material sense but in a universal biological one as well. Their 'passing' was graphic proof of evolution itself. Decline of the primitive races at the bottom of the scale gave promise of further progress of the more advanced at the top. The South Australian pioneer J.W. Bull remarked in 1884 that the question of 'the displacement of an aboriginal race has always been attended with great difficulties, but it is one of those necessary processes in the course of Providence to bring about the improvement of the human race'. In an article on the Aborigines in the *Melbourne Review* in 1878, the Victorian D. Macallister argued that the total extinction of these people, which seems, and is so certain, is not without an important significance to those who are conversant with the theory of 'Evolution'...for being admittedly on the very lowest link of the long chain embraced by mankind, we cannot fail to recognize in their extinction a decided widening of the chasm by which mankind is now cut off from its animal progenitors. Not only is the chasm thus widened, but the difficulty of its ever being bridged over becomes greater...Thus, then, we see a double process at work, by which is being effected the extinction of all traces of the unity of the organic chain. One, the dying out of the lowest races of men; the other, the steady forward movement by those races which are able to hold their own in their internal struggles and against natural changes.

But while the Aborigines continued to cling precariously to life's platform, they were of great scientific interest, representing for scientists the early stages of humanity, the childhood of the human race. The celebrated author Sir James Frazer wrote to the pioneer anthropologist Baldwin Spencer, telling him that the 'anthropological work still to be done in Australia is...of more importance for the early history of mankind than anything else that can now be done in the world'. A German ethnographer visiting Australia for several years in the first decade of the twentieth century observed that it was 'a proper thing from a scientific standpoint to preserve the Australian nature. We preserve our natural scenery, our natural beauty and it is our duty to preserve this beautiful document in the development of mankind'. Dr W. Ramsay-Smith, the leading medical scientist, told the 1913 Australian Association for the Advancement of Science Congress that the Aborigines were the 'most interesting and educationally the most valuable primitive race on the face of the earth today'.

In the late nineteenth and early twentieth century overseas scholars showed a keen interest in the Aborigines. Local ethnographers were consulted and their work read abroad; old pioneers were invited to give papers about their experiences with the blacks when they returned to Britain. For their part scientists and philosophers in the great metropolitan centres used as evidence the deeply prejudiced observations of settlers on the frontiers of the Empire; they gave them intellectual respectability, built them into theories and then shipped the finished product back to the colonies to confirm the settlers in their racism. At the same time collectors sought Aboriginal artifacts, bones and skulls, which found their way into the leading museums and universities in Europe and North America. During the 1880s an enterprising colonial entrepreneur took a troupe of Queensland Aborigines abroad and displayed them in all the major cities of the United States, Britain and the Continent. Members of the anthropological societies in Berlin, Paris, Brussells and St Petersburg subjected the blacks to more detailed and searching examinations. After five years of touring and the death of several members of the party, the three surviving Aborigines—an adult couple called 'Billy' and 'Jenny' and a boy known as 'Little Toby'—were displayed at a meeting of London's Anthropological Institute. They danced, sang, threw paper boomerangs and showed their ceremonial cicatrices to the distinguished audience. In subsequent discussion the Rev. W. Wyatt Gill, who spoke with the authority of colonial experience, said that he was about to return to Sydney where several scientists hoped to establish an anthropological society and as the blacks were dying out no time was to be lost 'in gathering up all that can possibly be known of their characteristics, habits, thoughts, worship and language'. History is silent on the fate of 'Billy', 'Jenny' or 'Little Toby' after their appearance before London's ethnographers. We don't know how much longer they were paraded before curious European audiences, nor do we know if they were ever able to return to their homeland and their kin in north Queensland.

Racism flourished in Australia in the nineteenth and in the early twentieth century. It shaped an orthodox view of the Aborigines which survived intact until the 1940s and 1950s, giving white Australians the conviction that they knew 'all about the abos'. Like many orthodoxies it was impervious to actual experience and people clung to it long after the ideas which gave it birth had been challenged and overthrown. Jean Devanny was struck by this aspect of white opinion while touring north Queensland after the Second World War. She wrote:

as time passed I was brought to marvel at the inability of the white [north Queenslander] to assimilate the evidence of their own senses in respect of the native people. The Aborigines were required to perform, and did perform excellently well, tasks arduous and courageous, tasks demanding skill and independent judgement, yet the inner meaning of this capacity to do and dare, the conclusions to be logically drawn from it, were completely lost upon the white Australians. At the completion of his skilful job the brown workman was required to reassume the status of an infant, or a dog, whistled to heel by men who in many cases, as the Aborigines could not but realize, were inferior to themselves in skill, endurance, physique and mental capacity.

The persistence of nineteenth-century ideas was well illustrated by references to the Aborigines in the official centenary history of Queensland, *Triumph in the Tropics*, published in 1959 and written by Cilento and Lack. Sir Raphael Cilento was, in his own right, a distinguished medical scientist. The authors observed that:

it is usual to assess the Aboriginals...by comparison with mature or, indeed primitive civilizations...[but]...they must be considered as nomads of the jungle or savannah or desert, comparable with the animal groups that inhabited those areas, for which they felt...an affinity. If their reactions are estimated along those lines, they become logical and understandable. Like other nomadic food gatherers...the Aboriginal ignored what he did not comprehend or showed indifference, rather than astonishment, when faced by something he failed to classify among his schedules of experience. Like his own half-wild dogs, he could be frozen into shivering immobility or put to frenzied flight by people or things that provoked impressions of terror...
Like his dogs, too, he could be cowed by direct and confident stare into a wary armed truce, but would probably attack with fury if an opponent showed signs of fear...These are primitive reactions common to many feral jungle creatures, and not uncommon to higher races.

Early scientific racism weakened the belief in racial equality in colonial Australia; social darwinism undermined it altogether. The emphasis in late-eighteenth-century philosophy on the influence of the environment on human behaviour was overwhelmed by the darwinians' supremely confident assertion of biological determinism. The challenge mounted to the literal truth of the Old Testament seriously diminished the philanthropist's main argument that God had created all men in his own image. The blacks were no longer brothers. They were distant ancestors who had overstayed their time on earth. Social darwinism carried a message of struggle, competition, violence. These were not only inevitable but necessary to progress itself. The Aborigines were beyond redemption. They could never be integrated into modern society and, after all, their time was short. They were doomed to extinction. The heightened interest in traditional culture, born of evolutionary philosophy, was little compensation for a disastrous intellectual legacy. Australian society was more racist in 1930 than it had been a century before. The missionaries and philanthropists of the early nineteenth century talked more sense about Aboriginal society than the pioneer anthropologists, their more systematic studies notwithstanding.

The growth of scientific racism was a European rather than a purely Australian phenomenon. A small colonial society had little chance of resisting the most powerful intellectual currents of the age. But it is equally true that racism furthered the material interests of most settlers. It made it so much easier to take Aboriginal land without negotiation or purchase, to crush resistance to the dispossession and then keep the survivors 'in their place'. Frontier squatters and other entrepreneurs could pursue their economic objectives, could invest their capital, free from restraint. Neither government action, nor the law, nor public opinion need obstruct the pursuit of profit. If necessary resident blacks could be expelled from their traditional lands, murdered and enslaved if they were needed for labour or sex. As long as the whites continued to believe the blacks were primitive savages it could all be done with a clear conscience. Another advantage for the entrepreneur was that racism prevented any significant development of working-class sympathy, let alone support, for the blacks. On the frontier it could be argued that all white men had an equal stake in the struggle both with the blacks and the land itself, even though most ended up with nothing while a few won principalities for themselves and their descendants. Once the frontier era was over it was unthinkable to accept alternative and more favourable views of the blacks. Too much had been done on the assumption that they were savages. There was blood on too many hands and profits in too many pockets. Any suggestion to the contrary had to be vigorously resisted. For compelling economic and psychological reasons the Aborigines had to remain underfoot.

The development of ideas about the blacks was thus only partly due to broader intellectual movements. The central fact was not that the Aborigines were savage but that they occupied the land and were therefore in the way of progress and personal enrichment. The question of land ownership, of the rights of the soil, must, therefore, now be considered.

—PART III—
The Land

– 6 –

The Rights of the Soil

Land has always been at the centre of conflict between black and white Australians. It was in 1788 and probably still will be in 1988 when Europeans celebrate the bicentenary of their first settlement. Debate about Aboriginal land rights is not new. The issue was vigorously canvassed between 1820 and 1850; problems widely discussed then have re-emerged 150 years later. In the course of the colonial debate few questioned the right of the British to claim sovereignty over Australia by right of discovery. But the implications of that declaration for Aboriginal land tenure was a matter of contention, some colonists arguing that as a result of annexation all indigenous rights to land were instantly wiped out, others claiming that sovereignty merely impaired the native title and that the tribes retained the right to occupy and use their land and to receive compensation if their title was extinguished by government action.

Despite a century-old land rights debate the issue did not reach the Australian courts until 1971 when Mr Justice Blackburn of the Northern Territory Supreme Court handed down a controversial judgment in the case *Milirrpum* v. *Nabalco* concerning ownership of land on the Gove Peninsula. Like numerous settlers before him, Blackburn argued that the original British claim of sovereignty extinguished all Aboriginal rights to property. The map was wiped clean of traditional tenure in 1788. Following that radical spring-cleaning the only source of property was the Crown. 'All titles, rights, and interests whatever in land which existed' after 1788 Blackburn asserted were the 'direct consequence of some grant from the Crown'. As there appeared to be no legislation which specifically created native title none existed; indeed it did 'not form and never has formed part of the law of any part of Australia'.

Native title

That might have been an end to the matter. But Blackburn's understanding of native title differed from the one which had evolved in the courts of other common-law countries—Britain, Canada, New Zealand and the United States—during the nineteenth and twentieth centuries. The concept was most authoritatively outlined by Chief Justice Marshall of the United States Supreme Court in 1823 in the case *Johnson* v. *McIntosh*. Marshall argued that there was no question of the right of European nations to assume sovereignty over Indian lands. Discovery gave title which could then be consummated by possession. Sovereignty allowed the colonising nation to exclude all other European powers and gave it the sole right of acquiring the soil from the natives. Radical title was held by the Crown, or the succeeding United States government, but the Indians did not lose everything on annexation. They retained a right of occupancy although they could only dispose of their land to the Crown. But it had never been contended that Indian title 'amounted to nothing'. Indeed their right to possession had 'never been questioned', they were

> in no instance entirely disregarded; but were admitted to be the rightful occupants of the soil, with a legal as well as a just claim to retain possession of it, and to use it according to their own discretion; but their rights to complete sovereignty, as independent nations, were necessarily diminished, and their power to dispose of the soil at their own will...was denied by the original fundamental principle that discovery gave exclusive title to those who made it.

Marshall's definition of native title was highly influential in all common-law countries during the nineteenth century and was affirmed in many later constitutional cases in America, Britain and the colonies. Native title was established in New Zealand in the 1840s, both by the Treaty of Waitangi, which was specific to that colony and, more significantly, by the common law, which had much wider application. In his judgment in the 1847 case *Symonds* v. *the Crown* Mr Justice Chapman wrote:

> Whatever may be the opinion of jurists to the strength or weakness of the native title it cannot be too solemnly asserted that it is entitled to be respected, that it cannot be extinguished...otherwise than by the free consent of the native occupiers. But for their protection, and for the sake of humanity, the Government is bound to maintain and the Courts to assert, the Queen's exclusive right to extinguish it. It follows, from what has been said, that in solemnly guaranteeing the native title, and in securing what is called the Queens preemptive right, the Treaty of Waitangi...does not assert, either in doctrine or practice anything new or unsettled.

It is important before considering the Australian situation to emphasise that native title was seen as arising from prior occupation and not from the actual use of the land. In America Indian title existed despite the fact that the tribes, in Marshall's view, were 'fierce savages, whose occupation was war, and whose subsistence was drawn chiefly from the forest'. The issue of land use arose in New Zealand in 1846, when the imperial government sought to limit Maori rights to those small areas actually in cultivation—said at the time to be less than 1 per cent of the whole—thereby leaving any other land open to alienation regardless of its status in customary law. But the government was forced to retreat in the face of pressure both from within the colony and from the missionary organisations in Britain and returned to the basic principles of native title that the Maoris had a right of occupancy on all land held under traditional tenure regardless of whether it was cultivated or not.

Native title in Australia

The situation in the Australian colonies was less clear-cut than in New Zealand or North America. There were no comprehensive statements of imperial policy, no treaties, no judicial decisions like those of Marshall in the United States or Symonds in New Zealand, although there were cases which related to the Crown's exclusive right to extinguish native title and the power of colonial courts to deal with offences committed within Aboriginal communities. There was public debate about the morality of settlement and the British assumption of sovereignty, but neither issue impinged directly on the question of native title. However, it is possible to assemble a number of statements made by imperial and colonial officials between the late eighteenth century and the middle of the nineteenth which show that there was a much greater awareness—and acceptance—of native title than previous accounts have suggested. Admiralty instructions given to Cook before his voyage into the Pacific were directly relevant to the question of native title. He was told to annex the land if it was uninhabited; if not he was to take possession of convenient situations in the country 'with the consent of the natives'. There was a clear distinction between occupied and uninhabited territory. The expedition could exercise the European's right of discovery by taking possession of convenient locations but the inhabitants had to agree to the transaction. They were not without rights even if their title was impaired as a result of 'discovery' by white men. An even more pertinent document dates from 1807. Governor King prepared a confidential memo for his successor Bligh. Under a section entitled 'Respecting Natives' he explained that he had never been willing to force the blacks to work because he had 'ever considered them the real Proprietors of the Soil'. Similar sentiments were expressed by Governor Brisbane in 1821. While discussing the Aboriginal question with a pioneer missionary he remarked; 'we have taken the land from the Aborigines of the country, and a remuneration ought to be made.' After experiencing several years of open warfare Tasmania's Governor Arthur offered a number of suggestions to the imperial government in the hope that violence could be avoided elsewhere in Australia. He proposed, in 1832, that the utmost care should be taken to give the Aborigines presents

> for whatever land is taken possession of by the British settlers; for each tribe claims some portion of territory, which they consider peculiarly their own, they should be in some formal manner satisfied for bartering it away; a negotiation which they perfectly comprehened. Had this system been early adopted in Van Diemen's Land, many deplorable consequences, I have no doubt, would have been averted.

A few years later F.C. Irwin, the commandant and sometimes

acting Governor of West Australia, argued that the settlers, having gained a sufficient knowledge of the Aboriginal languages, should enter into a formal treaty with the local clans as a 'measure of healing and pacification'.

The attempt by John Batman to purchase 600000 acres from the Port Phillip clans in 1835 raised the question of the rights of Australian Aborigines. The government's rejection of the so-called treaty did not indicate that the Aborigines were without rights, rather it illustrated that the Crown alone could extinguish native title. This was borne out when the question was referred by Batman's company to three of Britain's leading constitutional lawyers. In his comments on the case William Burge, one-time Attorney-General of Jamaica and 'in all matters of colonial law...one of the first authorities', referred directly to Marshall's dicta and observed that it had been

> a principle adopted by Great Britain as well as by the other European states, in relation to their settlements on the continent of America, that the title which discovery conferred on Government by whose authority or by whose subjects the discovery was made, was that of the ultimate dominion in and sovereignty over the soil, even whilst it continued in the possession of the Aborigines. This principle was reconciled with humanity and justice towards the Aborigines, because the dominion was qualified by allowing them to retain, not only the rights of occupancy, but also a restricted power of alienating those parts of the territory which they occupied.

Governor Gipps advanced similar arguments in a speech to the New South Wales Legislative Council in 1840. He explained that

> the uncivilized inhabitants of any country have but a qualified dominion over it, or a right of occupancy only; and that, until they establish amongst themselves a settled form of government, and subjugate the ground to their own uses, by the cultivation of it, they cannot grant to individuals, not of their own tribe, any portion of it, for the simple reason, that they have not themselves any individual property in it.
>
> Secondly that if a settlement be made in any such country by a civilized power, the right of preemption of the soil, or in other words, the right of extinguishing the native title, is exclusively in the government of that power, and cannot be enjoyed by individuals without the consent of their government.

Gipps referred extensively to American discussion of Indian title, quoted liberally from Marshall, and asserted that the principles outlined by American jurists were not only United States law 'but also the law of England, and founded both on the law and practice of nations'. The twin principles of native title and the Crown's exclusive right of alienation were, he concluded, 'fully admitted', and indeed 'received, as political axioms'.

Knowledge accumulates

Growing knowledge and understanding of traditional society was just as important for the Aboriginal cause as were calls for land rights. With more information about Aboriginal society sympathetic colonists were able to undermine many of the cruder misconceptions about tribal ways and especially the view that they merely ranged over the land and had no sense of property. The continuing Aboriginal occupation of large areas of the continent was in itself an inescapable feature of colonial life. Their prior ownership of the land was officially recognised in New South Wales in the 1830's, the government noting that the blacks were the 'Aboriginal possessors of the soil'. South Australia's Governor Gawler went further, referring to the land over which, 'from time immemorial', the Aborigines had exercised 'distinct, defined and absolute rights of proprietary and hereditary possession'. Such views appear to have become widely accepted in the community in the 1840s, the author of a book on Port Phillip noting that the blacks' 'priority of proprietorship [was] on all sides acknowledged'.

Widespread resistance underlined in blood the Aboriginal sense of property. One of the leaders of the Roving Bands, dispatched to catch Tasmanian Aborigines, reported to Governor Arthur in 1828 that the blacks had ideas 'of their natural rights which would astonish most of our European statesmen'. Aborigines voiced their own protest, struggling with English to make their point. G.A. Robinson met an old man who stamped on the ground vehemently exclaiming: 'the country belonging to [me], belonging to me, my country'. Returning from a journey through Victoria's Western District in 1843 he noted in his journal the complaints of the blacks he had met: 'They were poor now. White men had taken their good country, they said, no ask for it but took it. Black man show white man plenty grass and water and then white man say be off come be off and drive them away and no let them stop.' A South Australian settler met a local Aborigine in 1837 who said to him: 'damn your eyes, go to England, this my land.' Bishop Broughton told a House of Commons committee that the blacks had a 'conception of our having excluded them from what was their original property. Certainly that idea is prevalent among them...they frequently said to me that such a part was their property, but that it was all assigned now to Europeans'.

Europeans who took an interest in the Aborigines appreciated their strong relationship with the land. They were, a pioneer missionary observed, 'a most bigoted race of people to the ground on which they were born'. Explorer George Grey believed that every black 'knew the limits of his own land and could point out the various objects which mark his boundary'. The West Australian settler G.F. Moore described the behaviour of his Aboriginal companion Coondebung while travelling with him in 1836 beyond the fringes of white settlement. 'We were,' Moore wrote, 'now passing through his own country, over his native soil, and as he bounded along with a buoyant look and an elastic step, he appeared as if glorifying in his vigour and exulting in his independence.' The Tasmanian historian West described the reaction of an island black who returned from Flinders Island in 1847 and immediately went to Cataract Gorge near Launceston because 'it was a station of his people'. As he approached his destination 'his excitement became intense; he leaped from rock to rock, with gestures and exclamations of delight'.

After much experience of Aborigines Edward Eyre emphasised how strongly they felt for their land, writing in 1845:

> It was generally been imagined but with great injustice, as well as incorrectness, that the natives have no idea of property in land, or proprietary rights connected with it. Nothing can be further from the truth than this assumption, although men of high character and standing, and who are otherwise benevolently disposed towards the natives, have distinctly denied this right, and maintained that the natives were not entitled to have any choice of land reserved for them out of their own possessions, and in their respective

districts. As far as my own observation has extended, I have found that particular districts, having a radius perhaps of from ten to twenty miles, or in other cases varying according to local circumstances, are considered generally as being the property and hunting-grounds of the tribes who frequent them. These districts are again parcelled out among the individual members of the tribe. Every male has some portion of land, of which he can always point out the exact boundaries.

The level of understanding of traditional society achieved by the 1830s was illustrated in a letter written by John Dunmore Lang in answer to a query from a missionary organisation in Britain as to whether the Aborigines had any idea of property in land. The whole race, he replied,

is divided into tribes, more or less numerous according to circumstances, and designated from the localities they inhabit; for although universally a wandering race, with respect to places of habitation, their wanderings are circumscribed by certain well defined limits, beyond which they seldom pass, except for purposes of war or festivity. In short, every tribe has its own district, the boundaries of which are well known to the natives generally; and within that district all the wild animals are considered as much the property of the tribe inhabiting, or rather ranging on, its whole extent, as the flocks of sheep and herds of cattle that have been introduced into the country...are held by European law and usage the property of their respective owners...But particular districts are not merely the property of particular tribes; particular sections or portions of these districts are universally recognized by the natives as the property of individual members of these tribes...I have often heard natives myself tell me, in answer to my own questions on the subject who were the Aboriginal owners of a particular tract of land now held by Europeans; and indeed this idea of property in the soil, for hunting purposes is universal among the Aborigines...[y]ou may take it as certain...that the Aborigines of Australia have an idea of property in the soil...Indeed, the infinity of the native names of places, all of which are descriptive and appropriate, is of itself a *prima facie* evidence of their strong ideas of property in the soil.

By the 1840s the more perceptive settlers were aware that the Aboriginal relationship with the land was much more complex than theories about wandering savages suggested. They could see that clans carefully and systematically exploited the food resources of their territory; 'every forest...every valley, every plain and sheet of water furnished its number of repasts at the proper season'. The Aborigines' profound knowledge of the bush was widely appreciated and exploited in all frontier districts and on practically every inland journey. Settlers made extensive use of networks of paths, associated waterholes and man-made dams. Aboriginal employment of fire to shape and manage the environment was increasingly understood, Leichhardt noting that regular firing was 'connected with a systematic management of their runs, to attract game to particular spots, in the same way that stock holders burn parts of theirs in the proper season'. Observant settlers came to see how narrow was the gulf between Aboriginal gathering and European agriculture. George Grey found extensive yam fields in Western Australia which stretched as far as the eye could see in a district where 'far more had been done to secure a provision from the ground by hard manual labour' than he had believed it 'in the power of uncivilized man to accomplish'. G.A. Robinson discovered in Victoria's Western District far-flung earth works created to control river flow and harvest the eels as they travelled down to the sea. They resembled 'more the works of civilized than of savage men. They were of considerable extent one continuous treble line measured 500 yards in length, 2 feet in width and from 18 inches to 2 feet in depth. These treble watercourses led to extensive ramified trenches. The whole covered an area of at least 10 acres and must have been done at great cost of labour to the Aborigines'.

Humanitarian support

Colonial philanthropists strongly supported Aboriginal land rights in the 1830s and 1840s. The Port Phillip Protector E.S. Parker argued in favour of 'the right of the Aborigines to the soil and its indigenous productions'; his colleague Robinson thought they should have a 'reasonable share in the soil of their Fatherland'. Robinson had a stormy breakfast with a squatter with whom he had stayed overnight as they argued about the 'rights of the natives to the soil'. A few days later he came upon the body of a black shot by the settlers, forcing him into 'deep and painful reflection'. He later wrote in his journal: 'I thought of the rights of these people—the rights of the soil.' Methodist missionary Joseph Orton believed that colonisation should be conducted with 'sacred reference to all rights to the original occupants of the soil'. He believed that 'this great principle of British jurisprudence the rights of man has, with regard to the Aborigines of this country been overlooked and grossly violated by the intruders utterly regardless of any right of property in the lands of their nativity on which and by which they have been supported since time immemorial'. He referred approvingly to the recent establishment of the Port Phillip Protectorate, but even in that initiative there was 'little if any reference to right'. It was, he wrote, 'an important truth which has been designedly or ignorantly overlooked but which demands consideration viz. that the Aborigines of this country though an erratic race of savages they have decidedly a property in the land of their birth which right is recognized and held sacred by themselves in their respective relations of tribes, families and individuals'. A generation later the Catholic missionary Duncan McNab told the Queensland Minister for Lands that if the local blacks were to survive the 'essential requisite' was land. They had 'the first and best right to it' because it was 'their own country which they have always occupied and used and never renounced or alienated'.

Concern in Britain

While the colonists debated the issue of land ownership there were important developments in official policy as the British government came increasingly under the influence of the humanitarians whose power had been augmented in the House of Commons after the passage of the Reform Bill in 1832. The new attitude towards the Empire's indigenous people found expression in a Select Committee on native people which issued reports in 1836 and 1837. Chaired by T.F. Buxton, the committee was particularly interested in the question of land rights. In his report of the proceedings Buxton observed that

> it might be presumed that the native inhabitants of any land have an incontrovertible right to their own soil; a plain and sacred right, however, which seems not to have been understood. Europeans have entered their borders uninvited, and, when there, have not only acted as if they were undoubted lords of the soil, but have punished the natives as aggressors if they have evinced a disposition to live in their own country.

While the committee's focus was Empire-wide, members looked

closely at Australia, noting that within the recollection of many living men 'every part of this territory was the undisputed property of the Aborigines'. However in the establishment of the colonies it did not appear that 'the territorial rights of the natives were considered'. In fact the Aborigines' claims, 'whether as sovereigns or proprietors of the soil, have been utterly disregarded. The land has been taken from them without the assertion of any other title than that of superior force'.

One witness who had been in Australia, the Reverend W. Yate, was closely questioned by Buxton:

Buxton: Do the natives in the interior possess any land; have they any idea of property?

Yate: There are certain very large districts which they claim as belonging to different tribes, but which the English took possession of, without taking any notice of their claims.

Buxton: Then, as our settlements have extended, we have continued to deprive the natives of what unquestionably belongs to them, without affording them any compensation?

Yate: Yes; and if they have been found upon their own property, they have been treated as thieves and robbers.

Buxton: Then, when a new station is established, no question is ever entertained as to the right of the natives?

Yate: I have never heard of its being entertained.

The English missionary organisations and the Aborigines Protection Society were actively concerned with the question of native land rights in the Empire at large and in Australia in particular. The Society of Friends called for a 'Magna Charta for Indians, Caffres, Zoolahs and Australian Aborigines' (*sic*) in order to achieve recognition of their right to 'some portion of the territories once wholly theirs'. The occupancy of land by Aboriginal tribes, the Quakers argued, 'appears to imply a possession on their part, the proofs of the invalidity of which seems to be required of those who directly or indirectly take it from them. The natives consider themselves the real owners of the soil; and even in South Australia, where their condition is the most abject...

the more intelligent often assert that the land belongs to the black men'.

In 1838 the Aborigines Protection Society set up a sub-committee on Australia which reported that Britain had long oppressed the Aborigines by taking their land 'without treaties or consent founded on sufficient compensation'. Two years later the society published an *Outline of A System of Legislation for Securing Protection to the Aboriginal Inhabitants of all Countries Colonized by Great Britain* which took particular notice of the rights of property, urging that in future 'it be a fundamental principle in colonization, that no settlement shall be made on any land possessed or claimed by its aboriginal inhabitants, without their consent, formally obtained by treaty or otherwise substantially acknowledged by them'. The society was particularly concerned with developments in South Australia where, despite official statements recognising Aboriginal rights, the local clans were being relentlessly swept aside. As the nonexistence of any land rights was 'strongly insisted upon by many worthy and conscientious persons', the investigation of the native title was a point of primary importance. The society argued that the rights of the original possessors were 'not at all affected by Acts of Parliament or Commissioners' Instructions: their right rests upon the principle of justice. It is impossible to deny the right which natives have to the land on which they were born, and which from age after age they have derived support and nourishment, and which has received their ashes'.

Land rights in South Australia

The act of the British parliament which established South Australia in 1834 gave no recognition to Aboriginal land rights. Both the legislation and the charter incorporating the South Australian Colonizing Commission referred to the territory in question as 'waste and unoccupied lands which are supposed to be fit for the purposes of colonization'. The act declared that all lands in the province were to be regarded as public lands which were open to purchase by settlers and investors. Land remaining unsold was to become security for the colonial debt. But within a short time of the passage of the legislation voices in both Britain and the colony called for reconsideration of the question of native title. Governor George Arthur responded to news of the settlement by writing to the Secretary of State for the Colonies on how to avoid the bloodshed experienced in the colony in the previous decade. 'Every effort', he argued should be made to come to an understanding with the natives of South Australia' about the land question before the settlers arrived. His Tasmanian experience had convinced him that in the occupation of the colony it was a great oversight that a treaty was not, at that time, made with the natives, and such compensation given to the chiefs as they would have deemed a fair equivalent for what they surrendered...and that feeling of injustice which I am persuaded they always have entertained would have had no existence'. Arthur spoke with authority. After eleven years in Tasmania he had more experience of white–Aboriginal relations than anyone else in the colonial service. The incoming Secretary of State for the Colonies, Lord Glenelg, sent his letter to the South Australian Commissioners and subsequently warned them of the necessity 'for averting from the Aborigines that part of N[ew] Holland the calamities which that race of men have been overwhelmed by in the other British settlements in Australia'.

Humanitarian influence over colonial policy greatly increased in the months between the passage of the South Australian Act and the issue of the Letters Patent in March 1836 with the coming to office of Lord Glenelg as Secretary of State for the Colonies, Sir George Grey as his parliamentary under-secretary, and the elevation of James Stephen to assistant under-secretary in 1834 and permanent under-secretary two years later. All three had strong links with the Anti-Slavery cause and the mission societies. Stephen and Glenelg were committee members of the Church Missionary Society; Grey sat on the 1836–37 House of Commons Select Committee on Natives in the British Colonies and was a member of the Aborigines Protection Society.

The South Australian Commissioners were quickly made aware

of the new administration's concern for Aboriginal rights. Grey sent them a copy of a recent House of Commons address to the King praying 'that measures be taken to secure to the natives of the several Colonies the due observance of justice, and protection of their rights' and conveyed Glenelg's admonition that the subject could not 'but be regarded as of the first importance' in the formation of the new colony.

The Colonial Office showed concern over the large size of the projected colony. In a memo to Glenelg, Stephen noted: 'H.M. is to fix the boundaries of the Provinces. How this is to be done in a Terra incognito I cannot imagine, nor how it can be done at all with any due regard to the rights of the present Proprietors of the Soil or the rulers of the Country.' Writing to the Commissioners Glenelg argued that if the colony was allowed to occupy all the land encompassed within the boundaries established by the enabling legislation the definition of those boundaries was

> an object of very serious importance. This is more especially evident when it is remembered that the Act of Parliament presupposes the existence of a vacant territory and not only recognizes the Dominion of the crown, but the proprietary right to the soil of the Commissioners or of those who shall purchase lands from them, in any part of the Territory...Yet if the utmost limits were assumed within which Parliament has sanctioned the erection of the Colony it would extend very far into the interior of New Holland, and might embrace in its range numerous Tribes of People whose proprietary title to the soil we have not the slightest ground for disputing.

The humanitarian concerns of the Colonial Office were expressed in the Letters Patent, issued on the eve of the departure of the first settlers and containing the clause that no other provision should 'affect or be construed to affect the rights of any aboriginal natives of the said Province to the actual occupation or enjoyment in their own Persons or in the Persons of their Descendants of any lands therein now actually occupied or enjoyed by such Natives'. Before the issue of the Letters Patent, and under pressure from the Colonial Office, the Commissioners drew up a plan for 'the protection of the rights of the Aborigines in the Province of South Australia' which was especially concerned with the land question and included the clauses:

> The Colonial Commissioner after having completed the survey of any

portion of Public Land shall, before declaring the same open to sale, give notice to the Protector of Aborigines, whose duty it will be to ascertain, whether the lands thus surveyed or any portion of them, are in the occupation or enjoyment of the natives...Should the Protector of the Aborigines find that the Lands, or any portion of them...are occupied or enjoyed by the Natives, then the lands which may be thus occupied or enjoyed shall not be declared open to public sale, unless the Natives shall surrender their right of occupation or enjoyment, by a voluntary Sale made to the Colonial Commissioner...Should the Natives occupying or enjoying any lands... not surrender their right to such land by a voluntary sale, then, in that case, it will be the duty of the Protector of the Aborigines to secure to the Natives the full and undisturbed occupation or enjoyment of their lands and to afford them legal redress against depredators and trespassers.

The Colonial Office clearly believed that the Aborigines should receive compensation for land occupied by the settlers. Stephen explained that Glenelg did not think that the Commissioners should be the judges of the compensation 'they are to pay the Natives for the lands to be taken from them'. A draft bill prepared to amend the South Australian Act included the clause:

That it shall be lawful for the said Commissioners to assign or allot any Part of the Lands of the said Province to the Aboriginal Natives thereof free of any Price...and also to make such Compensation to the said Aboriginal Natives as the said Commissioners shall deem just in Compensation for their Interests in any Lands now occupied by them in the said Province; and any such Compensation shall and may be paid out of the Produce of Lands sold...by the Commissioners in the said Province.

Aboriginal land rights were strongly supported in the colony itself by Governor Gawler and his Land Commissioner Charles Sturt. In 1840 they came into conflict with a group of prominent colonists demanding the prior right of selection of land purchased in advance of settlement. Gawler and Sturt argued that it was impossible to regard any rights possessed by the Europeans 'as preliminary to those of the aboriginal inhabitants' who had 'natural indefeasible rights...vested in them as their birthright'. Before settlement the blacks had 'possessed well understood and distinctly defined proprietary rights over the whole of the available lands in the Province'. The colony itself was 'publicly known to have been founded on principles of the strictest regard to the original rights of the aboriginal inhabitants'. The rights of the Aborigines could be protected during the process of colonisation by giving them 'an absolute right of selection prior to all Europeans who have settled in it during the last four years, of reasonable portions of the choicest land, for their especial use and benefit, out of the very extensive districts over which, from time immemorial, these Aborigines have exercised distinct, defined and absolute rights of proprietary and hereditary possession'. The invasion of these 'ancient rights by surveys and land appropriations of any kind' was justifiable only on the ground that the colonial authorities would 'at the same time reserve for the natives an ample sufficiency for their present and future use and comfort, under the new state of things into which they are thrown—a state in which we hope they will be led to live in greater comfort on a small space than they enjoyed before it occurred on their extensive original possessions'.

Gawler's plan to select land for the Aborigines received the endorsement of Stephen and Russell, the new Secretary of State for the Colonies, who merely observed that given 'the very small portions of land assigned to the Aborigines out of extensive districts...a more liberal provision should have been made for their support'. In a memo on Gawler's dispatch, which enclosed newspaper reports of his conflict with the settlers, Stephen made the telling observation: 'It is an important and unexpected fact that these Tribes had proprietary and unsuspected rights in the Soil—that is, in particular sections of it which were clearly defined & well understood before the occupation of their country.'

In the event Gawler's scheme for reservations was judged to be illegal under the terms of the original South Australian Act, and colonial opinion turned sharply against the Aborigines with news of conflict on the fringes of the colony. But the idea of granting land in recognition of native title survived. The 1841 House of Commons Select Committee on South Australia passed the resolution: 'That it is expedient, that Her Majesty should be authorized to reserve, and set apart within the said Province, for the use of the Aboriginal Inhabitants thereof, any lands which it may be found necessary so to reserve and set apart for the occupation and subsistence of such Aboriginal Inhabitants.' In the same spirit the Australian Waste Lands Acts, passed in the

British Parliament the following year, and applying to all the colonies, allowed for the reservation or disposal of land 'for the use and benefit of the aboriginal inhabitants of the Country'.

The policy of reserving land for the Aborigines grew from a recognition and acceptance of their prior ownership of the land. It was an endorsement, not a denial of native title. Writing of the policy in 1839 the editor of the *South Australian Gazette* observed:

> We have not been charitable; the natives have received no charity at our hands; they have received nothing but what they are justly entitled to—they have received in fact but a miserable instalment of the debt of justice we still owe them...we met them upon the footing of British subjects—their claim of property in the soil distinctly recognized by our Sovereign and the Parliament of England. Had they been adequately instructed in the value of their land or had they been, like their New Zealand brethren, sufficiently informed to demand a treaty previous to cession, it is abundantly clear that the local government could not have dared and would not have been justified in taking possession of it without complying with that demand. But our poor natives had no such ideas. They received us as friends, without suspicion and without dread, we took their land without ceremony, we destroyed and extirpated their natural food without compunction, we occupied their plains with our flocks and herds without permission.

Squatters and protectors

'Philanthropists' in both Britain and Australia realised that the squatting movement advanced over both the bodies and the property of the Aborigines, that without official recognition of land rights prospects for the blacks were bleak. Even their survival as a people was threatened. 'In its bearing on the colonization of uncivilized nations,' an English humanitarian argued in 1847, 'the right of property in land is a fundamental point, and second in importance to none other. Indefinite and unjust ideas on this subject have been the radical cause of many of the injuries inflicted on Aboriginal tribes.' The Quaker James Backhouse believed that Australian colonisation as a whole had been 'based upon principles that cannot be too strongly reprobated and which want radical reformation'. The blacks, he wrote in 1834, had seen 'wholesale robbery of territory committed upon them'. The

Methodist missionary Joseph Orton believed that it was 'a base system of Colonization' which deprived 'so large a portion of our fellow creatures of their land and food'. After more than a decade on the fringes of European settlement the missionary L.E. Threkeld wrote:

> As a nation we have placed ourselves in a position that has compelled the Aborigines to become our neighbours, because we...dispossess the few Blacks of their rights of birth, which convey to them a certain district in which they seek and obtain their means of subsistence. Our might deprives them of this right...by taking away the common hereditary privileges which they have possessed from time immemorial. The place of their birth is sold to the highest bidder. They are excluded from the soil, being found generally prejudicial to the pecuniary interests of the purchaser, and that exclusion works their death.

The clash between the pastoral industry and the humanitarians over the question of Aboriginal land was highlighted during the 1840s with the establishment of the Port Phillip Protectorate. Robinson, the Chief Protector, wrote constantly about the acute problems faced by the Aborigines as a result of the occupation of their country. Soon after he arrived in Melbourne he complained that

> many of the Squatters with their twenty and forty square miles of country absurdly imagine that a ten pound license to squat confers on them the power to expel the primitive inhabitants from the land of their forefathers. It was a common occurrence but a short time since for these people to be coerced and chased by horsemen from their homes and their native fires. At that time squatters would openly avow their sentiments on this head, boasting that they never allowed an Aboriginal to appear on their run.

Robinson's concern increased after a case in the Supreme Court in Melbourne in 1841 which greatly strengthened the hand of the squatters. A settler named Bolden was arraigned for whipping and shooting blacks to drive them off his station. During the trial Mr Justice Willis declared that 'if a party receives a license from Government to occupy a run, and any person white or black come on my run for the purpose of stealing my property, I have a right to drive them off by every lawful means in my power... The blacks have no right to trespass unless there is a special clause in the license from the Government'.

Robinson continued to plead the Aboriginal cause, arguing in his annual report for 1846 that every acre of the black's native soil would 'shortly be so leased out and occupied to leave them, in a legal view, no place for the soles of their feet'.

Native title and pastoral leases

The Colonial Office responded to Robinson's account of the Aboriginal plight in February 1848. By then the Port Phillip Protectorate was regarded as a failure and Robinson was shortly to be dismissed, while the squatters had been given security of tenure on their runs. Earl Grey, the Secretary of State for the Colonies rejected a plea by Robinson for further Aboriginal reserves, but in doing so offered a far more radical solution to the conflicting claims of squatters and Aborigines. In a dispatch to the Governor of New South Wales he wrote:

> the very difficulty of thus locating the Aboriginal Tribes apart from the Settlers renders it the more incumbent on Government to prevent them from being altogether excluded from the land under pastoral occupation. I think it essential that it should be generally understood that leases granted for this purpose give the grantees only an exclusive right of pasturage for their cattle, and of cultivating such land as they may require within the large limits thus assigned to them but that these leases are not intended to deprive the natives of their former right to hunt over these districts, or to wander over them in search of subsistence in the manner to which they have been accustomed, from the spontaneous produce of the soil, except over land actually cultivated or fenced in for that purpose.

The importance of Grey's proposals has been seriously under-estimated. They warrant detailed analysis. The imperial government had accepted in 1847–48 that pastoral expansion would continue, but in so doing it sought to limit the rights of the settlers and to define and defend those of the Aborigines. The area in question was enormous. The proposals were immediately concerned with those large parts of Victoria and New South Wales occupied in the previous twenty years and held under pastoral lease. By implication all future settlement was to be governed by the principles spelt out by Grey and indeed they were embodied in all pastoral leases let in Queensland, Western Australia and the Northern Territory during the second half of the nineteenth century.

The squatters' rights were tightly circumscribed. They were far less than those of a freeholder, less than those allowed to a leaseholder by Justice Willis in 1841. The pastoralist had only an exclusive right to pasturage or the right to exclude other squatters and their animals. He was permitted to enclose and deny access to any land actually under cultivation, but in most of Australia such areas were likely to be very small. Aboriginal rights were more extensive. On any but enclosed and cultivated land they could come and go as they pleased, they could camp where they chose and pursue all their normal economic activities. But the sum was much greater than the parts, for what Grey had done was to recognise the right of Aborigines to continue to pursue their traditional life style undisturbed by the European presence. He had given a legal right to all who 'evinced a disposition to live in their own country'. It was less a matter of granting anything new, more a matter of recognising what had always been. The proposals established that Aboriginal rights had not been extinguished in 1788. They were impaired but they remained. Grey had recognised native title in very much the way that it was understood in North America and New Zealand. The Aborigines had been given a right of occupancy, a right of usage; they had what the nineteenth-century American jurist Storey called 'a present right of occupancy or use in the soil'; what New Zealand's Justice Chapman described as the right to 'all the enjoyment from the land' which had existed before settlement. Native title—the right of use and occupancy—was recognised to exist over most of the continent. The Crown had clearly exercised its right to extinguish that title in those comparatively small areas which were held as freehold in 1848. On crown land occupied under lease—both existing and prospective—Aboriginal rights of occupancy were to remain. If they existed on crown land held under lease they also existed on land still unoccupied by Europeans and that covered more than half the continent.

An examination of the historical context of Grey's 1848 proposals confirms the foregoing interpretation. Throughout the 1830s and 1840s strong concern was expressed in Britain about the fate of the indigenous people of the Empire. The Select Committee of 1836−37, of which Grey was a prominent member, was the most obvious expression of that interest. Concern centred in missionary and humanitarian organisations but spread from there into parliament and especially into the Colonial Office headed by James Stephen between 1836 and 1847 and still under his influence until 1850. When the English humanitarians spoke of Aboriginal rights they were particularly interested in land tenure. And their concern was Empire-wide. The Society of Friends wanted land rights for Indians, Kaffirs, Zulus, Australian Aborigines and all other 'coloured peoples'. The 1837 committee insisted that the 'native inhabitants of any land have an incontrovertible right to their own soil'. Australia did not appear unique when viewed from the centre of the Empire, nor did the Aborigines. That was a colonial not an imperial idea. Native title had been confirmed in the courts of both the United States and New Zealand between 1823 and 1847. The relevant decisions of Chief Justice Marshall were well known in legal circles in Britain and the colonies. An attempt to restrict Maori rights to land actually under cultivation had been given up by the Colonial Office at exactly the same time that the Australian pastoral leases were being considered. For twenty years before 1848 influential British humanitarians—people with strong links with the Colonial Office—had been concerned with racial conflict in Australia. The Colonial Office itself was alarmed at the incessant violence on the frontier. Earl Grey warned Governor Fitzroy in 1850 'how deeply the honor' of the colonists was involved in providing 'that no efforts have been wanting on their part to avert the destruction of the native race'. There was wide agreement that a major source of trouble was that Aboriginal rights to land had never been officially defined. Given the attention focused on the question of native rights in the Empire during the 1830s and the 1840s, it would have been surprising if the Colonial Office had not moved to recognise the existence of native title in Australia sometime before 1850. The Select Committee of 1836−37 noted that in the formation of the Australian colonies the 'territorial rights' of the Aborigines were not considered. 'Such omissions,' the report concluded, 'must surely be attributed to oversight.' That oversight, widely recognised in the 1830s, was remedied in 1848.

Grey's proposals may not have won wide acclaim, but they were not imposed on an incomprehending colony. The concept of native title had been widely discussed for a decade or more. Senior colonial officials—King, Arthur, Brisbane, Irwin, Gipps, Gawler and Sturt—had conceded that the Aborigines were the prior owners of the country and retained rights of occupancy under the aegis of the Crown. Land rights were discussed during negotiations which preceded the foundation of South Australia and were embodied in the Letters Patent establishing the colony, while the Colonial Office accepted that tribes living beyond the boundaries of South Australia had a 'proprietary right to the soil'. But during the 60 years between 1788 and 1848 the imperial government failed to define the nature of Aboriginal tenure. As the historian West remarked in 1852, it 'left undefined the obligations it seemed to confess'. In his 1971 judgment Blackburn took this to mean that native title had never existed in Australia. But it is probably more significant that it was never officially rejected. The question was taken up by the British politician Sir Howard Douglas in a speech in the House of Commons in 1843 in which he argued that if the concept of native title, as known in North America, had been abandoned in Australia it had been 'abandoned tacitly'. 'It does not appear,' he said, 'that any servant of the Queen was found openly to deny or disavow that policy.' Douglas reflected the contemporary view that native title was entrenched in the common law and had been since the eighteenth century; it was, in his view, the 'old and righteous principle' which had 'anciently guided the Colonizing operations of Britain'. Legal decisions in a number of common-law countries suggest that without deliberate and specific extinction by legislation native title survives. Inaction, as in Australia in the early nineteenth century, preserves the status quo. Silence strengthens rather than weakens the case for native title. The task for historians, jurists and politicians, then, is not to prove that native title existed in Australia; rather it is to show that it was ever extinguished.

The Rights of the Soil

The squatters respond

Pastoral leases issued during the second half of the nineteenth century and covering vast areas of the continent embodied the proposals in Grey's 1848 dispatch. In Western Australia they provided 'full rights' to the Aborigines 'at all times to enter upon any unenclosed but otherwise unimproved land' for the purpose of seeking their subsistence 'in their accustomed manner'. Queensland blacks were allowed free access to any part of a lease 'and to the trees and water thereon as will enable them to pursue the animals, birds, fish and other foods on which they subsist'. The South Australian–Northern Territory leases went into greater detail, allowing the Aborigines

> full and free right of ingress, egress and regress into upon and over the said Waste Land of the Crown...and in and to the Springs and surface water thereon and to make and erect such wurlies and other dwellings as the said Aboriginals have been heretofore accustomed to make and to take and use for food birds and animals...in such manner as they would have been entitled to if this demise had not been made.

In practice these provisions were ignored. Within a few months of receiving Grey's dispatch the colonies began to prepare for self-government, and after 1856 land policy and Aboriginal affairs became colonial rather than imperial concerns everywhere except Western Australia. Patterns of behaviour, already two generations old, were too deeply entrenched to be changed by an edict from London and especially one which threatened the most powerful economic interests in the country. Hostility to the Aborigines and to those who defended them was rampant and squatters continued to behave as they pleased on 'their' land. Some were paternalistic and came to terms with neighbouring clans, but rarely in a manner which conceded Aboriginal rights to anything. The majority drove the blacks away with guns and whips because they frightened the cattle, burnt the grass, drank the water, worried the whites or were just in the way.

The squatters and the imperial government were each defending a different concept of property. Grey foreshadowed a system similar to that common in traditional European rural society where different groups of people had overlapping use-rights to the same piece of land. The typical squatter was totally committed to the ascendant concept of an absolute and exclusive right to land even though he was normally only a lessee of the Crown. Most pastoral expansion after 1848 was carried out in a way that totally disregarded Aboriginal rights and, therefore, the law itself. On hundreds of stations, across vast stretches of country, the Aborigines were driven away or shot if they 'evinced a disposition to live in their own country'. A Queensland squatter told the journalist A.J. Vogan in the 1890's: 'Curse their black hides, I've tried kindness, and I've tried the other thing; but curse me if I aint got less trouble to clear them off first thing—I've always found it so, instead of having to shoot 'em in compartments afterwards.' An old drover, recalling his outback experiences in the late nineteenth and early twentieth centuries, observed that 'to make friends with wild blacks required plenty of patience and cold nerve'. Most pastoralists preferred 'to shoot them off the stations...it seemed quicker and easier to do the job that way'.

Pioneers openly boasted how for years on end they had 'kept the blacks out'. Yet throughout 60 or 70 years of murderous dispossession the law was impotent. Further research may eventually turn up a relevant case or two, but it is reasonable to assume that no colonial court ever defended the Aboriginal right of occupancy. Without enforcement there was no litigation. Without litigation there were no judicial attempts to define Aboriginal rights; no dicta; no precedents; no case law. It is not surprising that in the late twentieth century jurists can assert that native title never existed in Australia. But in so doing they rest their case not on what the law actually said but on a record of abject failure to enforce it.

If the provisions in the pastoral leases providing for Aboriginal rights had been respected by squatters, enforced by police and upheld in the courts the history of land settlement after 1848 would have been very different. The distribution of power between black and white would have been transformed. Life would have been more difficult for the pioneers. There would have been a need for negotiation and diplomacy rather than brute force. Many more clans would have presumably stayed on their own land;

traditional economic and social life would have been bolstered and fewer blacks would have been forced to work for Europeans in situations of gross exploitation. The frontier squatters who developed the most successful, and peaceful, relations with neighbouring clans adopted policies which grew out of assumptions very similar to those of Grey's proposals. There were a number of cases where squatters negotiated with blacks to allow for a sharing of the land and water, for a balancing of the needs of hunting and pastoralism. The Queensland pioneer Robert Christison came to terms with the blacks resident on his Lammermoor station, saying to one of the leading clansmen: 'Very good Barney. Country belonging to you; sheep belonging to me.' In southern Queensland the Archer family avoided the conflict endemic on most runs, acting on the premise that all the Europeans could claim was the grass for their herds. David Archer considered 'the Black as the hereditary owner of the soil and that it is an act of injustice to drive him from his hunting ground'.

Official impotence

Colonial officials occasionally drew attention to the enormous gap between legality and reality. In Queensland after the passing of the Aborigines Protection Act in 1897 the newly appointed protectors attempted to encourage respect for regulations which had been ignored for 50 years. The Chief Protector wrote in 1904 that

> notwithstanding the efforts of myself and other Protectors to combat it, the assumption continues to prevail that because a large area of land is held from the Crown on lease, license or other tenure, the lessee has the legal right to prevent aboriginals roaming or hunting over it; even living on it...[T]he principle must be rigidly instilled that the aboriginals have as much a right to exist as the Europeans, and certainly a greater right, not only to collect native fruits, but also to hunt and dispose of the game upon which they have been vitally dependent from time immemorial.

In his annual report for 1887 the Government Resident in the Northern Territory considered the problems of continuing conflict between squatters and Aborigines. He conceded that the rights of the blacks to as much land—'the best of the land'—as was necessary for their sustenance and tribal life were 'indisputable'. He referred to, and quoted from, the relevant clauses in pastoral leases but noted that they were observed 'rather in a poetic than a practical sense'. What, he asked, was the usual course of events on the frontier?

> A capitalist or a syndicate applies for or buys at auction the leases for a certain number of hundreds or thousands of square miles of country, carefully following the permanent watercourses, and including the permanent lagoons and waterholes. The Aborigines who have the vested interest of hoary antiquity are only considered by the State to the extent of the above recited clause in the pastoral lease. Afterwards the squatter or his manager, comes on to the country with his overland herds...In nearly all cases the early result of the white mans intrusion is a permanent feud between the blacks and whites. The blacks frighten and spear the cattle and hold themselves in readiness to attack the boundary rider and stockman, or to make a raid upon outstations or storeroom. The whites look well to their Winchesters and revolvers, and usually proceed on the principle of being on the safe side. It is an affection of ignorance to pretend not to know that this is the condition of things throughout the 'backblocks' and the 'new country' of Australia.

Blackburn v. Marshall

In his 1971 decision in *Milirrpum* v. *Nabalco* Mr Justice Blackburn determined that native title had never existed in Australian law; all Aboriginal rights were extinguished in the eastern half of Australia in 1788, and because no subsequent grant from the Crown could be discovered native title had never been recognised. Despite the detailed consideration given to relevant cases in other countries it is clear that on several crucial points Blackburn's interpretation runs directly against the overwhelming weight of case law which has been accumulating since the early nineteenth century.

The mainstream view has been that native title arose from the incontrovertible fact of occupation, that it was recognised both in the common law and the 'law of nations'. When Marshall said in 1823 that it had never been contended that native title amounted to nothing be did not mean that nobody had ever put forward that view. No doubt many settlers had done so in every colonial society. What he argued was that it had never been contended in law that indigenous people lost everything on annexation. Native title was not called into existence by statute or executive action and it continued to exist until the Crown exercised its undoubted right to extinguish that title. But it was not extinguished because it was neglected or ignored. It required specific and precise legislation. In the absence of such clear and unequivocal action native title continued to exist.

Many of these issues were raised in Canada at the same time that Blackburn was sitting in judgment on *Milirrpum* v. *Nabalco*. The case in question, *Calder* v. *Attorney General of British Columbia*, came before the provincial Court of Appeal in May 1970 and the Canadian Supreme Court in January 1973, eighteen months after Blackburn had handed down his judgment. The case had many features relevant to Australia. Calder was a representative of the Nishga Indians of the Nair Valley of north British Columbia who sought recognition of their native title. The Nishga had been hunters and gatherers and numbered about 2000 before extensive contact with Europeans. They could point to no official recognition of their land rights. The royal proclamation of 1763 which recognised Indian rights of occupation in the east of what was to become Canada and the United States had no direct relevance to the west coast. No treaties had been signed with British Columbia Indians in contrast to the situation east of the Rockies. The colonial government, before entry into the confederation in 1871, acted in the manner of contemporaneous Australian ones. It gave no recognition to Indian land rights and legislated to throw open the land to European pioneers as though they didn't exist.

For these reasons the British Columbia court held that the Nishgas had no title at all. They could not point to any legislation or executive action which recognised their rights. And at the same time the colonial government exercised 'absolute sovereignty over all the lands of British Columbia, a sovereignty inconsistent with any conflicting interest, including one as to Aboriginal title'. The result was that if there 'ever was such a thing as aboriginal or Indian title...such has been lawfully extinguished in toto'.

Blackburn regarded the first Calder case as an important and relevant one, which, while not binding on his court, was 'weighty authority' for his two crucial propositions:

1   In a settled colony there is no principle of communal native title except such as can be shown by prerogative or legislative act. . .
2   In a settled colony a legislative and executive policy of treating the land of the colony as open to grant by the Crown, together with the establishment of native reserves, operates as an extinguishment of native title, if that ever existed.

The Canadian court's discussion of the source and recognition of native title was particularly important. It decisively rejected the view that native title only existed as a result of specific enactment. Mr Justice Hall referred directly to Blackburn's judgment and his agreement with the British Columbia courts. The essence of Blackburn's concurrence, Hall argued, 'lies in his acceptance of the proposition that after conquest or discovery the native peoples have no rights at all except those subsequently granted or recognized by the conqueror or discoverer. That proposition is wholly wrong as the mass of authorities. . .establishes'. The court discussed the nature of native title, Mr Justice Judson observing that when the settlers arrived in British Columbia the Indians were there, 'organized in societies and occupying the land as their forefathers had done for centuries'. That, he concluded, 'is what Indian title means'. Justices Hall, Spence and Laskin argued that the lower court had erred

in accepting the proposition that, after conquest or discovery [the Indians] had no rights at all except those subsequently granted or recognized by the conqueror or discoverer. There is an aboriginal Indian interest usufructuary in nature which is a burden on the title of the Crown, and is inalienable except to the Crown and extinguishable only by a legislative enactment of the Parliament of Canada. This aboriginal title does not depend on treaty, executive order or legislative enactment but flows from the fact that the owners of the interest have from time immemorial occupied the areas in question and have established a pre-existing right of possession. In the absence of an indication that the sovereign intends to extinguish that right aboriginal title continues.

The Rights of the Soil

The belief that native title amounted to nothing was unacceptable to many people in colonial Australia, as the foregoing discussion has shown. It is untenable today within Australia, even more so in the outside world. Eventually Australian courts will be forced to move out of their provincial backwater and contend with the mainstream common-law tradition regarding indigenous rights. The view of Chief Justice Marshall enunciated in *Johnson* v. *McIntosh* over 150 years ago will eventually prevail in Australia as it did long ago in the courts of comparable countries overseas. Comments made by Mr Justice Deane of the High Court in a recent case suggest that change is in the air. He said:

> The almost two centuries that have elapsed since white settlement have seen the extinction of some Aboriginal clans and the dispersal, with consequent loss of identity and tradition, of others. Particularly where the clan has survived as a unit living on ancestral lands however, the relationship between the Aboriginal peoples and their land remains unobliterated. Yet, almost two centuries on, the generally accepted view remains that the common law is ignorant of any communal native title or other legal claim of the Aboriginal clans or peoples even to ancestral tribal lands on which they still live. If that view of the law be correct, and I do not suggest that it is not, the common law of this land has still not reached the stage of retreat from injustice which the law of Illinois and Virginia had reached in 1823 when Marshall C.J. accepted that, subject to the assertion of ultimate dominion... by the State, the 'original inhabitants' should be recognised as having 'a legal as well as just claim' to retain the occupancy of their traditional lands.

– 7 –

This Whispering in Our Hearts

Richard Windeyer, barrister and defence counsel in the Myall Creek Trials in 1838, was one of the ablest apologists for European colonisation. In a paper delivered in Sydney in 1844 he mounted a powerful attack on the idea that the blacks retained rights to the land, referring, in the course of his argument; to such standard authorities as Vattels' *The Law of Nations*, Blackstone's *Commentaries on the Laws of England* and Locke's *Of Civil Government*. But even when he had completed a forceful analysis of the question his conscience still troubled him. 'How is it our minds are not satisfied?' he asked. 'What means this whispering in the bottom of our hearts?'

A sore subject

Many white Australians have had the same problem over the last 200 years. 'This right to Australia is a sore subject with many of the British settlers,' observed a Port Phillip settler in the 1840s, 'and they strive to satisfy their consciences in various ways.' Few colonists commented openly on the morality of settlement, a second Victorian pioneer noted in 1845, but he detected 'an uneasiness in dealing with the subject', indicating that many thought 'our title is bad'. The South Australian, Francis Dutton, went further, arguing, in that same year, that the claims of the blacks were 'superior to ours', although we are 'too eager on all occasions, by casuistical reasoning, to persuade ourselves that such is not the case'. The Aboriginal problem was an 'inexhaustible and standard question' with the 'civilized and humane portion of the Australian public' during the 1850s; it gave rise 'to more argument than almost any other' in Queensland in the 1860s. A young emigrant, writing home from a frontier station in Queensland in 1844, described an animated discussion with three companions about the 'moral right of a nation to take forcible possession of a Country inhabited by savages', explaining that:

> John and David McConnell argued that it is morally right for a Christian Nation to extirpate savages from their native soil in order that it may be peopled with a more intelligent and civilized race of human beings etc. etc. F. McConnell and myself were of the opposite opinion and argued that a nation had no moral right to take forcible possession of any place. What is your opinion on the subject? Don't you think it a most heinous act of any Nation however powerful, however civilized and however christianized that Nation may be—to take possession of a country peopled by weak and barbarous tribes?

More exalted colonists worried about the same problem. 'The stain of blood is upon us,' Bishop Polding told his flock in a pastoral letter in 1869, 'blood has been shed far otherwise than in self-defence—blood, in needless and wanton cruelty.' It was a question of 'crime against humanity', thundered the missionary William Ridley in 1865, 'involving national guilt and disgrace'. John Cook, a north Queensland miner, raised a fundamental issue in a letter to the colonial government in 1891. The blacks were, he argued, the rightful owners of Australia 'for even if we are born in Australia we are only usurpers here for if we take away the peoples property without paying for it it does not matter how much we beautyfully [*sic*] try to cloak it it is and always must remain stolen property'.

An unwelcome obelisk

Many of these questions arose in 1884 when James Dawson, a pioneer of Victoria's Western District, decided to erect a monument in the Camperdown cemetery to commemorate the local Aborigines. He had been interested in the blacks for many years, had written a book about them, and was for some years honorary protector of the districts' Aborigines. Returning from a trip to Britain he found that the last member of the local clans—his friend and confidante Wombeetch Puuyuun or 'Camperdown

George'—had died in his absence. When he visited the cemetery he found 'no mark of respect beyond burial in a big hole...and that outside the boundaries of the White Man's ground, as if the black man was a brute'. He was outraged and began a collection to build a 20-foot obelisk modelled on one he had seen in Oban in Scotland, eventually digging the body up himself and reburying it at the base of the monument which he had inscribed with the epitaph 'In Memory of the Aborigines of this District'.

In order to raise money for the venture Dawson wrote to the local landowners, 'all of the olden time', for donations, but received little support despite follow-up letters. He told an officer of the Aborigines Protection Board:

> You would be amused if you read some of the letters I hold from some of those who are powerful in prayer as they are mean in charity and good deeds, their excuses are contemptible, and in two or three instances accompanied with religious advice. Religious advice from men holding Magnificent Estates from which the Aboriginals were expelled and massacred wholesale.

Some of the landowners who answered Dawson's letters expressed conventional hostility towards the Aborigines, one explaining that he had 'always looked on the blacks as a nuisance' and hoped the trustees would forbid the erection of the monument. But others betrayed continuing unease about the dispossession although they had been secure on their properties for 40 years. 'I decline to assist in erecting a monument,' one correspondent explained, 'to a race of men we have robbed of their country.' A second believed the obelisk would 'point for all time to come to our treatment of this unfortunate race—the possessors of the soil we took from them'.

The moral foundations

Australians troubled with a whisper in their heart have often taken comfort from the history of the first years of settlement when, so the argument runs, Governor Phillip and his officers pursued a policy of amity and kindness towards the clans around Sydney Harbour. At least, it is felt, the original intentions were good, the moral foundations were sound. But how valid is this view? A major problem is that the apologists take the official expression of benevolence at its face value. But could anything else have been expected? Invasions are usually preceded with statements of goodwill towards the people targeted for submission. Usurpers rarely admit to evil intent. The history of European colonisation abounds with sentiments like those expressed by the British in 1788. Two hundred years earlier Phillip II of Spain issued an ordinance concerning expansion in the Americas. Discovery, he insisted, 'must be made with all the peace and charity we desire. We do not wish to give occasion or pretext for force or injury to the Natives'.

Was it realistic to think that the Aborigines could be conciliated in the midst of imposition and expropriation? It is true that little was known about them, but by 1788 the Europeans already had the benefit of 250 years of colonial experience. British relations with the indigenous people of the Caribbean and North America would have provided scant evidence to support prospects for a peaceful result in New South Wales. The likely outcome of the expedition to Botany Bay was foreshadowed by a correspondent writing in London's *Morning Herald* in September 1786. 'The voyages of our late Navigators,' he recalled,

> are full of shocking instances of murder, and show us how improbable it is that any plantation can be made upon the lately discovered islands of the continent, without a cruel disregard for the lives of the natives...[B]ecause they are justly and naturally jealous of such invasion [the natives] must be destroyed by the armed force which is sent out with the convicts, to support the occupancy of lands not their own.

The officers of the First Fleet might have reflected on the words of Francis Bacon in his essay 'Of Plantations', published almost 200 years before they shipped for the Antipodes. 'I like a plantation in a pure soil,' he explained, 'that is, where people are not displanted to the end to plant in others, for else it is rather an extirpation than a plantation.'

A fundamental contradiction

A more serious problem with British policy in 1788 was the fundamental contradiction between treating the indigenes with 'amity and kindness', avoiding 'interruptions to their several occupations', while at the same time taking their land. The difficulty was compounded by the fact that the Aborigines became British subjects in 1788 and, as in other colonies of settlement, all English laws were, in the authoritative words of Blackstone, 'immediately there in force'. What is more, those laws were overwhelmingly concerned with protecting property. It need only be recalled that most convicts were transported for crimes against property, that men and women were hung for theft in both Britain and New South Wales. John Locke, a seminal influence on eighteenth-century political thought, defined power as the 'right of making laws, with penalties of death, and consequently all less penalties, for regulating and preserving of property'. Indeed Locke argued that men entered society in the first place in order to protect their possessions. 'The great and chief end, of men entering into commonwealths,' he believed, was 'the preservation of their property.' No government could 'take from any man any part of his property without his consent'. The state could legitimately take a man's life but it could not confiscate his estate. The proposition that anyone could actually lose their property as a result of entering society was, in Locke's view, 'too gross an absurdity for any man to own'.

The position of the Aborigines in 1788 was beset by anomalies. The government professed benevolence; the blacks were British subjects under a legal system whose primary function was the protection of property, yet their property rights were disregarded. The Pole Strzelecki observed in 1845 that the blacks had been 'declared by law, or by rather, sophistry of law, to be illegitimate possessors of any land which they do not cultivate...The Christianity which was offered to him was stripped of its charity, and the civilization embraced no recognition of his rights of property'. Policy so tangled with contradictions could not hope to succeed. It is scarcely surprising that the colonists took their cue, with respect to the blacks, from what the authorities did rather than what they said. How could the average settler take Aboriginal rights seriously? If their property could be confiscated, why respect their persons, why respect their lives? A Queensland frontiersman observed in 1857, while defending frontier violence: 'Say—an argument often used—they are under our laws, subject to our laws, and therefore we cannot, we must not punish the innocent for the guilty, this is, indeed, hypocrisy. If they are under our laws, why not protect their property? What business have we with their land?—with their hunting grounds?'

Terra nullius?

Some settlers resolved the contradictions concerning the place of the Aborigines in European society by assuming that Australia had been, before 1788, 'waste and uncultivated', a *terra nullius* or land without owners. The blacks themselves, it was asserted, were living in a state of nature; they lacked any idea of ownership and entered European society without any property at all. Such ideas, stemming principally from Locke, were commonplace in early-nineteenth-century Australia, the editor of the *Sydney Herald* arguing in 1838 that land in Aboriginal society 'belonged generally to every body but particularly to nobody...the ground was in common and no part of it was the permanent property of any particular man'. The blacks wandered at will over the face of the country without permanent resting places. They merely ranged over the land; 'the right of possession continued no longer than the act of possession lasted'. What was the difference, the editor asked, 'between taking possession of a country without inhabitants, and taking possession of a country of which a comparatively few wandering inhabitants make no use? Such a country is a *desert* for every purpose involved in this question, and may be justly occupied by civilized man'. People like the Aborigines had no property rights at all, 'Fidelis' argued in the *Sydney Gazette* in 1824:

> Any doubt, therefore, as to the lawfulness of our assuming the possession of this Island, must arise from the opinion that it was the *property* of its original inhabitants. Such opinion, however, would be incorrect; for the very notion of property, as applicable to territorial possessions, did not exist among them. Which tribe, or which individual, could with propriety be considered as the proper owner of any particular district? Each tribe wandered about wheresoever inclination prompted, without ever supposing that anyone place belonged to it more than to another. There were the

inhabitants, but not the proprietors of the land. This country then was to be regarded as an unappropriated remnant of common property; and, in taking possession of it, we did not invade another's right, for we only claimed that which before was unclaimed by any.

If Fidelis' basic premise was accepted it was a cogent and logically consistent argument. But the state of nature did not exist outside the European imagination. Without it the justification for occupying Aboriginal land was seriously weakened and the concept was increasingly difficult to defend as knowledge of Aboriginal society grew and the Aborigines' attitude to land became more generally understood. The fact that the blacks were the prior owners of Australia was accepted by many settlers and received official recognition in both Britain and the colonies in the 1830s. The most decisive statement was one made by Lord Glenelg in a letter to the South Australian Colonizing Commissioners, and referred to earlier, in which he wrote of the Aborigines living in the interior of the new colony whose 'proprietary title to the soil' the government had not 'the slightest ground for disputing'. The implications of this statement were both clear and important. The land in question had been annexed by Britain either in 1788 (up to the 135th line of longitude) or by Captain Bremer in 1824. Despite the obvious fact of annexation the Colonial Office clearly recognised that the Aborigines retained a proprietary title to their land which had not been extinguished by the claim of sovereignty. The concept of native title had been officially accepted. Glenelg's statement also made it clear that the imperial government had abandoned the concept of *terra nullius*. The Aborigines were the original proprietors, their interest remained after annexation and did so until it was formally extinguished.

Sovereignty and native title

There is little doubt that international law of the late eighteenth century allowed the British to claim sovereignty over eastern Australia by right of discovery. They could also, with some show of legality, assert the right to settle at specific locations where they intended to establish colonies and cultivate the soil. But it has been usual to claim much more than that; the common view, endorsed by Blackburn in *Milirpum* v. *Nabalco* in 1971, is that on 26 January 1788 all Aboriginal rights to land in eastern Australia disappeared. It was, by any measure, an extraordinary claim. Occupation and ownership, arching back in time over 40 000 years and more, was wiped out in an instant. Fifteen hundred generations amounted to nothing. For their part Governor Phillip and his officers knew little about the people expropriated or the land claimed. For a generation after 1788 the settlers huddled close to the coast. In 1838 the Aborigines still occupied most of the continent; even in 1888 many blacks had not seen a white man. Aboriginal communities continue to live on their traditional land in many parts of Australia.

When addressing this question white Australians have generally concluded that while British actions in 1788 might be difficult to justify by modern standards they were fully endorsed by the theory and practice of contemporary European colonisation. That is, at best, only partly true. In justifying the dispossession of the Aborigines the settlers frequently referred to such standard works of international law as Vattel's *The Law of Nations* which did, indeed, establish the right of Europeans to plant colonies in the New World and to occupy land sufficient to support the settlers. Vattel argued, in a much-quoted passage:

> There is another celebrated question, to which the discovery of the new world has principally given rise. It is asked if a nation may lawfully take possession of a part of a vast country, in which there are found none but erratic nations, incapable, by the smallness of their numbers to people the whole? We have already observed in establishing the obligation to cultivate the earth, that these nations cannot exclusively appropriate to themselves more land than they have occasion for, and which they are unable to settle and cultivate. Their removing their habitations through these immense regions, cannot be taken for a true and legal possession; and the people of Europe, too closely pent up, finding land of which these nations are in no particular want, and of which they make no actual and constant use, may lawfully possess it, and establish colonies there.

But the settler's study of international law was very selective; they quoted those passages which bolstered their cause and ignored the rest. Much of the difficulty arose over the precise nature of a claim of sovereignty by right of discovery. The principal objective of such a claim was to forestall counter-claims by other Europeans, Mr Justice Marshall explained in his 1823 judgment in *Johnson* v. *McIntosh*, that the accepted principle was that 'discovery gave title to the government by whose subjects, or by whose authority, it was made, against all other European governments, which title might be consummated by possession'. Sovereignty gave the nation the 'sole right of acquiring the soil from the natives and establishing settlements upon it'. It did not of itself deliver up, unencumbered, all land held by the indigenes. The question of what happened to native rights had to be resolved afterwards. And in that process it was never assumed that the indigenes were without rights. Marshall insisted in 1823 that their right to continued occupation—their native title—had never been questioned. Vattel believed that they could be 'confined within narrower limits' but not dispossessed. While they had no right to 'keep to themselves the whole of a vast continent', the colonists were to make sure that 'sufficient land was left to the Indians'. 'Wandering tribes' were not to be stripped of all their rights as a consequence of European intrusion. 'Still, no other nation,' Vattel insisted, had the right to 'restrict their possessions, unless it is in absolute need of land; for, after all they are in possession of the country, they make use of it after their own fashion; they obtain from it what they need for their manner of life, as to which no one can dictate to them.' Nor could Europeans lay claim to larger areas of land than they actually needed. While they might settle 'in certain parts of the region' their ambitions should not be boundless. 'It is questioned,' Vattel wrote, 'whether a Nation can thus appropriate, by the mere act of taking possession lands which it does not really occupy, and which are more extensive than it can inhabit or cultivate. It is not difficult to decide that such a claim would be absolutely contrary to the natural law.'

The belief that native title disappeared completely at the moment of annexation may continue to be upheld in Australian courts, but the proposition had little support in the legal and political writing of the late eighteenth and early nineteenth centuries or in the courts of other common-law countries. It appears, for better or for worse, to have been a home-grown product, unique to Australia. The West Australian pioneer, R.M. Lyon, observed in 1833 that his fellow colonists were 'determined to disregard every other principle of justice', and had resolved 'to consider the king's proclamation a sufficient title to their lands'.

Subdue the earth

The most enduring justification for the settlement of Australia was the argument that Europeans made better use of the land than did Aborigines. The editor of the *Port Denison Times* argued in 1866 that 'the only tenable argument that will justify us white men in Australia for taking possession of the country, and holding it against its prior occupants is that we improve the ground more than they do, that under our occupation it will produce more and be more beneficial to the human race than it would under theirs'.

Biblical texts bolstered the argument and especially God's injunction to man to 'go forth and multiply, subdue the earth and replenish it', which was taken as an indication of divine approval of colonial endeavour. A writer in the Sydney *Atlas* in 1844 explained: 'We are bound in duty to our country, as well as commanded by our faith to increase, multiply and replenish the earth.' In his history of Victoria, published in 1858, McCombie concluded that it 'could never be intended by a wise providence that fine continents, capable of maintaining millions of inhabitants in comfort, should be abandoned to the support of a few savages'. The editor of the *North Australian* claimed in 1861 that 'the right, the duty of civilization to occupy and subdue the soil...is not an open question'. The Reverend J.D. Lang developed a similar argument while addressing a meeting of the Moreton Bay Friends of the Aborigines Society in 1856. In confiscating Aboriginal land,

> he did not think they had done any thing wrong. God in making the earth never intended it should be occupied by men so incapable of appreciating its resources as the Aborigines of Australia. The white men had indeed, only carried out the intention of the Creator in coming and settling down in the territory of the natives.
>
> God's first command to man was 'Be fruitful and multiply, and replenish and earth'. Now that the Aborigines had not done, and therefore it was no fault in taking the land of which they were previously the possessors.

As the colonies developed the settlers became increasingly confident that their material success was sufficient to drown out any whispers in the heart. Economic growth was its own justification. 'No man,' wrote West in his *History of Tasmania* in 1852, 'can witness the triumph of colonization, when cities rise in the desert, without being gladdened by the change.' Fifty years later in his *A History of the Colony of Victoria* H.B. Turner argued that the 'substitution of more than a million of industrious and peaceful people for a roaming, fighting contingent of 6000 cannot be said to be dearly purchased'. In 1843 the Reverend W. Pridden argued:

> One of the greatest efforts to which the industry and powers of man can be directed is to change a lonely and uncultivated wilderness into an enclosed and fruitful country—to occupy with civilized human beings and comfortable dwellings those wilds which have hitherto been nearly deserted, or at best scantily occasionally inhabited by savage barbarians. The colonisation of New South Wales by the English has been one of the most successful of these efforts, and certainly never before did the change effected by industry so rapidly make itself visible in the face of the new country.

But even if it were true that the land belonged morally to those who cultivated it, the embarrassing fact was that very little of Australia was ever brought under the plough. Even now less than 10 per cent of the land surface is under crop or sown grass. The extensive open-range grazing of pioneer squatters neither met the expectations of European philosophers nor did it differ all that much from the way in which the Aborigines used the land. The Commissioner of Crown Lands on the Clarence River in 1848 noted that 'like the native', the squatter 'occupies without possessing the soil, he has never appropriated it by agriculture'. The editor of the *Brisbane Courier* argued, in 1865, that the person who merely grazed stock upon the natural grasses had 'no greater claim upon the soil than the Aborigines who merely hunt thereon the animals indigenous to it'.

Was the earth open to all?

If Britons' claim to Aboriginal land rested on their ability to 'subdue the earth', what justification was there for immigration restriction, especially when so much of the continent remained empty and undeveloped? It was a question often posed by those who resisted the growth, from the 1850s, of the White Australia policy. During debate in the New South Wales parliament in 1857, on a bill restricting the entry of Chinese, William Forster asked his colleagues:

> By what right or authority had the people of this country to occupy the land? Not by the right of conquest from the aboriginal population, but by the right to civilize and put the land to some use...If that were the right upon which they possessed the land, by what right did they attempt to prevent the Chinese from coming here to join the colonists in the work of usefulness and civilization?

The editor of the *Queensland Guardian* argued in 1862 that while he was personally opposed to the Chinese, 'we cannot shut our eyes to the fact that even our own title to the land in which we now dwell is founded on the broad cosmopolitan principle that the earth is open to all'. During debate in the South Australian parliament in 1888, on a bill to further restrict Chinese immigration, Robert Caldwell remarked:

> This colony was only fifty years old. It was inhabited by several savage tribes before we came here. It was not an uninhabited piece of territory...and it appeared to him that we were assuming a great deal more than as representatives of the human race we had any right to assume. The British came here and took possession of a considerable territory to the exclusion of, and ignoring the rights of the original inhabitants...It seemed to him that the only arguments we used was [sic] that we were masters of this country, we exercised rights over the whole of it, and we were going to say who should not come here. He granted that we were justified in taking possession of this country in the name of civilization, and we were justified in taking a fair share of the territory, but we had no right to be selfish and prevent other people coming here...The Australians were not capable of monopolizing and turning to the best possible account the country which they had claimed as their own.

The argument about the mission to develop the continent eventually came full circle. In 1902 Senator Stewart addressed a meeting on Thursday Island, a community which had benefited considerably from Japanese immigration. Defending the recently imposed White Australia Policy, he argued that rather than accept Asian migration, 'he would see it remain a desert. There was no particular hurry about developing the resources of this continent'.

Part III: The Land

Humanitarian doubts

Humanitarian critics in both British and Australia questioned the conventional justification of colonisation and particularly the argument that Europeans could legitimately confiscate land lying 'waste and unproductive'. In 1844 William Duncan, the editor of Sydney's *Morning Chronicle*, argued that such a proposition 'upsets all our previous ideas of justice, and expunges it from the volume of all human ethics—in short it is the philosophy of brigands, or buccaneers, and would justify the Russian aristocrat in his oppression of the Poles, or any oppression whatsoever'. Other 'philanthropists' pointed out that while neglect or misuse of land might be frowned upon in British or Australian society it was not an excuse for confiscation. A writer in the journal of the Aborigines Protection Society remarked in 1839 that before sanctioning the operation of such principles in respect to native people, it would be appropriate 'to enquire into the situation of landholders even in this country, when land is left uncultivated... There are... many acres of land wholly appropriated to the propagation and preservation of wild animals... and yet there is, perhaps, no portion of the land of which the possession is more immovably fixed in the hands of the proprietors and their descendants, than some of these apparently waste and neglected districts'. G.A. Robinson made the same point in Australia in 1849. 'Improvable lands,' he wrote, 'are it is said too valuable, as they [the Aborigines] do not cultivate, and such lands are of great value to the White settler, but if considerations of this sort were held to justify a compulsory transfer of property then would there soon be an end to the rights of all property'. In 1876 the Catholic missionary Duncan McNab put a similar argument in a letter to Queensland's Minister of Lands. He wrote:

> Some fancy that the occupation of the country by the blacks for fishing and hunting does not amount to the exercise of a right of property in the soil; but their opinion must be erroneous as such occupation has been deemed sufficient in other barbarous countries and even in those that are civilized. In Scotland I have seen waste tracts of land inherited, or bought at a great price, and possessed by gentleman for no other purpose, and such use of them is acknowledged as an exercise of the right of property; and only he who possesses such a right can lawfully use or let the shootings and fishings.

An English critic of colonial policy suggested in 1839 that the land should be held in trust for the Aborigines. Even if they were unable to immediately develop their country's resources they should be treated like children who were heirs to large fortunes and who were

> possessed of capital which, for the present, is as respects them, in a state of dormant and unproductive investment. This surely is no plea for the abstraction of such capital but should induce us to watch against its dissipation, and to take every care that their present necessities and future claims are effectively provided for. The idea that the want of disposition or ability on the part of the natives, in their present condition, to take advantage of the natural resources and treasures of their country, is a sufficient plea for their being deprived for the benefit of others... only needs to be fully sifted and examined to be exploded by the conscientious and thinking portion of society.

The right of conquest

Frontier settlers often answered their critics by referring to rights established by conquest. 'It is evident that New Holland is only held by right of might,' a New South Wales colonist asserted in 1843. 'We have a right to our Australian possessions,' a West Australian settler argued in 1847, 'but it is the right of Conquest; and we hold them in the grasp of Power.' Similar sentiments were expressed in Queensland, a writer in the *Moreton Bay Courier* explaining in that same year, 'we have seized this country by the right of might, and by the right of might the whites will continue to possess it'. 'We hold this country by the right of conquest,' a contemporary wrote in the same paper in 1848, 'and that right gives us a just claim to its continual possession.'

But if anything there were more problems for those who talked of the rights of conquest than for their fellows who continued to argue that Australia was a colony of settlement. Appeals to force did not resolve the fundamental moral problems, as an examination of such standard, and widely used, authorities as Locke and Vattel will indicate. The first difficulty to overcome was that if in fact the British had waged war on the Aborigines it could not have been a just war. Vattel observed that if a nation 'takes up arms when it has not received any injury and when it has not been threatened it wages an unjust war'. War fought to 'usurp the property of another' lacked 'even a semblance of right'. Indeed such action was not warfare at all but brigandage. Another difficulty for the tough-minded settlers was that conquest—even achieved in course of a just war—did not give the victor the right to confiscate property, not in the eighteenth century nor at any time since. A lawful conqueror, Locke explained, had 'an absolute power over the lives of those engaged in warfare but not over their possessions'; the right of conquest extended only to the lives of those who joined in the war, but not to their estates. The conqueror, argued Vattel, 'takes possession of the property of the State and leaves that of individuals untouched. The citizens suffer only indirectly by war, conquest merely brings them a change of sovereign'. Some writers, Vattel explained, 'have dared to assert the monstrous principle that the conqueror is the absolute master of his conquest, that he can dispose of it as his own property'.

And while settlers claimed what they believed to be fruits of conquest they were unwilling to concede to the Aborigines the rights allowed to the conquered. Resistance against an unjust attack was not only a right, according to Vattel, but a sacred duty. Land acquired by conquest did not become the legitimate property of an invader merely by the passage of time. Locke explained that the inhabitants of any country 'who are descended and derive a title to their estates from those who are subdued, and had a government forced upon them, against their free consents, retain a right to the possessions of their ancestors...[T]hey have always a right to free themselves from the usurpation or tyranny the sword hath brought in upon them'. The struggle to regain land unjustly taken could legitimately proceed generation upon generation'. 'If it be objected,' Locke wrote, 'that this would cause endless trouble, I answer, no more than justice does, when she lies open to all that appeal to her.'

Occasionally these unpleasant truths were driven home in the colonies. In an address to a gathering of settlers at Guilford in Western Australia in 1833 R.M. Lyon told a far from enchanted audience:

> If ye have taken their country from them and they refuse to acknowledge your title to it, ye are at war with them; and, having never allowed your

right to call them British subjects, they are justified by the usages of war in killing you whenever they have an opportunity. Ye are the aggressors. The law of nations will bear them out in repelling force by force. They did not go to the British Isles to make war upon you. You are the invaders of their country.

The blood is on every hand

A common response of frontier settlers to doubts about the morality of settlement was to argue that once the original decision had been made to establish colonies there was no way to reverse the inexorable advance of the white man. 'They are a hard used race,' admitted the Queensland pioneer Edward Palmer in 1874, 'but we have to occupy the country, and no two races can inhabit the same country, but the weaker must go to the wall.' It was 'simply a question of whether the natives are to have the country or the whites', Francis Connor, member for East Kimberley told the West Australian parliament in 1893, 'that is what it comes to. It is simply a question of whether we or they are to have this country'. If the Native Police Force couldn't control the blacks, a north Queensland settler told the Police Commissioner in 1904, 'there is only one alternative, to let them have all the country again'. Alexander Harris, the author of *Settlers and Convicts*, made a similar observation half a century before. If we want a league of peace of equal grounds, he argued, 'really there is no road to it but that we give up their land and foresake their country; for this and this only is the true source of aggravation... The blacks cannot be conciliated unless by giving up their country'.

Humanitarian critics of frontier violence were humbugs, the outback settlers cried, they were hypocrites who accepted all the advantages of colonial life while refusing to face the fact that their well-being was built on the ruins of Aboriginal society. 'It is useless now to speak about our right to come to New Holland and appropriate a part of it for our subsistence,' a South Australian settler remarked in 1839. 'It is now in vain to talk about the *injustice* of dispossessing the natives of part of their territories... [E]very one of us by coming here, has, in reality, said that we either had such a right—or, not having the right, that we, at least, have the might, and resolved to exercise it.' Everyone who came to the colonies was implicated; all had some share or responsibility. 'Let us therefore hear no more about the *right* or *justice* of our proceedings,' he argued, 'or let every sincere objector on this ground, prove his sincerity, by at once leaving the country which he thinks he has so unjustly taken from another.' A generation later a north Queensland frontiersman remarked that if the 'philanthropists' had the 'courage of opinions they would not stop on in a colony built up on bloodshed and rapine'. Hide it as you will, he wrote,

> our policy towards the black is bad, but it is only the game we play all over the world; and it starts with the original occupation of the country, and any other policy would be equally outrageous that entailed the taking of the land from the blacks...We all want to get on here, and we all want to get somebody else to do the work needful [*sic*]; and if there is any dirty work necessary we are the first to cry out against it—when we are in a position to do so. This is the black question, as put forward by the protectors of the poor savage. I know full well that I shall hear of atrocities, of barbarities, and other disgraceful proceedings committed by the whites; but that does not touch the point at issue. The unanswerable fact remains that by over-running this or any other country we expose the natives to the chances of suffering the rigours of guerilla warfare—always the cruellest and and worst—and, knowing that, we come here and take up our quarters with our eyes open; by our very presence in the land justifying the act of every white ruffian in the outside country...[T]he recital of all the atrocities going, of all the shooting and slaying by the Native Police, never alters the fact that, once we are here, we are committed as accessories, and that to prove the fidelity of our opinions we should leave the country.

While accepting the necessity for violence some settlers came to see the tragedy inherent in the whole colonial situation. In a letter to the *Port Phillip Patriot* in 1842 'A Colonist' observed: 'the irretrievable step of taking possession of a country, infers many minor wrongs to its inhabitants, besides the first great act of spoliation; but he who would govern in a country so situated, must steel his breast to their wrongs which are unanswerable.'

What actually happened when the British claimed sovereignty over eastern Australia has been an important and a controversial question since the early years of settlement. There have been two competing interpretations of that event. The minority view has been that despite the Crown's claim of overall sovereignty native title remained, giving the Aborigines rights of use and occupation over their traditional lands. This impaired title rested, not on legislation or other official recognition but on the irreducible fact of prior ownership. In 1972 the Canadian Supreme Court judges summed up ideas which had been evolving since the early nineteenth century:

> This aboriginal title does not depend on treaty, executive order or legislative enactment but flows from the fact that the owners of the interest have from time immemorial occupied the areas in question and have established a preexisting right of possession.

For those who believed that the Aborigines retained rights to their land the nature of white land tenure was, at best, uncertain. G.A. Robinson expressed his doubts in a letter to a friend in 1832. He was, he remarked, at a loss 'to conceive by what tenure we hold this country for it does not appear to be that we either hold it by right of conquest or right of purchase'. Some settlers believed that despite claims to the contrary the Aborigines remained the rightful owners of Australia. This view was taken by people as widely separated in time, space and social position as Governor King and John Cook, miner on the Fanning Reefs.

The conviction that native title survived 1788 inevitably coloured the interpretation of the nature of European land settlement. Aboriginal land rights were extinguished not by official edict but by force, district by district, over many decades. 'We hold it neither by inheritance, by purchase, nor by conquest,' observed Colonel Mundy in the 1850s, 'but by a sort of gradual eviction. As our flocks and herds and population increase and space is required, the natural owners of the soil are thrust back without treaty, bargain, or apology.' The gradual eviction has gone on throughout Australian history. It has continued up to the present. The moral responsibility for the dispossession was not the burden of any one group or even a particular period of Australian history. It is shared by all generations of white Australians. The modern land rights movement embodies the same moral dilemmas as those faced by early governors and officials. Time has passed but we have not escaped from our history.

The alternative interpretation—that all Aboriginal rights to land disappeared on the assumption of sovereignty—leads the argument in an entirely different direction. The blacks were dispossessed in a decorous official ceremony. The only shots fired were those dispatched into the air by the guard of honour. It was bloodless and instantaneous. The moral responsibility for the expropriation belonged to the British government of the period and the small group of officials who stood around the flag-pole at Sydney Cove. The colonists themselves did not take any land from the blacks. It was granted, leased or sold to them by the imperial government, and it all happened so long ago that it is pointless to reopen old wounds and old arguments. Frontier conflict, though perhaps regrettable, was not about land ownership. That issue had been decided in advance of settlement. Consequently, the bloodshed had no real political significance. The petty warfare which raged around the fringes of white settlement was as peripheral to the real story of Australia as it was remote from the main centres of population.

There were great advantages in believing that all Aboriginal property rights disappeared in 1788. Merely by the occupation of a few hectares at Sydney Cove the British were able to gain by 'settlement' legal title to land which no conqueror could legitimately acquire even after expending blood and treasure in a just war. It was the ultimate confidence trick—vast in scope, breathtaking in ambition. The settlers embraced all the advantages of acquisition by settlement while avoiding most of the attendant obligations towards the dispossessed. For the Aborigines the situation was reversed. They suffered all the disadvantages of invasion while receiving few of the benefits of settlement. The law which defended property with unparalleled vigour provided no protection for their land. Although they were British subjects 20–30 000 died under the foot of the pioneer. Only a handful of whites were ever brought to trial for killing Aborigines. By becoming British subjects the blacks lost everything. Even the 'sacred duty' of resisting an invader was denied them. In European eyes they could be criminals and bandits, never patriots or freedom fighters.

Locke, the most influential thinker of eighteenth-century Britain, declared that men entered into society in order to protect their property. The thought that the opposite could be true, that anyone could actually lose their property as a result of incorporation, was 'too gross an absurdity for any man to own'. Yet that absurdity is still defended and maintained by many of the most powerful forces in Australian society.

Conclusion

I

Governor Phillip's instructions, issued to him in April 1787, included a paragraph about the Aborigines. He was told

> to endeavour by every possible means to open an intercourse with the natives, and to conciliate their affections, enjoining all our subjects to live in amity and kindness with them. And if any of our subjects shall wantonly destroy them, or give them any unnecessary interruption in the exercise of their several occupations, it is our will and pleasure that you do cause such offenders to be brought to punishment according to the degree of the offence.

Three months after Phillip was handed his instructions the new United States Congress passed the North-West Ordinance dealing with the government of territory beyond the boundaries of the foundation states of the union. Article 3 dealt with the Indians, much of it echoing the sentiments expressed in the British document. The 'utmost good faith' was to be observed towards the Indians, laws 'founded in justice and humanity' were to be made 'from time to time...for preventing wrongs being done to them, and for preserving peace and friendship with them'. But while there were similarities the differences were more significant. There was no mention of land at all in Phillip's instructions whereas the Congress determined that the Indians' land and property would 'never be taken from them without their consent, and in their property, rights and liberty' they would never be 'invaded or disturbed, unless in just and lawful wars authorized by Congress'.

In recognising Indian land rights the Congress was not doing anything new. The Royal Proclamation of 1763 relating to North

America specified that the Indians 'should not be molested or disturbed in the Possession of Such Parts of our Dominions and Territories as, not having been ceded or purchased by us, are reserved to them...as their hunting grounds'. While considering the question of native title in 1847, New Zealand's Mr Justice Symmonds observed that 'the practice of extinguishing native title by fair purchase is certainly more than two centuries old'. The recognition of indigenous land rights was, then, well established in Britain's North American colonies before the settlement of Australia and was further strengthened in the nineteenth century in both Canada and the United States. It was reaffirmed when New Zealand was settled, both by the Treaty of Waitangi and the Land Claims Ordinance of 1841 which allowed for 'the rightful and necessary occupation and use' of land 'by the aboriginal inhabitants'.

The Admiralty's instructions to Cook in 1768 were, then, fully in accord with both international law and contemporary colonial practice; those given Phillip eighteen years later were not. The Admiralty tacitly recognised native title by insisting that while 'suitable locations' might be occupied it must be with the consent of the indigenous people. Why were Phillip's instructions mute on the matter of land? The question has rarely been asked, let alone answered. Most Australian commentators have made the profound error of assuming that the issue of land tenure was resolved by the act of sovereignty and did not require any further investigation. Sovereignty was claimed and native title extinguished in one official gesture; to explain and justify one was to explain and justify the other. This was clearly not the case. The most that can be said is that the instructions of 1786 neither confirmed nor rejected native title. If anything they left the situation where it was. Given the widespread acceptance of the concept in both Britain and the colonies (and ex-colonies) it could well be argued that silence suggested that the status quo was maintained. On the other hand a reversal of established doctrine and practice would presumably have required a clear statement of both intent and justification. As the British politician Howard Douglas observed in 1843 no official in England or the colonies had openly denied or disavowed native title. If the 'old and righteous principle' had been abandoned it had been abandoned tacitly.

The problem has never been properly addressed by Australian scholars although there is a significant body of relevant North American case law. The United States Supreme Court has accepted for more than 60 years that native title existed, whether or not it had been officially recognised. Neither neglect, nor the passage of time, were sufficient to extinguish it. In the 1923 case, *Cramer* v. *the United States*, Mr Justice Sutherland determined that 'the fact that such right of occupancy finds no recognition in any statute or other formal government action is not conclusive'. This view was reaffirmed in 1941 in *United States* v. *Sante Fe Pacific Railroad* where the Supreme Court 'emphatically denied that a tribal claim to any particular lands must be based upon a treaty, statute or other formal government action'. In the more recent case of the *Lepan Apache Tribe* v. *the United States* Mr Justice Davis argued that 'Indian title based on Aboriginal possession does not depend on sovereign recognition or affirmative acceptance for its survival'.

Was the absence of any direct reference to native title in Phillip's instructions a mistake, an oversight? Did the officials who planned the First Fleet deliberately leave out any mention of Aboriginal rights to land or did they forget to include one? The last was certainly the assumption of the House of Commons Select Committee on Aborigines in the British Empire as they looked back in 1837 over the history of colonial expansion. Where land had been taken 'without any reference to the possessors and actual occupants' the committee concluded that it 'must surely be attributed to oversight'.

In the absence of any official guidance it was easier for the early governors and settlers to behave as though native title did not exist. In the early 1830s senior officials like Arthur and Irwin, as well as many lesser individuals, urged the imperial government to end the uncertainty surrounding the matter. But by then it was too late. Local traditions were already entrenched, attitudes were fixed, settlers were secure on their land and liked the way things were. They were willing to resist vigorously any threat to the status quo. For their part the blacks had shown that while they could harass the settler they could not halt settlement itself. They could terrorise whole districts but they could not force the colonial governments to the negotiating table. In South Australia expressions of goodwill, even official recognition of Aboriginal rights to 'the actual occupation or enjoyment' of traditional lands, were unable to prevent the new colony moving in the wake of Tasmania and New South Wales. The reaction in New South Wales to the growing humanitarian zeal in the Colonial Office in the late 1830s well illustrated the difficulty of changing policies and practices in place for half a century. Governor Gipps arrived to take up office in February 1838 carrying a dispatch which embodied the sentiments of the recently completed House of Commons Committee. But policies implemented by Gipps over the ensuing few years proved to be most unpopular. The establishment of the Port Phillip Protectorate was widely attacked; the trial, conviction and, above all, the execution of seven Europeans late in 1838 for murdering blacks evoked a whirlwind of protest. A month after arriving in the colony Gipps indicated that he planned to issue an official statement outlining the position of Aborigines in colonial society. It proved difficult to draft and did not appear until May 1839, fourteen months after it had been announced. Notwithstanding what was going on in South Australia, the problem for Gipps was to say something about Aboriginal rights without being too specific as to what they actually were 'lest we be called upon to acknowledge their right to possession of the soil'. Gipps was to show later that he was fully aware of the concept of native title and relevant American jurisprudence. When it suited his purpose he could declare that the native title was received as political axiom. But he had trouble enough with the appointment of protectors, even more trying to establish that it was murder to kill a black man. It was not in the realms of practical politics to declare that the Aborigines had rights to the land. But his wording 'lest we be called upon to acknowledge their right to the possession of the soil' is interesting. Gipps did not say that such rights did not or could not exist, rather that it was politically inexpedient at the time to admit them. Acknowledge means literally 'to admit the truth of', 'to recognize something that existed', 'to own to knowing', 'to admit as true'. The comment was far from being a denial of the Aboriginal right to the soil.

Earl Grey's regulations of 1848 had no more success in changing colonial opinion or practice than the humanitarian policies of the preceding decade. Yet their importance remains. They were designed to apply to most existing, and all future areas of pastoral expansion and, by implication, to all those parts of the continent where Aboriginal occupation of the land was still unchallenged. Grey attempted to provide a minimum of rights for the Aborigines. After 1848 no Aboriginal community should have been accorded less than the rights of use and occupation outlined in his dispatch. Native title—a usufructuary right to the soil—had been officially recognised. Policy towards native land in Australia had come closer to that in other parts of the Empire. While Aboriginal rights were limited to functions associated with their traditional lifestyle they could have provided a strong buffer against the fast-flowing tide of settlement.

In the United States such rights of occupancy and use have been expanded and strengthened by decisions of the Supreme Court over the last half-century. In two cases in 1938—*the United States* v. *the Shoshone Tribe* and *the United States* v. *the Klamath Indians*—the federal government argued that rights of use and occupation were limited to specific economic activities relating to traditional Indian lifestyle. But the argument was rejected. The American jurist Felix Cowen observed, in 1947, that with these decisions the Supreme Court 'delivered a death blow to the argument that aboriginal ownership extended only to products of the soil actually utilized in the [traditional culture] of the Indian tribes...The court took the view that original Indian title included every element of value that would accrue to a non Indian landowner'.

The failure to recognise any Aboriginal rights to the land until 1848 had far-reaching consequences. Injustice was thus cemented into the foundations of Australian society. The injustice was gross regardless of whether the Aboriginal circumstances were compared with those of the settlers or those of indigenous people in other Anglo-Saxon colonies of settlement—the Indians of Canada and the United States and New Zealand's Maoris—whose native title was recognised. The contrast was apparent to some colonists from the very early years of settlement. 'How different is the policy of Great Britain towards North America,' a New South Wales settler noted in the 1820s, 'there our Government seems to acknowledge the claims of the Aborigines; for they never take possession of the land without purchase. Why not extend the same show of justice to the Aborigines of New Holland. Their right is the same—their condition the same—their relation to us the same.'

The contrast between the respect accorded Aboriginal property rights and those of everyone else in early colonial Australia was even greater. The law of the period gave more protection to property than to life itself. Convicts—and marines as well—were hanged for theft while Sydney was still only a few months old. Hangmen and flagellators continued to enforce the sanctity of private property for the first two generations of settlement. A community with such priorities could not find a more decisive way to illustrate its fundamental disrespect for another society than to ignore its property rights. Even an enemy beaten in battle might receive more consideration. If the British *deliberately* ignored native title all references to amity and kindness were humbug, and Australian society stands on a foundation of hypocrisy. But whether by accident, oversight or design, the failure to give clear recognition to native title had serious long-term consequences. It was the single most important issue in the 200-year-old history of white—Aboriginal relations. Lacking any clear guide from government, the settlers felt there was no need to conciliate the blacks or negotiate with them. There was nothing to negotiate about. Aborigines could be driven away as trespassers and shot if they 'evinced a desire to live on their own country'. More than anything else, this attitude to land explains, if not the conflict itself, which had many causes, then certainly its bitterness, ubiquity, longevity. It also accounts for the persistent undercurrent of guilt among settlers—the whisper in the heart. In a society where government, church and courts all upheld the absolute sanctity of private property and vigorously condemned theft, it is not surprising that there was widespread uneasiness about taking what belonged to the original inhabitants. In turn that hidden guilt helps explain the fervour with which the settlers denounced the blacks, their refusal to consider evidence favourable to the Aborigines, their anger at the white 'philanthropists' whose criticism touched what has been for 200 years the most tender spot in the national psyche.

II

The settlement of the land has been one of the central motifs of white Australian history. Scholars have written widely on two land-related themes—the struggle with the land, and the conflict, between different groups of Europeans, for the land. In the past both were treated in isolation from the other great theme of settlement, the frontier conflict between encroaching whites and resident Aboriginal clans. Traditional historical accounts were premised on three assumptions: at the time of settlement Australia was an unchanged wilderness; if the Aborigines ever owned the land they lost it in 1788; violence was a minor feature of colonisation due to the personal characteristics of the blacks themselves and of outcast Europeans. With such assumptions in mind Queensland's Governor Bowen, and many subsequent writers, could argue that Australian settlement had seen 'victories without injustice or bloodshed, conquests not over man, but over nature'. The classical account of land settlement—S.H. Robert's *History of Australian Land Settlement*, published in 1924—dealt with the struggle between the Colonial Office and the settlers, between squatter and selector. The conflict of black and white was totally ignored. The Aborigines were not even mentioned in the index, neither in the original edition nor in the 1968 reprint. In his companion volume, *The Squatting Age in Australia* (first published in 1935, reprinted unchanged in 1964 and 1970), Roberts observed that it was 'quite useless to treat [the Aborigines] fairly because they were 'completely amoral and usually incapable of sincere or prolonged gratitude'. Meanwhile their grievances were 'usually the result of their own ungovernable dispositions'. The period covered by Roberts' books witnessed the most prolonged and serious conflict that has ever taken place within Australia, a conflict primarly about the ownership and control of land resulting in over 20 000 deaths. Such was the distorted vision of traditional Australian historiography!

What happens to our interpretation of land settlement if the Aborigines are brought into the story? Many changes must be made. Clearly the Europeans did not enter an empty land or a wilderness; rather they moved across a country shaped by thousands of years of firestick farming, turned a long-settled land to new uses and in the process were often heavily dependent on Aboriginal knowledge and expertise. Violence was endemic on the frontier—the pioneer was accompanied by a 'line of blood'. The Aborigines had to be physically removed and their title extinguished; the settlers fought the blacks before they fought the land. The gun accompanied the bullock dray and preceded the plough. The prolonged conflict was, by general consensus, a sort of warfare. Yet war is by no means a perfect analogy because most wars are not accompanied by a total transfer of land from vanquished to victor or by the complete overthrow of the existing economic and social order. White settlement was more like revolution than war.

It is important, while investigating this question, to consider which of the various aspects of European penetration proved most destructive to Aboriginal society. It was not the mere presence of the settlers, although their diseases obviously took a heavy toll in large areas of the country; nor was it their greater numbers, because the Europeans were far less evenly distributed than the blacks and on most occasions small groups of settlers were actually outnumbered by the local Aborigines. The idea of pioneer anthropologists that Aboriginal society disintegrated immediately after contact with European culture is clearly wide of the mark. Aborigines were resilient, adopting those things which suited them and ignoring the rest, emulating here, rejecting there. European use of the land was not, by itself, a decisive factor. The open-range pastoralism of the pioneer era was not necessarily destructive of Aboriginal economic life. The idea, often heard, that pastoralism and hunter-gathering are incompatible is disproved by many contrary examples in Australia and elsewhere. European racial ideology was a factor of considerable importance but the conflict was never solely a question of colour. From the very beginning the Aborigines were on both sides of the frontier. Blacks employed as trackers, guides and police troopers were a crucial factor in European success. On the other hand a minority of whites were always vehemently opposed to the course of settlement and dispossession.

Many things contributed to frontier conflict; they have been considered in detail in *The Other Side of the Frontier*. Perhaps the single most important element in a complex situation was the revolutionary concept of private property which the settlers brought with them from Britain along with the will and the weapons to impose it in Australia. For 200 years before the great expansion of settlement in Australia traditional concepts of property had been undermined in Britain both by parliament and the courts. The open fields had been enclosed, as had many of the commons. The ancient, customary rights to hunt and gather had been progressively restricted. The old idea of land being used for different purposes by different people, none of them with absolute right of possession, had been replaced by the concept of absolute and exclusive property rights. That great revolutionary document the *Code Napoléon* expressed it as 'the right of enjoying and disposing of things in the most absolute manner'.

Settlers arrived in the colonies with the desire to own the land and everything on it 'in the most absolute manner'. Most of them preferred to drive the blacks away whenever they were seen, both for security and to consummate that burning passion for property. Typically they prevented, as far as they could, Aboriginal hunting and gathering, stopped their burning of the country, shut off their access to water and punished with severity any attacks on the sheep or cattle. All this took place on land that was often only held under lease or license from the Crown. But the idea of absolute and exclusive property rights had taken such deep root in Australia by 1848 that Grey's attempt to impose a strictly limited form of tenure, allowing for coincident usufructuary rights, was almost completely ignored. Writing in 1852, of settler attitudes to Aboriginal concepts of property, the historian John West noted that they would 'not comprehend joint ownership, notwithstanding the once "common" property of the nation has been only lately distributed by law'. The more perceptive colonists appreciated that black and white society were premised on conflicting concepts of property. The West Australian settler R.M. Lyon explained to his fellows in 1833:

> Reflect that ye have to do with a people who are not less the antipodes of the British Isles in their manners, laws, and polity, than in their geographical position. The laws and polity of Britain contemplate all property as private property, and protect it in this character, restricting each individual to the enjoyment of their own particular portion. The laws and polity of New Holland are just the reverse. They contemplate all property as public property, and guard it as such, allowing the free unrestricted use of the whole to every person in the community.

When the land had been grasped and ideas of private property, theft and trespass imposed, much remained to be done to prepare the blacks for the subordination and deference required of powerless and propertyless outcasts in a class society. The passion to keep the blacks in their place was not due solely to the need to confirm the revolutionary expropriation of property but also to impose the social relations of the new order. The vulnerability of the blacks allowed Europeans to indulge themselves in personal brutality and enforced sexual encounters, but most violence had a social and political purpose. That is why it was so widely practised, and so generally accepted, by people who were not in their own sphere cruel or insensitive. The wielders of stockwhips and stirrup irons were not sadists so much as zealots. They 'chastised' the Aborigines not for pleasure but out of a sense of duty. As beneficiaries of the revolution they were committed to carrying it through to its logical conclusion.

If the blacks were unwilling to conform to the new order and become wage labourers, there were many who believed they should be placed in institutions—the reserves and missions which proliferated in the second half of the nineteenth century—to be re-educated, or they would have to 'go' altogether. A Queensland politician told fellow members of the local parliament in 1880 that it 'was not absolutely necessary that the aboriginals should go, if they could be taught the value of labour'. Karl Lumholtz often heard the colonists say: 'they are unwilling to work...and hence they are not fit to live.' Settlers spoke like that not always because they were racists or sadists, though some, no doubt, were both, but because they acted with the conviction of participants in a social revolution. The editor of the *Port Denison Times*, in a passage quoted at length in Chapter 3, wrote: 'Times of change from one system to another, that is of revolution, have in all cases their peculiar elements of danger. One of the first maxims of such periods is *principius obsta*—that is, check anything that appears likely to disturb the working of the new system at the outset.'

The vigour of European action against 'cheeky blacks' was aimed not at personal qualities of individuals but at the social relations of traditional society—at the fundamental equality, the lack of institutionalised deference, the shifting balance of reciprocity of a society based not on property but on kinship and sharing. The blacks, the Port Phillip Proctor E.S. Parker explained in the 1840s, had to be taught 'to have some idea of the respective relations of Master and Servant'. They did not 'know the restraint of being any thing like the servant of another', a West Australian settler explained in 1837, they showed an 'inborn obtuseness to the advantages they enjoy in servitude', another observer wrote in 1865. 'All members of the clan are held to be equal,' a South Australian missionary observed in 1879. Indeed the 'aversion to acknowledge superiority' was a 'great evil when the Aborigines come into contact with the colonists'. 'He did not understand exalted rank,' a Victorian clergyman noted a few years later, 'and, in fact, it is difficult to get into a black fellow's head that one man is higher than another.' The problems of enforcing what Governor Gipps called 'the restraints which are imposed on ordinary labourers', were discussed by the missionary James Gunther in a lecture on the Aborigines during which he explained that

> this peculiar form of government admitting of no distinction of rank, but allowing each man a share in their consultations and decisions as to any questions arising among them stamps a feeling of independence and even

Conclusion

haughtiness with an appearance of dignity on the character of the men rarely to be met among other differently governed natives. As they have no titles for distinction nor a proper name for a chief so they have neither a word in their language to signify a servant...no man has an idea of serving another. This idea of their own dignity and importance is carried so far that they hesitate long before they apply the term MR. to any European even though they know full well the distinction we make [between master and servant].

III

In his book *The Age of Revolution: Europe 1789–1848* the historian E.J. Hobsbawm observed that 'what happened to land determined the life and death of most human beings in the years 1789 to 1848'. Australia became part of the European world during those years, distance and isolation notwithstanding. The conflict of settlers and Aborigines over the vast plains of inland Australia was an offshoot of the bourgeois revolution which swept across the face of Europe during the late eighteenth and early nineteenth century. The revolution encompassed many things. But land was at the centre of it. Men struggled to determine who would own the land, under what tenure it would be held and how it would be used. Differences of race and culture have for too long obscured the fact that the Aborigines were in a similar situation to those groups in European society who were being dispossessed and displaced by the penetration of capitalism into traditional rural communities. Even if comparisons are restricted to the British Isles it is obvious that the Aboriginal situation can be profitably compared to that of the squatters on the shrinking commons, the foresters and men of the fens who struggled to maintain a traditional economy in opposition to an ever-growing official commitment to absolute property rights. Even closer to the Aboriginal experience was the fate of Celtic-speaking Scottish highlanders who were forced off their traditional lands by new landlords, and new tenants who brought commercial sheep farming from the south. The Cheviots advanced into the Scottish highlands only a few years before Merinos spilled out across inland Australia. After the clearances Celtic bards lamented that 'nothing was heard but the bleating of sheep and the voices of English speakers'; a Queensland settler looked forward ruefully to the time when 'the valleys and forests, the scrubs and mountains, will be untenanted and unroamed, save by the flocks and herds of the strangers'.

Australians regard the settlement of the land as the central experience of the nation, the landscape in the settled districts illustrating the struggle with nature—hard, heroic, but largely successful. The frontier settlers have traditionally been seen as explorers, overlanders, pioneers. But they were also revolution-aries, and the landscape reflects the success of revolutionary vio-lence. It shows that settlement proceeded without concessions to traditional culture, settlement patterns or land use. The survey lines and the fences could run straight for tens and even hundreds of miles as though they crossed vast sheets of blank paper. Neither survey line, nor furrow, fence, track, flock or herd need deviate because of sacred sites, camping grounds, bora rings, pathways or wells. All could be overridden, ploughed under or trampled by hard massed hooves. Even the rich and dense local nomenclature could be wiped from the earth. The anthropologist W.E.H. Stanner observed in 1939 that 'a few hundred towns are known by more or less corrupted versions of improperly preserved native names, spelt in barbarous phoenetics...Yet for every Woolloomooloo and Dee-Why there is a second hand Kensington and an imitation Kew'.

Settled Australia has a landscape reflecting sudden and dramatic change, the complete and violent overthrow of one social and economic system, one mode of production, by another. It is a landscape of revolution. It does illustrate the European conflict with and partial conquest of nature. But it also represents the success of the bourgeois revolution in Australia—one of the most prolonged, complete and successful in the world.

IV

Australia celebrated 150 years of white settlement in 1938. Many of those who watched blacks participate in official ceremonies and historical reenactments were convinced that the Aborigines were a dying race, that few if any would be there to celebrate the 200th anniversary in 1988. As the nation prepares to mark that event the role of the Aborigines will be one of the major unresolved questions. The bicentenary celebrates the events of 26 January 1788 which have figured prominently in this book. Their significance cannot be overlooked. It has been suggested above that the assumption of sovereignty by what was called the right of discovery was not surprising, nor was the establishment of a small settlement on the shores of Sydney Harbour. Even the violence of the frontier was unexceptional when compared with the manner in which governments in Europe and elsewhere put down rural insurgency and peasant rebellion. What was truly remarkable was the assumption that in one official ceremony all Aboriginal rights to their traditional land disappeared. Their history before 1788, their ancient achievements, their intimate association with the land, 'time out of mind', counted for nothing—and still count for nothing in the courts unless recognised by recent enactment. No statements of goodwill, no fashionable gestures of respect for 'the triumph of the nomads' or interest in traditional culture can overcome that fundamental cause of alienation. It has always been the 'true source of aggravation'.

Many white Australians believe that the political, legal and moral issues embedded in the land rights campaign will fade away if people stop brooding about the past and if more money is spent on education, health, housing. But such expenditure—welcome as it would be—will not touch the heart of the matter any more than blankets and engraved breastplates did in the nineteenth century. Indeed, a better-educated, more affluent black community may feel these issues more keenly once the pressing, and depressing, economic and social burdens are eased. Ancient injustice burns like a beacon across the generations. In black Australia the flame is fed by two of humanity's most keenly felt grievances—lost land and martyred kin. White Australians should not suppose that the Aborigines have forgotten the 'martyrs of their country', that they no longer remember the 'blood-red dawn of their civilisation'. The killing times are still in living memory in those parts of Australia where most blacks live. The deep fear of the frontier still stalks communities and individuals alike. A majority of Aborigines have at least one relative of their own, their parents' or their grandparents' generation who was gunned down, whipped, raped or for one reason or another taken away—often for ever—by white people.

White Australians have generally failed to appreciate the great weight of history which presses the land rights movement forward. Many suppose it to be a recent fad, a new cause thrown up out of the turbulent politics of the late 1960s and early 1970s, entering Australia as an alien issue with origins in the Third World or black American ghettos. But the 'rights of the soil' is the oldest question in Australian politics, launched on its long life on the first official day of white settlement. It has often been overlooked, sometimes for years or decades at a time, resting like an unexploded bomb under the foundations. The importance of the question was fully apparent to the settlers in the 1830s and 1840s. Current calls for land rights and compensation are no more radical—and no more 'advanced'—than those made by earnest Christian philanthropists six generations ago.

The present generation of politicians has failed to get the measure of the land rights movement. They have showed neither the intellectual nor the moral stature to deal with a question of such magnitude. They have been dwarfed by the issue. Small stop-gap measures are a totally inadequate response to a crusade carried forward on the tides of history. Against enormous odds the Aboriginal people have survived. Their great cause will live and flourish with them. To suppose that an issue which has already occasioned over 20 000 deaths will not again, unless resolved, lead to further violence is to ignore totally the lessons we can learn from the past. A West Australian pioneer warned his fellow colonists about these matters in 1833. He can be listened to profitably today. 'Think not,' he said, 'that the aboriginal inhabitants of Australia—offspring of the same parent with yourselves, and partakers of all the kindred feelings of a common humanity, can resign the mountains and the seas, the rivers and the lakes, the plains and the wilds of their uncradled infancy, and the habitations of their fathers for generations immemorial, to a foreign foe, without the bitterness of grief.'

Notes

Book, articles and other material which appear in the bibliography will be referred to in abbreviated form in the notes. For more detailed information see pp. 197—215.

CHAPTER 1: UNRECORDED BATTLEFIELDS

For the settlement-invasion question see *Kittle*, 7; *Launceston Examiner*, 26 Sept. 1831; *HRA*, 1, 19, 48—9; *Fison & Howitt*, 182; *Thirty Years of Colonial Government: A Selection from the Dispatches & Letters of...Sir George Ferguson Bowen*, Lond. 1889, I, 214.

The issue was addressed by the High Court in the case *Coe* v. *Commonwealth* (1979) A.L.J.R. 53.

Was it warfare?
This question was widely discussed in colonial society. See for instance *Tench*, 138; *Collins*, 1, 348; *Fremantle*, entry dated 5—11 Sept. 1832; R.M. Lyon in *Aboriginal Protection Society Papers*, 11,4 June 1841, 109; Threlkeld letter, 11 Sept. 1826 in *London Missionary Society: Australian letters 1833—44*; Frankland to Arthur, 25 Oct. 1828, *Arthur Papers* 19; *Arthur to Magistrates*, 1 Nov. 1828, *BPP* 1831, 259; Select Committee on Police & Gaols *NSWLCV & P*, 1839, 224; Mr Watts, MLA in *Queensland Guardian*, 4 May 1861; *Queenslander*, 15 Feb. 1879; *Queensland Figaro*, 3 Jan. 1885; Select Committee on Native Police *QVP*, 1861, 9. For the letter of the retired native police officer see *Queenslander*, 3 June 1899.

Martyrs of their country
See the letter of G. Robertson, a leader of the Roving Bands, to Governor Arthur, 17 Nov. 1828, Tas.Col.Sec. CSO/1/331; 7578/16 and letters in *Colonial Times*, 26 Feb. 1830; *The Colonist*, 4 May 1839; *Northern Territory Times*, 23 Oct. 1875. See also *Bartlett*, 78 and Annual Report of Government Resident, Northern Territory, *South Australian Parliamentary Papers*, 2, 1890 No. 28,9.

The enemy of everyday
Comparisons with conflict in other parts of the Empire were common, especially in Queensland and the Northern Territory. See *Moreton Bay Courier*, 23 March 1858, 7 May 1859; *Port Denison Times*, 1 May 1869; *Queenslander*, 8 March 1879, 11 April 1885, 26 Nov. 1887; *Rockhampton Bulletin*, 8 Nov. 1870; *Herberton Advertiser*, 17 Jan. 1885. For similar comments in other colonies see *Reilly*, 235; V.L. Solomon evidence to Select Committee on the Aborigines Bill, *South Australian Legislative Council Votes & Proceedings*, 1899, 88.

The guerilla mode of warfare
For early references see *Melville*, 26 and R.M. Lyon, *op. cit.*, 110. See also J.E. Calder papers in Mitchell Library, extract entitled 'Natives', 35; the comments of LaTrobe in *Port Phillip Patriot*, 31 March 1842 and of West the historian of Tasmania, *West*, 284.

Frontier

Constant dread

For evidence of frontier anxieties see the following newspapers. *Hobart Town Courier*, 13 March 1830; *Herberton Advertiser*, 11 April 1890; *Palmer Chronicle*, reprinted in *Herberton Advertiser*, 14 Jan. 1885; *Rockhampton Bulletin*, 5 Aug. 1865; *Moreton Bay Free Press*, 24 Aug. 1852; *Colonial Times*, 12 March 1830; *Northern Territory Times*, 19 June 1874; *The Tasmanian*, 11 April 1828; *Queenslander*, 14 Jan. 1899; *Cairns Post*, 11 April 1888.

For similar evidence see G.S. *Lang*, 77; *Sutherland*, 20; *Macpherson*, 13–14; W. Cox, *Memoirs*, Sydney 1901, 129; A. Hasluck, *Portrait with Background*, Melbourne 1955, 165; Fenwick, *Deary*, 29; R.B. Mitchell, *Reminiscences*, 100; P. Leslie letter to his parents, 2 March 1843 in WALLER, 85; E. Cuer to Governors of VDL Company, TSA, *VDL Papers*, 5/2, 262, 5/3, 108.

The blacks are coming

Evidence of these fears can be found in many sources but see *Tench*, 137–8; Stirling to Stanley, 1 Nov. 1834, Despatches to Colonial Office, 14, *B.L.*; *Brown, ed.* 110; E. Mayne evidence to Committee on Police & Gaols, *NSWLCV & P*, 1839, 23; *Moreton Bay Courier*, 5 April 1852; Petition of Kimberley settlers to Governor Broome, *WA Col.Sec.*, CSO, 3398/89; Letter of W.B. Brown, Daly River, 17 Dec. 1887, SA Archives, GRS/10/A/10,531; Mr Harte of Swanport, 28 March 1828, *Tas.Col.Sec.*, CSO/1/316,128; J. Demarr, *Adventures in Australia Fifty Years Ago*, London 1893, 122–3.

From the barrel of the gun

The evidence relating to firearms is voluminous. See for instance, *Jukes*, 57; *Waller*, 85; *Attwood*, 17; *Fremantle*, 91; *Plomley*, 218; Bonwick, *Port Phillip Settlement*, 515; *Queenslander*, 8 June 1878; *Australian*, 7 July 1840; Mr Torlesse to Magistrate Bothwell, 15 Feb. 1830, *Tas.Col.Sec.*, CSO/1/316, 422–3.

Evidence relating to north Queensland will be found in the *Cooktown Courier*, 5 Dec. 1874; the *Cleveland Bay Express* as quoted in the *Queenslander*, 20 Dec. 1873; *Queenslander*, 25 Dec. 1875; Royal Commission into the Alleged Killing...of Aborigines in East Kimberley, *West Australian Votes & Proceedings*, 1, 1921, 81,84; G.W. Broughton, *Turn Again Home*, Brisbane 1965, 33–4.

For the fortification of houses see *Le Souef*, 31; *Mann*, 13; *Grant*, 95; *Anning*, 123; *Richmond*, 84; P. O'Farrell (ed.) *Letters from Irish Australia*, Sydney 1984, 69; M. McManus, *The Early Settlement of the Maranoa District*, Brisbane 1913, 7; 'The Men Who Blazed the Track', *MacKay Mercury*, Jubilee Edition, Aug. 1912.

For evidence of women carrying guns see *Gray*, 69; R. Campbell-Praed, *My Australian Girlhood*, London 1904, 80. For stations which had no experience of conflict see McManus, *op. cit.*, 7; Charles Archer to his father, 23 Nov. 1844, Archer brothers Durundur Diary, 1843–4, Oxley Library; *Richmond*, 84. Information relating to the use of guns in pioneer towns will be found in: MacArthur notes, *Northern Territory Times*, 15 Sept. 1888; *Queenslander*, 27 June 1878; *Queensland Guardian*, 3 March 1863; *Rockhampton Bulletin*, 21 Feb. 1865; *Moreton Bay Courier*, 21 Nov. 1846; *Empire*, 30 Nov., 12 Dec. 1857; *Brisbane Courier*, 6 May 1922; *Courier Mail*, 18 Feb. 1939; Nesbit, *Reminiscences*, unpaginated; Police Magistrate, Normanton to Col. Sec., *Qld Col. Sec.* Col/A203, 2913 & 2949 of 1874.

Fear comes to town

Evidence of anxiety in pioneer towns will be found in the following: *Perth Gazette*, 8 June 1833; *Swan River Guardian*, as reported in the *Colonist*, 14 Dec. 1837; *Finlayson*, 45; *Knight*, 220; H. Fysh, *Taming the North*, Sydney 1950, p.142; *Queensland Guardian*, 24 April 1861; Moreton Bay correspondent of the *Empire*, 28 Jan. 1856; *Mackay Mercury*, 14 Feb. 1874; *Cooktown Herald*, 1 July 1874; Govt. Resident, Port Curtis to Col. Sec., *NSW Col.Sec. In Letters*, 2128 of 1856; Telegram, Land Commissioner, Normanton to Minister for Lands, 17 Dec. 1874; *QSA*, CCL/462.

For events at Port Lincoln see *Adelaide Examiner*, 7,14 Sept., 17,19 Oct. 1842; *South*

Notes

Australian Register, 2,16 April, 15 Oct. 1842; Journal of Events at Port Lincoln, SA. Archives, GRG/24/6 A(1842) 81; McLean, 66—92; M. Davies, 'Settlers & Aborigines at Port Lincoln 1840—45', *South Australiana*, 18,1 March 1979. Evidence relating to Cardwell can be found in: J. Moresby, *Discoveries and Surveys in New Guinea etc.*, London 1876, 41; Resident Magistrate to Col. Sec. *Qld Col.Sec. In Letters*, Col/A63, 157 of 1865; The Natives in the Far North, No. 7, *Sydney Morning Herald*, 1880 in ML, Aborigines: Newspaper Extracts 1, 1875—80.

For similar experiences in Maryborough see Walker, Aboriginal-European Relations in the Maryborough District, *Letterbooks of the Commissioner for Crown Lands, Wide Bay & Burnett*; Letterbook of W.H. Wiseman; Commissioner of Crown Lands, Wide Bay to Chief Commissioner, *NSW Col.Sec.*, 9967 of 1852; Mr Uhr, J.P. to Col. Sec. 30 Dec. 1852, *NSW Col.Sec.*, 472 of 1853; *North Australian*, 7 Jan. 1862.

For the desertion of Gilberton see Select Committee on the Claims of P.M. Corbett, *QVP*, 2, 1874; R.B. Brown, *Gilberton*; *Queenslander*, 14 Dec. 1872, 12 April 1879.

Plunder and penury
See letter from pioneer of Mt Buller, *Port Phillip Herald*, 3 July 1840; one from Cameron of Barcaldine Downs to Union Bank, Brisbane, *Qld Col.Sec.*, Col/A79, 1482 of 1866; and one from Cheyne to the W.A. Government quoted in M. Bignell: *The Fruit of the Country*, Perth, 1977, 66. For the Palmer River see Kirkman, 284—5.

Counting the cost
The compilations of Aboriginal 'depredations' can be found in: Aboriginal Tribes in British Possessions, *British Parliamentary Papers*, (hereafter *BPP*) 1834, 156—8; Aborigines (Australian Colonies), *BPP*, 1844, 213—4; Annual Report of Commissioner for Crown Lands, 28 Dec. 1855, CCL Wide Bay Letterbook, 1 Jan. 1855—13 Dec. 1857, *QSA*, 30/11.

Progress stalled
For concern about Queensland's future see: *North Australian*, 6 Dec. 1861, 23 March 1858; For Tasmania see: *Colonial Times*, 31 Dec. 1830; Arthur to Murray, 12 Sept. 1829, *HRA*, 1,15, 446—7; Petition of Clyde River settlers, 27 Feb. 1830 in *Desailly*, 44; *Colonial Times*, 24 Sept. 1830; Reports of Aborigines Committe in Copies of All Correspondence...*BPP*, 1831, 42; Aboriginal Tribes...etc. *BPP*, 1834, 154.

The death toll
Studies which have attempted to assess the death toll in frontier conflict include: *Loos*, especially 191—247; Ryan, *The Aboriginal Tasmanians*, Brisbane 1981; N. Green, *Broken Spears*, 226—231; Reynolds, *The Other Side of the Frontier* Penguin edition, Ringwood 1982, 121—5; *Attwood*, 64; *Kirkman*, 274—83.

CHAPTER 2: DEEDS OF BLOOD

The most important material on the early years of white settlement can be found in: *Tench, Hunter, Collins* and the early volumes of the *Historical Records of Australia* and the *Historical Records of New South Wales*.

An universal terror
For the events following the spearing of McEntire see *Tench*, 205—13; *Collins*, 1,117—9; *Hunter*, 326—8, 334—5; *Easty*, 123. For Phillip's attitude refer to *HRNSW*, 1,39,2,411; *Collins*, 1,36,121—2; *Tench*, 215.

The kindest piece of violence
For Phillip's account see Phillip to Sydney, 13 Feb. 1790, *HRA*, 1,1,159; *The Voyage of Governor Phillip to Botany Bay*, Sydney 1970, 79. See also *Tench*, 137. Phillip's despatch concerning the marines is in *HRA*, 1.1.161.

Frontier

A tradition develops

Relevant material will be found in *Bradley*; *Collins*, I, 122, 348; King to Portland, 2 Jan. 1800, *HRA*, 1,2,402; *Collins*, 2,26. For Brisbane's declaration of martial law see *HRA*, 1,11,409; for Atkins' opinion see *HRA*, 1,5,502−4.

Acts of decisive severity

For conflict on the Hawkesbury see *Collins*, 1,348. Macquarie's statements are in *HRA*, 1,9,54,139−42 and Brisbane's in *HRA* 1,11,431. For Governor Arthur see Van Diemens Land, Return to an Address...etc. *BPP*, 259, 1831, 9. For WA refer to *Hasluck*, 49 and *Irwin*, 27.

Vigorous measures amongst yourselves

For the development of vigilante action see: Journal of George Thompson, *HRNSW*, 2,797. The order of 1796 is in *HRA*, 1,1,688 and the one of 1801 in *HRA*, 1,3,250; Macquarie's announcement of 1816 is in *HRA*, 1,9,145 and Darling's is in *HRA*, 1,12,576. See also *Harris*, 221. For similar developments in WA and Tas. refer to *Hasluck*, 49; Van Diemens Land: Return to an Address...etc. *BPP*, 259, 1831, 43. Governor Gipps' comment is in *HRA*, 1/19/509−10 and James Stephen's Minute of 24 April 1838 is quoted in S.C. McCulloch, James Stephen and the Problems of New South Wales, *Pacific Historical Review*, 25, 1957. An account of Robinson's interview with Gipps is in G.A. Robinson Journal, 22 Sep. 1838, vol. 13, *ML* A7034.

By fear alone

The views of settlers can be found in a wide range of sources; see for instance the *Hobart Town Courier*, 2 Oct. 1830. Robinson account of his interview with a squatter is in his Journal for 18 Jan.−1 June 1840, vol.15, *ML* A7036/1. See editorial in *Hodgkinson Mining News*, 29 Dec. 1877 and letter by G. Hislop in *Queenslander*, 24 July 1897. See also *Carnegie*, 328. For the advocates of decisive action see the letter of W.S. Sharland, 25 June 1831, *Tas.Col.Sec.*, CSO/1/323,283; Inspector General of Police to Col.Sec., 25 Oct. 1855, *NSW Col.Sec.* 11068 of 1855 and W. Howitt to his mother in Mulvaney, 'The Ascent of Man etc.', 287.

A wanton and savage spirit

The views of the Tasmanian Aborigines Committee are recorded in Van Diemens Land. Return to an Address, etc. *BPP*, 259, 1831, 38. For Backhouse's views see *Hasluck*, 180. The *Northern Argus* is quoted in *Queensland Times*, 27 Dec. 1864; for Wiseman see his letterbook for 5 Jan. 1856, *QSA*, CCL7/61.

For settler views of Aboriginal resistance see *Cooktown Independent*, 19 Nov. 1890; Sutherland *Pioneering Days*, 13, *Queenslander*, 14 Jan. 1899.

For the European belief that the Aborigines were compulsive killers see *West*, 276; a letter from a squatter in the *Moreton Bay Free Press*, 8 July 1852, the *North Australian*, 17 Nov. 1857, *Hodgkinson Mining News*, 29 Dec. 1877, *Northern Territory Times*, 4 Oct. 1884, *Northern Public Opinion*, 30 March 1895 and the Journal of an Expedition of Maitland Brown, *Inquirer*, 31 May 1865.

The settler's conviction that the blacks were the aggressors can be seen in *Hodgson*, 79; *Sydney Morning Herald*, 24 April 1839; *Hodgkinson Mining News*, 29 Dec. 1877.

An intensity of hatred

For Governor King's views see his memo to Bligh, King Papers, 2, *ML* C/189. James Stephen's memo is quoted by S.C. McCulloch, *op.cit*. See also R.J. Sholl quoted in *Hasluck*, 171; The Natives in the Far North, *Sydney Morning Herald*, 1880 in Aborigines Cutting Book, I, 1875−80, M.L. Expressions of racial hatred will be found in the following: J. Docker, 19 Jan. 1841, Port Phillip, 1841, *NSW Col.Sec.*, ML; De B. Cooper, 91, *G. Windsor-Earl*, 117; *Harris*, 205; *Moore*, 167. Robinson, Journal 1839−40, ML, A7035.

Notes

An animal craving for revenge
See F. Eldershaw, *Australia As It Realy Is*, London 1854, 63–73; G.S. Lang, 42, *Colonial Times*, 25 May 1831; *Jukes*, 1, 70–113. For the reaction to Aboriginal resistance in Qld refer to *Moreton Bay Courier*, 14 Nov. 1857, 19 Nov. 1861; *Queensland Guardian*, 6,9 Nov., 11,21 Dec. 1861; W.H. Wiseman to Chief Commissioner Crown Lands, 16 Nov. 1857, *NSW Col.Sec.*, 4319 of 1857.

Doing the needful
For settler reprisals in central Qld see *Reid*, and *Wright*. See also *Rockhampton Bulletin*, 30 May 1865; *Northern Miner* as quoted in *The Bulletin*, 9 June 1883. The Attorney General was reported in *Queensland Guardian*, 22 July 1861. For other comments see letter by C.G. Heydon in *Sydney Morning Herald*, 7 Jan. 1874; *Cairns Post*, 4 May 1887; *Queenslander*, 23 Dec. 1876; *Eyre*, 1, 170.

Fiery young gentlemen
See the following: *Mundy*, 1, 230–5; evidence of Polding to Select Committee on Aborigines, *NSWLCV & P*, 1845, 952; Dredge, *Diary*, 9 Oct. 1838; *Bartlett*, 65–6; J.B. Gribble letter to Anti-Slavery Society, 5 March 1881, *Anti-Slavery Papers*, G101; E. Thorn, 'A White Australia—The Other Side', *United Australia*, 25 Oct. 1901. Sir Arthur Gordon is quoted by Knaplund in 'Sir Arthur Gordon on the New Guinea Question 1883', *HS* 7, 1955–7, 330–1.

A pleasurable excitement
For relevant evidence see *West*, 271; *Mundy*, 1, 230; *Hodgson*, 13, *De B. Cooper*, 67, Robinson, Letterbook, 1845–8, ML A7050; *Queensland Figaro*, 3 Jan. 1885.

Counting the bodies
See *Evans* et al., 62; Reynolds: *The Other Side*, 121–7. Since writing the above I have read far more extensively among the diaries and journals of the missionaries and Aboriginal Protectors in NSW and Vic. I think that the evidence there strongly suggests that the death-rate in the period 1820–50 was considerably higher than I had previously thought and approached that in Queensland in the second half of the century.

Was it genocide
For long and widespread debate about extermination refer to the following. For Tas. see the views of Curr and Barnes in *Tas.Col.Sec.*, COL/1/323 and of Sherwin in the *Tasmanian*, 26 Feb. 1830. For WA see despatch by Stirling to Aberdeen, 10 July 1835, BL; for NSW see the *Sydney Morning Herald*, 26 Dec. 1836, 24 Oct. 1838; for Vic. refer to the papers of William Thomas including letters of 21 June and 6 Aug. 1839 and the journal of G.A. Robinson, 18 Jan. – 2 Feb. 1840, 86. Queensland material will be found in *Evans* et al., 80, *Lumholtz*, 153, *Queenslander*, 28 Feb. 1874, *Moreton Bay Courier*, 8 May 1858; *Peak Downs Telegram* as reported in *Queenslander*, 31 March 1866; *Queensland Guardian*, 27 July 1861; *Rockhampton Bulletin*, 6 July, 10 Aug. 1865, 6 Aug. 1867. The SA Clergyman expressed his views in a letter to the Anti-Slavery Society on 8 Dec. 1850, *Anti-Slavery Papers* S.18/159. The Jesuit missionary's views are reported in *O'Kelly*, 86, those of James Stephen are in Knaplund *op.cit.* and Collier's will be found in *The Pastoral Age in Australia*, London 1909, 129–30.

CHAPTER 3: GENERATIONS HARDENED AGAINST THE NATIVES

The views of the Kimberley correspondent, reported in the *North West Times*, 10 Feb. 1894 were typical of much frontier opinion.

A tradition of brutality
For atrocities and conspiracies of silence see W.H. Traill, 'Historical Sketch of Queensland', A. Garran (ed.) *Picturesque Atlas of Australia*, 3 vols. Melbourne, 1880, 2, 362–7;

letter from A Squatter, *North Australian*, 10 July 1860; letter 'Killing No Murder', *Moreton Bay Courier*, 19 Nov. 1861; letter 'The Raid of the Aborigines', *Moreton Bay Free Press*, 15 Sept. 1859; letter 'A Squatter', *Moreton Bay Courier*, 2 April 1861; *Harris*, 211. *Colonial Intelligencer and Aborigines Friend*, 1860, 163; report of Commissioner of Crown Lands, Bligh referred to in *Grey to Fitzroy*, 10 Feb. 1850, ML A1310. The most meticulously researched account of violence and atrocity will be found in *Evans* et al., 27–145.

For the development of a tradition of brutality see *Backhouse*, 558; Robinson, *Journal*, Jan.–Feb. 1840, 64, ML, A7036/1; The *Adelaide Examiner*, 1 April 1843; letter of R.W. Newland to Anti-Slavery Society *op.cit.*; Threlkeld in *Second Annual Report of Aborigines Protection Society*, London 1839, 14; *Meyrick*, 136–8; letter 'The Raid of the Aborigines', *Moreton Bay Free Press*, 15 Sept. 1859; *Sadlier*, 27; *Rockhampton Bulletin*, 25 June 1867, 19 April 1876.

For concern about colonial children see 'The Question of the Day…', *Rockhampton Bulletin*, 24 Aug. 1865; 'The Recent Outrage on the Blacks', *Ibid.*, 25 June 1867; Vice-Admiral Sir George Tryon in *Evans*, 78.

For examples of European guilt see J.A. Palmer (ed.), *William Moodie : A Pioneer of Western Victoria*, Maryborough, Vic, 1973, 167; *Farwell*, 160; R. Campbell-Praed, *Australian Life : Black and White*, London 1885, 27–8; *Plomley*, ed. 219; *Willey*, 15.

Letting the blacks in
See the *Port Denison Times*, 12 June 1869; *Rusden*, 2, 235; *Queenslander*, 25 Feb. 1888; Inspector Drewry to Police Commissioner, 15 Dec. 1894, WA Police Dept. 3548/97, *B.L.*; Inspector Lamond to Police Commissioner, 4 July 1897, *QSA*, Col. 140.

Such extraordinary terrorism
See letter by Constable R.C. Thorpe to Govt. Resident, Northern Territory, 5 March 1898; Select Committee on Aborigines Bill, *SA Parlt. Papers*, 1897, No. 77, 113–14; A. Meston to Col. Sec. on Aborigines West of the Warrego, 27 June 1900, *QSA*, Col/144; Meston, 27 June 19; *Queenslander*, 5 June 1880.

For Aborigines in fringe camps see H. Reynolds, 'Townspeople and Fringe-dwellers,' in *Race Relations in North Queensland*, Townsville 1978, 167–178.

For the killing of the Aboriginal girl see Curr, *Australian Race*, 3, 21.

Keeping them in their place
For justification of personal violence towards the Aborigines see: *Moreton Bay Courier*, 29 Jan. 1863; *Queenslander*, 12 Jan. 1884; letter from a gentleman, 1826, Methodist Missionary Society, In Correspondence—Australia, 1812–26.

For outback attitudes see, *Willey*, 6; *Devanny*, 185, 230, *Queensland Parliamentary Debates*, 1945-6, vol. 187, 204.

For the use of whips consult: S. Burt, *Parlt. Debates*, 2, new series, 1892, 398; *Carnegie*, 121–2; J. Matthews, 'The Australian Aborigines', *J. & P. of Royal Society NSW*, 23, 1889, 390; A.H. Palmer in *Qld Parlt. Debates*, 33, 1880, 1137–8; Harper in *WA. Parlt. Debates*, 19, 1901, 638; *Attwood*, 79; Walker in *WA. Parlt. Debates*, 28, 1905, 319; Harold Meston to Protector of Aborigines, 20 Dec. 1902, *QSA*, Col/144; *Hasluck*, 193; *North West Times*, 10 Feb. 1894.

Wild animals or impulsive children
See editorial comment in *Northern Argus*, Rockhampton, as reported in *Queenslander*, 23 June 1866; D. McAllister, 'The Australian Aborigines', *Melbourne Review*, 3, 1878, 139; *Carnegie*, 153; *Devanny*, 185; Burt in *WA. Parlt. Debates*, 2, 1892, 398; *North West Times* quoted in R. McGregor, Answering the Native Question, B.A. Hons thesis, James Cook, 1985, 111; A.R. Richardson, *Early Memoirs of the Great Nor-West*, Perth 1914, 21.

Black velvet
There is much material about sexual relations between European men and Aboriginal

Notes

women but see for instance the report of the Protector of Aborigines at Normanton, Annual Report of Chief Protector, *Qld Parlt. Papers*, 1904, 864; 'The Case of the Aboriginal', *Queenslander*, 2 Dec. 1899; letter of Constable Thorpe to Govt. Resident, NT, *op. cit.*; W.E. Parry-Okeden, Report on the North Queensland Aborigines, *Queensland Votes & Proceedings*, 2, 1897.

Catch 'em young
Kidnapping was widespread and evidence is plentiful. See for example letter of Chatfield of Natal Downs to Police Magistrate Bowen, *QSA*, Col/A1483; Report of Assistant Commissioner of Police, *Queensland Votes & Proceedings*, 1872, 1494; telegram from Police Magistrate, Normanton to Col. Sec. 29 Sep. 1874, *Qld Col.Sec.*, 2913 of 1874; *Queenslander*, 13 Jan. 1894; T. Peutzcke to Col. Sec., 25 Dec. 1893, *Qld Col.Sec.* Col/A758, 492 of 1894; Protector Galbraith, Normanton in Annual Report of Northern Protector of Aborigines, *Queensland Votes & Proceedings*, 1904, session 1, 871.

Their hidden nature
Discussions of the blacks' 'hidden nature' can be found in *Queensland Times*, 14 Feb. 1865; *Queenslander*, 2 Jan. 1897; evidence of J. Low to Select Committee on Native Police, *Queensland Votes & Proceedings*, 1861, 8; *Queenslander*, 2 Jan. 1897; C. Scallon, Aborigine Hereditary Ingratitude, *Science of Man*, 21 Aug. 1901, 115. For the fear of walking in front of an Aboriginal see, H. Holthouse, *S'Pose I Die*, Sydney 1973, 57. The story can also be found in *Lumholtz*, 45, 100; E. Rowan, *A Flower Hunter in Queensland & New Zealand*, Sydney, 1898, 84; F. Hives, *The Journal of a Jackeroo*, London 1930, 91.

The black bandits
Refer to Reynolds, *The Other Side of the Frontier*, Ringwood 1982, 118−121; *Mackay Mercury*, 13 Feb. 1894; *Markus*, 73−79; E. Fry (ed.), *Rebels and Radicals*, Sydney 1983, 1−26; B. Davies, *The Life of Jimmy Governor*, Sydney 1978; *Sydney Morning Herald*, 24,25 July,29 Oct.,23 Nov. 1900; *The Mudgee Guardian*, 23,26 July,10 Sept.,1,4,25 Oct. 1900; *The Gulgong Advertiser*, 21 Sept.,12 Oct. 1900; *The Dubbo Liberal*, 25,28 July,1,22 Aug. 1900.

For Pigeon see *H. Pedersen, McGregor, op.cit.*; *Northern Public Opinion*, 23 March 1897; *The Pilbara Goldfields News*, 19 March 1897.

For modern fears see M. Reay, 'A Half-Caste Aboriginal Community in North West New South Wales', *Oceania*, 25, 1944−5, 297−323.

CHAPTER 4: BLACK BROTHERS

There were a number of observers who discerned a sharp polarisation of opinion about the Aborigines in colonial society. See for instance *Bartlett*, 65−6.

Moral outrage
For the views of missionaries and other philanthropists see: Threlkeld, half-yearly report, 21 June 1826, Bonwick Transcripts, 53, *M.L.*; Tuckfield to Wesleyan Missionary Society, 13 May 1839, Methodist Mission Society Correspondence 1827−37; Tuckfield to Wesleyan Mission Society, 30 Sept. 1840, Bonwick Transcritps, *op.cit.*; James Dredge letter, 10 May 1841, Letterbook, LaTrobe Library, MSS. 421961; G.A. Robinson, Journal, Jan.−Feb. 1840, *op.cit.*; *Plomley*, 155.

Divine vengeance
Among many warnings of divine retribution see: W. Thomas, Journal, 1845, *M.L.* uncat. 214/3; Dredge letter 10 Mar. 1841, La Trobe Library, MSS. 421961; Tuckfield letter, 13 May 1839, Methodist Mission Society *op.cit.*; Mark Butler letter in *Colonial Intelligencer & Aborigines Friend*, 1860, 162; McKillop, 'Anthropological Notes', 264.

Emotional commitment
See J. Orton, Letterbook, ML A1719; Gribble, *Black but Comely*, 17; Gribble letter, 26

March 1887, Anti-Slavery Papers, S22/G101; D. Matthews, An Appeal on Behalf of the Australian Aborigines, Matthews papers ML, 9; *Plomley*, 276.

The great tide of opposition

For the pioneer missionaries see Threlkeld letter, 4 Sept. 1826, Bonwick Transcripts, Box 53, M.L.; J.C. Handt letter, 30 July 1832, Church Missionary Society Papers, C.N. 051; G.A. Robinson letter, 25 Aug. 1832, G.A.R. Papers ML, A7056, 35. For the fate of L. Giustiniani see: N. Green, 'Aborigines and White Settlers in the Nineteenth Century', in C.T. Stannage, *A New History of Western Australia*, Perth 1981, 72–123. See also W. Thomas Journal 18 Dec. 1839–4 Jan. 1840, ML, *op.cit.*

For philanthropists in the second half of the C19th see D. McNab to Minister of Lands, 2 Sept. 1876 in *Queensland V&P*, 3, 1876, 166; Gribble letter, 5 March 1885, to Anti-Slavery Society, *op.cit.* Other letters at same source are those of A. Vogan, 4 Sept. 1891, Robert Short, 29 March 1870, 10 July 1869 and a series from David Carly between 1884 and 1891. For more detail about the vicissitudes of J.B. Gribble see, Sue-Jane Hunt, The Gribble Affair : A Study of Aboriginal Labour Relations in North-West Australia during the 1880s, B.A. Hons., Murdoch 1978.

The eyes of England

Appeals to English opinion were common, see for instance: Orton letter to Wesleyan Mission Society, 5 Jan. 1841, Bonwick Transcripts, Box 53, *op.cit.*; letter on 'The Aborigines', *Port Phillip Gazette*, 22 April 1840; R.W. Newland letter to Anti-Slavery Society, 8 Dec. 1840, *op.cit.*; at the same source see letters by Rev. J.A. Fawcett, 6 Dec. 1882; J.B. Gribble, 21 Jan. 1887 and M.M. Bennett, 10 Feb. 1934.

Scruples on the frontier

For Daniel Cameron see his letter to the Colonial Secretary, 19 Oct. 1861, Qld Col.Sec., 2814 of 1861. Other viewpoints are illustrated in, letters of Samuel Davenport, 1842–49, *South Australiana*, 6 March 1967, 10 March 1971, 43; *Meyrick*, 137; *G.S. Lang*, 77; E. Thorn, A. White Australia—The Other Side, *United Australia*, 25 Oct. 1901, 14.

Humble protectors

There may have been many such people all over the continent. Few have left any record of their views. But see: the letter of T. Peutzcke, 25 Dec. 1893 to Col.Sec., *Qld Col.Sec.*, COL/A758, 492 of 1894 and at the same source those by John Cook, Col/A674, 11522 of 1891 and J.C. Hogflesh, Col/A595, 9567 of 1889. For the story of Sergeant Bennett see the journal of W. Thomas, 19 Aug. 1845, *op.cit.*

Of one blood

Phrases like this one run through much of the discussion about the Aborigines; see for instance : E.S. Parker, 1; T. Atkins, *Reminiscences*, Malvern 1869, 64; Rev. J. Innes in the *Inquirer*, 25 Dec. 1867; *Plomley*, 276; sermon of Rev. Saunders transcribed in William Thomas Diary 1839, Thomas papers, *op.cit.*; P. O'Farrell, *Letters from Irish Australia 1825–1929*, Sydney 1984, 76.

Enlightenment philosophy

For a discussion of these ideas see, H. Reynolds, 'Racial Thought in Early Colonial Australia', *Aus. J. Politics & History*, 20, 1, April 1974, 45–53. See also *Labillardiere*, V.; *Tench*, 294, *Dawson*, 194, 268, 332. P. Cunningham, *Two Years in New South Wales*, Sydney, 1966, 202.

The noble savage

For Cook see *Captain Cook's Journal During the First Voyage Round the World*, facsimile edition, Adelaide 1968, 323. For later comments refer to: O. Fry, Commissioner Crown Lands, Clarence River to Col. Sec., 20 Nov. 1848 in despatch Fitzroy to Grey, 25 Nov. 1849; Broughton in evidence to Select Committee on Aborigines, *BPP* 1836, 17., *Breton*, 242; *Cunningham*, *op.cit.*; *Dawson*, *op.cit.*; C. Rolleston, Commissioner Crown Lands, Darling Downs, Colonial office, CO1/201/442.

Notes

Personal experience
For the comments of Strele see O'Kelly, 87, and for Matthews, *RGSSA*, 1898-1900, 4, 44. See also *Wilson*, 167, Curr, *Recollections*, 93; A letter from a gentleman in N.S.W., Methodist Mission Society, In Correspondence—Australia, 1812–26; F. Bonney, 'On Some Customs of the Aborigines of the River Darling, NSW', *JAI*, 14, 1885, 124–5, W. Thomas, Language and Customs of the Australian Aborigines, Thomas Papers, *op.cit.*, 21, 153.

Brilliant intellects
See Grey as reported in *Aboriginal Protection Society Reports*, 2,4, Dec. 1841, 171; F. Dutton, *South Australia and Its Mines*, London 1846, 329; R.W. Newland to Anti-Slavery Society, 8 Dec. 1840, Anti-Slavery Papers, *op.cit.*; *Adelaide Examiner*, 22 April 1843; W. Watson Journal, 4 Dec. 1832; Polding in P.F. Moran, *History of the Catholic Church in Australasia*, Sydney, 1896, 410.

A real commonwealth
For appreciative comments about Aboriginal society see Thomas papers, vol.22, 436–7, Journal, 31 July 1844, Small Diary Oct.—Dec. 1840; H.E.A. Meyer, *Manners & Customs of the Aborigines of the Encounter Bay Tribe*, Adelaide 1846, 1; Leigh, Account of the Natives of New South Wales, Bonwick Transcripts, 52; M.M. Bennett, 79.

Craft and cunning
See letter by 'Outsider', *Hodgkinson Mining News*, 3 June 1877; *Colonial Times*, 16 July 1830, 1 June 1831; *Hobart Town Courier*, 11 Sept. 1830.

Linguistic lessons
Many colonists showed an interest in Aboriginal languages and collected lists of words. The missionaries were often the most serious students of language. See for instance Tuckfield to Wesleyan Mission Society, 30 Sept. 1840, Bonwick Transcripts, 53; For the Jesuit missionaries see *O'Kelly*, 87–94 and Report of Government Resident for Northern Territory, *SA Parlt Papers*, 2, 1888, No.28. See also J. *Dawson*, 1V.

Bushcraft
For appreciation of black skills see comments by D. Bunce in the *Argus*, 31 Aug. 1850; Mitchell, *Tropical Australia*, 412; J.E. Hammond, *Winjan's People*, Perth, 1933, 76–7; G.C. McCree, 'The Early Settlement of the Eastern Shore of Port Phillip Bay', *Victorian Historical Magazine*, 1, 1919, 25.

Adaptability
See Thomas, Language & Customs of Australian Aborigines, Thomas Papers, 21; E. Curr, *The Australian Race*, 1, 26; W. Cowan, 'The Natives of Western Australia', *Colonial Intelligencer & Aborigines Friend*, 1867–71, 53.

The impact of ideology
For general comments see H. Reynolds, Racial Thought in Early Colonial Australia, *op.cit.*, pp. 51–53. See also John Saunders in *The Colonist*, 17 Nov. 1838; W. Thomas, Language & Customs of the Australian Aborigines, *op.cit.*, 153; L.E. Threlkeld, Annual Report of the Mission to the Aborigines, 1838, Threlkeld Papers; *Dredge*, 10.

The claims of capital
Most of these comments were made in letters to the Anti-Slavery Society – Davidson, 1 Oct. 1870, Fawcett, 10 May 1883, Carly, 22 Oct. 1884, and Gribble, 28 May 1886. See also Threlkeld letter to London Missionary Society, 10 Aug. 1826, LMS Papers; R.B. Mitchell, Reminiscences, 102–4; letter of 'Fidelio' in *Sydney Gazette*, 19 Aug. 1824.

CHAPTER 5: SAVAGES

For a general survey see: H. Reynolds, *Racial Thoughts in Colonial Australia, op.cit.* and see also M.T. Hodgen, *Early Anthropology* in *The Sixteenth and Seventeenth Century*,

Uni. of Pennsylvania Press, n.d. For colonial views of savages see: *Journal of Daniel Paine, 1794–7*, (eds.) R. Knight & A. Frost, Sydney 1983, 39; *Turnbull*, 87, 96; *Hobart Town Gazette*, 8 April 1825; *Eipper*, 9; Ridley in *Moreton Bay Courier*, 19 Jan. 1856; Select Committee on Native Police, *Queensland V&P*, 1861, 4; White in *Rockhampton Bulletin*, 6 July 1865; Willshire, 28; *The Journal of Arthur Bowes Smyth*, Sydney 1979, 58.

The great chain of being
C. White, *An Account of the Regular Gradation in Man*, London 1799, 1, 33. For colonial exponents see, *Arden*, 98; *Byrne*, 321; *Henderson*, 152; *Cunningham*, 202.

For comments on the theory see: *Grey*, 2, 367; M. Levy, *Governor George Arthur*, Melbourne 1952, 104; *Dredge*, 9; letter from a gentleman in New South Wales, Methodist Missionary Society, *op.cit.*

Comparisons with monkeys were made by *Dawson*, 332; *Hodgson*, 253; *J.D. Lang*, 310; Wentworth in *Sydney Morning Herald*, 21 June 1844.

The smallest brains
For specific references in this section refer to Reynolds, *Racial Thought in Early Colonial Australia*, op. cit., 48–9.

Phrenology
See Reynolds, *Racial Thought*, op.cit. 50.

Mental poison
A letter from a gentleman in NSW, 1826, Methodist Mission Society, *op.cit.*; Threlkeld, Annual Report for the Mission to the Aborigines, Threlkeld Papers; *Henderson*, 2, 168; *Stokes*, 1, 89; Sturt, *Central Australia*, 2; Threlkeld letter to London Missionary Society, 10 Oct. 1825, *LMS Letters : Australia 1833–44*.

Evolutionary philosophy
C.C. Henderson, 'The Mutation Theory of Evolution in History', *AAAS*, 1912, 390; A. Lane-Fox Pitt Rivers, *The Evolution of Culture*, Oxford 1906, XV.

Living fossils
For the views of Drummond ad Haekel see G. Spiller, 'The Mentality of the Australian Aborigines', *The Sociological Review*, 6, 1913, 348–53. See as well: P. Pulleine & H. Wollard, 'Psychological and Mental Observations on the Australian Aborigines', *Royal Society of S. Aus. Proceedings*, 54, 1930, 62; *Bennett*, 102.

Ape-like characters
For the exposition of these ideas see T.H. Huxley, *Evidence As to Man's Place in Nature*, London, 1863, 78, 151–5; J. Bonwick, 'The Australian Natives', *JAI*, 16, 1887, 202; W. Ramsay Smith, 'The Place of the Australian Aboriginal in Recent Anthropological Research', *AAAS*, Adelaide 1908, 574.

The childhood of the race
See *JAI*, 1, 1872, 74–84. For Lubbock's views see pp. 462–5, and for Spencer see *The Principles of Sociology*, 2 vols., London 1876, 1, 62–103. See also Spencer, *Northern Territory*, 38–9 and Gregory as quoted in G. Kearney, et. al., *The Psychology of Aboriginal Australians*, Sydney 1973, 9.

Survival of the fittest
Such an influential idea found expression in many places but see for instance, K. Pearson, *National Life from the Standpoint of Science*, London 1901, 24; the views of Barron are reported in *SA Parlt. Debates*, 1866, 54; those of Barnard were aired in a paper entitled 'Aborigines of Tasmania', *AAAS*, 2, Melbourne 1890, 597; and Meston wrote in his Report on the Scientific Expedition to Bellender Ker Range, *Qld V&P*, 5, 1889, 1213.

Notes

Pitiless nature

See J. Collier, *The Pastoral Age in Australia*, op.cit., 135; *Sutherland*, 1, 29; *Age*, 11 Jan. 1888; 'Our Black Brothers', *Queenslander*, 30 Oct. 1875, 8 May 1880; *Age*, 13 Jan. 1881.

For belief about Aboriginal susceptibility to pain refer to: R.W. Felkin, 'The Differences of Sensibility between Europeans and negroes', *British Association*, 1889, 787; for Robart's paper see *AAAS*, 14, 1913, 445 and for those of Pitts refer to p.55.

A dying race

For theories before 1859 see *Stokes*, 2; P.de. Strzelecki, *Physical Description of New South Wales etc.*, London 1845, 344; *Merivale*, 540; *Darwin*, 520.

For the impact of evolutionary theory refer to the work of Alfred Russell Wallace: 'Natural Selection Applied to Anthropology', *Anthropological Review*, 16 Jan. 1867, 103—5; 'The Action of Natural Selection on Man', *Half Hours with Modern Scientists*, New Haven, 1873, 2—60, *Australasia*, London 1879.

For more recent Australian material see: J.B. Cleland, 'Disease Amongst the Australian Aborigines', *Journal of Tropical Medicine and Hygiene*, 31, 5, 15 Feb. 1928, 53; J.W. Bleakley, 'Can Our Aborigines be Preserved', *Australian Quarterly*, 7, Sept. 1930, 61—77.

A malign influence

See the *Queenslander*, 5 June 1880; *Lumholtz*, 348.

It is well

For the celebration of progress see J.S. Dunnett, 'Evolution in Australia', *The Empire Review*, 14, 1907—8, 132. The passage from Ida Lee's book will be found on pp. 239—40., and that from Semon's on 237. For the paper of J.J. Wild see *AAAS*, 1, Sydney 1889, 446. See also W. Bagelot, *Physics and Politics*, London 1872, 207—8; K. Pearson, op.cit., 61—2; D. McAllister, 'The Australian Aborigines', *Melbourne Review*, 3, 1878, 157; *Sutherland*, 29; Curr, *Recollections*, 179; *Bull*, 72; Macallister, op.cit., 158.

For the letter of Frager to Spencer see *Walker*, 223. See also interview with Professor Klaatsch in *Brisbane Courier* in cutting book of Australian Presbyterian Board of Missions, ML mss 1893, box 3; W. Ramsay-Smith, 'Australian Conditions & Problems', *AAAS*, 14, Melbourne 1914, 374. For the appearance of the Aboriginal party in London see *JAI*, 17, 1888, 83—5.

For the persistence of such ideas see *Devanny*, 188 and R. Cilento & C. Lack, *Triumph in the Tropics*, Brisbane 1959, 179.

CHAPTER 6: THE RIGHTS OF THE SOIL

For *Milirrpum* v. *Nabalco* (1971) F.L.R, 13 Oct. 17, 141—293.

Native title

For Johnson v. McIntosh see *The Constitutional Decisions of John Marshall*, 2 vols., New York, 1969, 2, 2—35. Chapman's judgement in *Symonds* v. *the Crown* is printed in Papers Relating to New Zealand, 1847—50, *BPP*, 64—7.

Native title in Australia

For Cook's instructions see *The Explorations of Captain James Cook*, ed. A.G. Price, Sydney 1958, 19; King's comments are in the King Papers, 2, *ML*, C/189; Brisbane was reported by Walker in a letter of 29 Nov. 1821, Bonwick Transcripts, 52, and Arthur's letter will be found in Aboriginal Tribes in British Possessions, *BPP*, 1834, 163. See also *Irwin*, 28.

For the views of Gipps and the legal opinion of Burge see Correspondence Relating to the Colony of New Zealand, *BPP*, 1842, 70.

Frontier

Knowledge accumulates

See the official opinions in S.G. Foster, 'Aboriginal Rights and Official Morality', *Push From the Bush*, 11 Nov. 1981, 69; *The South Australian Gazette*, 23 July 1840, and for public opinion at Port Phillip see *Arden*, 99. Aboriginal reactions are reported in Ryan, *The Aborigines in Tasmania*, 99; G.A. Robinson Letterbooks, 1841–5, 1845–8; letter of J. Herbert, 21 Oct. 1838, *Aborigines Protection Society Papers & Proceedings*, 5, 1839, 140; Select Committee on Aborigines, 1836, *op.cit.*, 19.

For the European appreciation of Aboriginal land use consult *Grey*, 2, 112, 252; *West*, 273; *Eyre*, 2, 296–7; *Leichhardt*, 354–5. See also Tuckfield's Journal, 174 and the letter of J.D. Lang in *Tracts Relative to the Aborigines*, London 1843, 10–12 and G.A. Robinson Letterbook, 1841–5, *op.cit.*

Humanitarian support

See letter of Parker to Robinson, 1 April 1840; Port Phillip Protectorate Papers, Box 11; Annual Report of Chief Protector, 1 Jan. 1849, G.A. Robinson Papers, vol. 61; Orton Journal, 28 Jan. 1842; Duncan McNab letter, 2 Sept. 1876, *Queensland V&P*, 1876, 3, 167.

Concern in Britain

See the Reports of the Select Committee on Aborigines, *BPP*, 1836, *op.cit.*, 203, 1837, 425; *Tracts Relative to the Aborigines*, *op.cit.*, 1843, 7; *Aborigines Protection Society : Report of Sub-Committee on Australia*. London 1838, 3; S. Motte, *Outline of a System of Legislation...etc.*, London 1840, 15; *Aborigines Protection Society Papers & Proceedings*, 5, 1839, 129–60.

Land rights in South Australia

The Act establishing the colony was 4 & 5 Will IV C.95; Arthur's letter was published in the Report of the Select Committee on Aborigines, *BPP*, 1837, *op.cit.*, 121. The considerable correspondence between the Colonial Office and the South Australian Colonizing Commissioners will be found in the Colonial Office files 396/1, 13/3, 13/4, 13/5, 13/6, 13/7. The affairs of South Australia were also reported in the British Parliamentary Papers, 1836, 36, 491; 1837–8, 97, 24; 1839, 225, 17; 1841, 129, 17. The conflict between Gawler and the settlers is reported in *The South Australian Register*, 1 Aug. 1840. See also the *South Australian Gazette*, 12 May, 1839.

Squatters and protectors

The view of the English Humanitarian are reported in the *Colonial Intelligencer*, 3 May 1847. The Backhouse letter was published in the report of the Select Committee on Aborigines, *BPP* 1836, *op.cit.* 680. Threlkeld's comments were in his 1838 Annual Report on the Mission to the Aborigines, op.cit. For Robinson's attitude to the pastoralists see his 1846 Chief Protectors Report, Colonial Office, CO201/382; *HRA*, 1, 26, 224; *Port Phillip Gazette*, 4 Dec. 1841; letter to La Trobe, 12 Dec. 1839, Robinson Papers, 25, *op.cit.*

Native title and pastoral leases

See in particular Grey to Fitzroy, 11 Feb. 1848, *HRA*, 1, 26, 225 and 10 Feb. 1850, dispatch No. 26, Dispatches from England, ML A1310. For the views of Sir H. Douglas see W. Martin, *England and the New Zealanders*, Auckland, 1847, 24–5.

The squatters respond

For the pastoral leases see Leases of Runs, *QSA*, LAN/01, 35/1213; Fraser to Government Resident, Derby 16 Aug. 1888, *WA Col. Sec.*, 2315/88; *Milirrpum* v. *Nabalco*, *F.L.R.*, *op.cit.*, 260. See also *Vogan*, 103; *Willey*, 98, *Bennett*, 68; Charles Archer to William Archer, 29 April 1845, Archer Papers : Some Letters Mainly from Australia, 1833–53.

Official impotence

The comments of the two government officials are in *Queensland Parliamentary Papers*, 1904, 870; *South Australia Parliamentary Papers*, 3, 1888, 17.

Notes

Blackburn v. Marshall
For *Calder et.al.* v. *Attorney General of British Columbia*, Dominion Law Review, 34, (3d), 1973, 145—226; for the comments of Deane, J., see *Australian Law Journal*, 59, 4 April 1985, 346.

CHAPTER 7: THIS WHISPERING IN OUR HEARTS

Windeyer's lecture on the Rights of the Aborigines of Australia is in the Mitchell Library, mss. A1404.

A sore subject
See *Griffith*, 170; *Howitt*, 277; *Kennedy*, 65; F. Dutton, *South Australia and its Mines*, London, 1845, 323; P. O'Farrell, *Documents in Australian Catholic History*, London 1969, 414; *Moreton Bay Courier*, 4 April 1857; *Rockhampton Bulletin*, 28 Aug. 1865; McConnell Papers, Oxley Library; John Cook to Colonial Secretary, 26 Aug. 1891; *Qld Col.Sec.*, 11522 of 1892.

An unwelcome obelisk
Dawson discussed his obelisk in the *Town & Country Journal*, 7 Aug. 1886 and in a letter to the Anti-Slavery Society, 26 Jan. 1886.

The moral foundations
Phillip II quoted in S. Zavala, *The Political Philosophy of the Conquest of America*, Mexico City 1953, 35; letter quoted in A. Atkinson, 'The Ethics of Conquest', *Aboriginal History*, 6, 1982, 87; *Essays of Francis Bacon*, London 1906, 104.

A fundamental contradiction
See W. Blackstone, *Commentaries on the Laws of England*, 4 vols. London 1765 (University of Chicago facsimile, 1979), 1, 104; J. Locke, *Two Treatises of Civil Government*, London 1955, 118, 180, 187; P.E. de Strzelecki, *Physical Description of New South Wales and Van Diemens Land*, London 1845, 348; letter from 'An Inhabitant of the Northern Districts', *Queensland Times*, 15 Dec. 1857.

Terra Nullius
See the *Sydney Morning Herald*, 5 Dec. 1838; *Sydney Gazette*, 19 Aug. 1824.

Sovereignty and native title
E. de. Vattel : *The Law of Nations*, Washington 1916, 85, 91, 142—3; *The Constitutional Decisions of John Marshall*, op.cit. 2,4.

Subdue the earth
These ideas were very common but see the *Port Denison Times*, 16 May 1866; *Moreton Bay Courier*, 9 Jan. 1856; *North Australian*, 5 July 1861; *Brisbane Courier*, 15 Dec. 1865; *West*, 332; H.B. Turner, *A History of the Colony of Victoria*, 2 vols., Lond. 1904, 1, 239; *Pridden*, 186; Fry to Col. Sec., 20 Nov. 1848 in Fitzroy to Grey, Colonial office, CO201/413.

Was the earth open to all
See the *Sydney Morning Herald*, 21 May 1858; *Queensland Guardian*, 5 March 1862; *Torres Strait Pilot*, 15 Nov. 1902; *SA Parlt. Debates*, 1888, 338.

Humanitarian doubts
See the *Morning Chronicle*, 15 June 1844; *Aborigines Protection Society Papers & Proceedings*, 5, 1839, 142—3; Report of the Chief Protector for Aborigines, 1 Jan. 1849; G.A. Robinson Papers, 61; *Queensland Votes & Proceedings*, 3, 1876, 167.

The right of conquest
For colonial comment see *Bartlett*, 78; *Landon*, 188; *Moreton Bay Courier*, 16 Jan. 1847, 9

Dec. 1848; R.M. Lyon, *op.cit.* 115. For international law refer to Vattel, *op.cit.*, 246, 309–10; *Locke*, 206–7.

The blood is on every land

See the *Queenslander*, 25 July 1874, 8 May, 1880; *Port Phillip Patriot*, 30 May 1842; *West Australia Parliamentary Debates*, 1893, 1050; letter to Police Commissioner, 31 July 1904, QSA, POL/J21, 413 M; *Harris*, 224; *Calder* v. *Attorney-General of British Columbia*, *op.cit.*; *Mundy*, 1, 48; Robinson to Whitcomb, 10 Aug. 1832, Robinson Papers, 35.

CONCLUSION

Phillip's instructions will be found in *HRA*, 1,1, 13–14; the Northwest Ordinance can be consulted in H.S. Commager, *Documents in American History*, 6th. edn New York, 1951, 128–31. The problems of Governor Gipps are outlined by S.C. Foster in 'Aboriginal Rights and Official Morality', *The Push From the Bush*. 11 Nov. 1981, 68–98. For comment on American jurisprudence see, F. Cohen, 'Original Indian Title'. *Minnesota Law Review*, 32, 1947, 55. The comparison between policy towards the Aborigines and the Indians appeared in A Letter From a Gentleman in NSW, Methodist Missionary Society, *op.cit.*

For the views of S.H. Roberts see *The Squatting Age*, 333. West's assessment of his contemporaries attitude to common property is in his *History of Tasmania*, 272. R.M. Lyon is reported in the Proceedings of the Aborigines Protection Society, *op.cit.*, 117. For attitudes to Aboriginal labour see Mr Jordan, *Qld Parlt. Debates*, 1884, 88; *Lumholtz*, 347; E.S. Parker in Port Phillip Protectorate Records, Box 12; Mr Collie in evidence to Select Committee on Aborigines, *BPP*, 1837, 129; *Transportation : The British Convict in Western Australia*, London 1865, 28, in B.T. Haynes et.al., *WA Aborigines, 1622–1972*, Perth 1972, 22; Taplin, *The Folklore*, 12 *Bulmer*, 30; J. Guanther, Lectures on the Aborigines, Gunther Papers, *ML* mss. B505; Address by Gipps to Legislative Council, 8 June 1841, in Aborigines, Australian Colonies, *B.P.P.* 1884, 119.

For the comments of W.E.H. Stanner see 'The Aborigines', J.C.G. Kevin (ed.), *Some Australians Take Stock*, London, 1939, 6. For the concluding quotation see R.M. Lyon. *Aborignes Protection Society Proceedings*, *op.cit.*, 116.

Select Bibliography

Abbreviations

AAAS	*Australian Association for the Advancement of Science, Papers and Proceedings*
BL	Battye Library
HRA	*Historical Records of Australia*
HRNSW	*Historical Records of New South Wales*
HS	*Historical Studies*
JAI	*Journal of the Anthropological Institute of Great Britain*
JRAHS	*Journal of the Royal Australian Historical Studies*
JRGS	*Journal of the Royal Geographical Society*
ML	Mitchell Library
NSW Col. Sec.	New South Wales Colonial Secretary, In Letters
NSWLAV&P	New South Wales Legislative Assembly Votes and Proceedings
NSWLC	New South Wales Legislative Council
NSWLCV&P	New South Wales Legislative Council Votes and Proceedings
Qld Col. Sec.	Queensland Colonial Secretary, In Letters
QSA	Queensland State Archives
QVP	Queensland Votes and Proceedings
RGSSA	*Journal of the Royal Geographical Society of Australian, South Australian Branch*
SA Col. Sec.	South Australian Colonial Secretary, In Letters
SMH	*Sydney Morning Herald*
Tas. Col. Sec.	Tasmanian Colonial Secretary, In Letters
THRA	*Tasmanian Historical Research Association, Papers and Proceedings*
TSA	Tasmanian State Archives
VPRO	Victorian Public Records Office
WA Col. Sec.	Western Australia Colonial Secretary, In Letters
WAHS	*Journal of the West Australian Historical Society*
WALCV&P	West Australian Legislative Council Votes and Proceedings

Official Printed Sources

BRITAIN
House of Commons, Sessional Papers
1831, 19, No. 259: Van Diemen's Land. Return to an Address...for Copies of all Correspondence between Lieutenant-Governor Arthur and His Majesty's Secretary of State for the Colonies, on the Subject of the Military Operations lately carried on against the Aboriginal Inhabitants of Van Diemens land
1831, 19, No. 261: New South Wales. Return to an Address...dated 19 July 1831 for Copies of Instructions given by His Majesty's Secretary of State for the Colonies, for

Promoting the Moral and Religious Instruction of the Aboriginal Inhabitants of New Holland or Van Diemens Land

1834, 44, No. 617: Aboriginal Tribes (North America, New South Wales, Van Diemen's Land and British Guinea)

1836, 7, No. 538: Report from the Select Committee on Aborigines (British Settlements)

1837, 7, No. 425: Report from the Select Committee on Aborigines (British Settlements)

1839, 34, No. 526: Australian Aborigines...Copies or Extracts of Despatches Relative to the Massacre of Aborigines of Australia...

1843, 33, No. 141: Port Essington: Copies or Extracts of Any Correspondence Relative to the Establishment of a Settlement...

1843, 32, No. 505: Papers Relative to the Affairs of South Australia, (especially pp. 267–340)

1844, 34, No. 627: Aborigines (Australian Colonies)...Return to an address...for Copies or Extracts from the Despatches of the Governors of the Australian Colonies, with the Reports of the Protectors of Aborigines...to illustrate the Condition of the Aboriginal Population of said Colonies...

1897, 61, No. 8350: Western Australia: Correspondence Relating to the Abolition of the Aborigines Protection Board

NEW SOUTH WALES

Legislative Council, Votes and Proceedings

1838: Report from the Committee on the Aborigines Question

1839, 2: Report from the Committee on Police and Gaols

1841: Report from the Committee on Immigration with...Replies to a Circular Letter on the Aborigines

1843: New South Wales (Aborigines). Return to an address by Dr Thomson...comprising details of Government Expenditure on Aborigines, 1837–43, and a large collection of correspondence relating to the protectorate and the missions

1844, 1: New South Wales (Aborigines). Return to an address by Sir Thomas Mitchell...for numbers of whites and Aborigines killed in conflicts since the settlement of the Port Phillip District

1845: Report from the Select Committee on the Condition of the Aborigines

1850, 1: The Native Police, Report of the Commandant to the Colonial Secretary

1852, 1: Letter from Mr F. Walker, Commandant, Native Police

1853, 1: Return of Murders by Aborigines in the Northern Districts

1855, 1: Report of Board of Enquiry Held at Moreton Bay regarding Commandant F. Walker

Legislative Assembly: Votes and Proceedings

1856–57, 1: Report from the Select Committee on the Native Police Force

1858, 2: Report from the Select Committee on Murders by the Aborigines on the Dawson River

SOUTH AUSTRALIA

Parliamentary Papers

1857–58, 2, No. 156: Explorations of Mr S. Hack

1857–58, 2, No. 193: Northern Exploration

1858, 1, No. 25: Northern Exploration: Reports etc of Explorations...by Babbage, Warburty, Geharty and Parry

1878, 4, No. 209: Journal of Mr Barlay's Exploration

1884, 3: Quarterly Report on the Northern Territory

1885, 4, No. 170: Report on the Pursuit of the Daly River Murderers

1888, 3, No. 53: Government Residents Report on the Northern Territory for 1887

1890, 2, No. 28: Government Residents Report on the Northern Territory for 1889

Bibliography

1892, 3, No. 129: Report on the Mai-Nini Murder Trial
1892, 3, No. 181: Government Residents Report on the Northern Territory for 1891
1899, 2, No. 77a: Report from the Select Committee on the Aborigines Bill
1899, 2, No. 77: Minutes of Evidence on the Aborigines Bill
1900, 3, No. 60: Justice in the Northern Territory; Letter from Mr Justice Dashwood
1901, 2, No. 45: Government Resident's Report on the Northern Territory for 1900
1913, 2, No. 26: Report from the Royal Commission on the Aborigines

TASMANIA
Legislative Council Journals and Papers
1863, No. 48: Half-Caste Islanders in Bass's Straits, Report by the Venerable Archdeacon Reibey
1881, No. 75: First Discovery of Port Davey and Macquarie Harbour by Captain James Kelly in...1815–16 and 1824

VICTORIA
Legislative Council: Votes and Proceedings
1858–59, No. D8: Report on the Select Committee of the Legislative Council on the Aborigines
Parliamentary Papers
1877–78, 3, No. 76: Report of the Royal Commission on the Aborigines
1882–83, 2, No. 5: Report of the Board Appointed to Inquire into and Report Upon...the Coranderrk Aboriginal Station
1873–84: Ninth to Twentieth Reports of Board for the Protection of Aborigines in the Colony of Victoria, presented to both Houses of Parliament

QUEENSLAND
Votes and Proceedings of the Legislative Assembly
1860: Report of Select Committee on the Police
1861: Report of Select Committee on Native Police Force
1863: Papers Regarding the Dismissal of J. Donald Harris of the Native Police
1867, 1: Copies of Correspondence...concerning the inquiry into the case of C.J. Blakeney, late Lieutenant of Native Police
1867, 1: Charges Against the Native Police under the command of Mr Sub-Lieutenant Hill
1867, 2: Alleged Massacre of Blacks at Morinish Diggings
1872: Report of Acting Commandant of Police for 1871
1874, 2: Enquiry into the Claims of Patrick Corbett
1875, 1: Report of Commandant of Police for 1874
1876, 3: Report of the North-Western Exploring Expedition
1876, 3: Report of Expedition in Search of Gold...in the Palmer District by Mulligan and Party
1878, 2: Report of the Aborigines Commissioners
1881, 1: Report of Explorations in Cape York Peninsula by R.L. Jack
1881, 2: Further Reports on the Progress of the Gold Prospecting Expedition in Cape York Peninsula
1883–84: Report of Police Magistrate, Thursday Island on Pearl Shell and Bêche de Mer Fisheries in Torres Strait
1885, 2: Reports of Mr Douglas's Cruise Among the Islands of Torres Strait
1886, 2: Visit of Inspection of Various Islands in the G.S.S. *Albatross*
1888, 3: Annual Reports of the Gold Fields Commissioners
1889, 3: Annual Reports of the Gold Fields Commissioners
1890, 3: Report on the Pearl and Pearl Shell Fisheries of North Queensland by W. Saville-Kent

1890, 3: Annual Report of the Government Resident at Thursday Island
1894, 2: Annual Report of Government Resident at Thursday Island
1896, 4: Report on the Aborigines of North Queensland by Mr A. Meston
1897, 2: Report on the North Queensland Aborigines and the Native Police by W. Parry Okeden
1900–1904: Annual Reports of Northern Protectorate of Aborigines
1902, 1: Report of the Southern Protector of Aboriginals
1903, 2: W.E. Roth: North Queensland Ethnography Bulletin No.5

WESTERN AUSTRALIA
Votes and Proceedings of the Legislative Council
1871, No. 2: Information Respecting the Habits and Customs of the Aboriginal Inhabitants of Western Australia
1872, No. 5: Despatches between the Governor and the Secretary of State for the Colonies
1875–76, No. 12: Correspondence Relative to the State of Affairs on the North-West Coast
1880, No. A16: Report of the Government Resident, Roebourne on the Pearl Shell Industries of the North-West Coast
1882, No. 33: Reports from the Resident Magistrate...in the Murchison and Gascoyne Districts
1884, No. 32: Report of a Commission to Inquire into the treatment of Aboriginal Native Prisoners of the Crown
1885, No. A15: Report of the Select Committee...Appointed to Consider and Report Upon...the Treatment and Condition of the Aboriginal Natives of the Colony
1888, No.27: Papers Respecting the Necessity of Increased Police Protection for the Settlers in the Kimberley District
Parliamentary Papers of Western Australia
1901, 2, No.26: Report on Stations Visited by the Travelling Inspector of Aborigines
1902–3, 2, No. 32: Report of the Aborigines Department
1903–4, 2, No. 32: Report of the Aborigines Department
1905, No. 5: Report of the Royal Commission on the Condition of the Natives

DOCUMENTARY COLLECTIONS
Historical Records of Australia, Series One, 1–25 and Series Three, 1–6
Historical Records of New South Wales, 1–7

Official Manuscript Sources

ARCHIVES OFFICE OF NEW SOUTH WALES
Colonial Secretary's Correspondence: In Letters (special bundles)
Aborigines, 4/7153
Aborigines 1833–35, 4/2219.1
Aborigines 1836, 4/2302.1
Aborigines 1837–39, 4/24433.1
Aborigines 1849, 4/1141
Aborigines 1849, 4/2831.1
Aborigines 1852, 4/713.2
Aborigines and the Native Police 1835–44, 4/1135.1
Aboriginal Outrages, 2/8020.4
Port Phillip Papers, 1839, 4/2471
Port Phillip Papers, 1840, Part 1, 4/2510
Port Phillip Papers, 1840, Part 2, 4/2511
Port Phillip Papers, 1841, Part 1, 4/2547

Bibliography

Port Phillip Papers, 1842, Part 1, 4/2588 B
Port Phillip Papers, 1842, Part 2, 4/2589 B
Port Phillip Papers, 1846, 4/2745−2
Letters Received from and about Wide Bay, 1850−57, 4/7173
Raffles Bay, 4/2060.2
Reports on the Border Police, 1843−46, 4/7203
Letters from Moreton Bay, 1843, 4/2618.1
Bathurst 1815−23, 4/1798
Bathurst 1824, 4/1800
Bathurst 1826, 4/1801
Bathurst 1824−26, 4/1799
Supreme Court Records
Papers Relating to the Aborigines, 1796−1839, 1161

Mitchell Library
Aborigines MSS A/611
Letters from Government Officials, MSS A/664
Queensland Native Police: Answers to Questionnaire, 1856, MSS A467
Letterbook, Commissioner of Crown Land, Darling Downs 1843−48, MSS A1764−2
Somerset Letterbook No. 1, MSS B1414

Tasmanian State Archives
Papers Relating to the Aborigines, 7578
Reports on the Murders and Other Outrages Committed by the Aborigines, CSO/1/316
Records Relating to the Aboriginals, CSO/1/317
Reports of Mr G.A. Robinson Whilst in Pursuit of the Natives, CSO/1/318
Papers of the Aborigines Committee, CSO/1/319
Reports of the Roving Parties, CSO/1/320
Suggestions Relative to the Capture of the Natives, CSO/1/323
Papers Relating to the Black Line, CSO/1/324

Battye Library, Perth
Swan River Papers, 9, 10
Colonial Secretary: In Letters, Volumes concerned with the Aborigines
53, April, May 1837
54, June, July 1837
56, October 1837
89, 1840
95, 1841
108, 1842
173, 1848

State Library of South Australia
Governors Despatches GRG/2/6/1
Letterbook of the Government Resident, Port Lincoln 3/379
Report of Attack on Barrow Creek Telegraph Station GRG/24/6/1874 Nos. 332, 347
Colonial Secretary: In Letters, 1837−41, GRG/24/1; 1842−45, GRG/24/6
Colonial Secretary's Letterbooks, GRG/24/4/3; GRG/24/4
Protector of Aborigines Letterbook 1840−57, GRG/52/7

Victorian Public Records Office
Records of the Port Phillip Aboriginal Protectorate, especially the boxes—Westernport, North-Western District, Mainly In-Letters, Mt Rouse

Frontier

QUEENSLAND STATE ARCHIVES

New South Wales Colonial Secretary, Letters Received Relating to Moreton Bay and Queensland, 1822–1860

Microfilm copies of material from State Archives of NSW, Reels A2/1—A2/48 including the special bundles and A2/48 which contains Commissioner of Crown Lands re Aborigines in the District, 1854 Government Resident, Moreton Bay re complaints about the Native Police 1857

Correspondence concerning the police firing on the Aborigines

Native Police: Moreton Bay 1857, Reels A2/47

Native Police Papers QSA/NMP 48/100, 48/111, 48/120

Government Resident, Moreton Bay, QSA/RES/2 and 3 48/101, 48/102

Letterbook of Commissioner for Crown Lands, Wide Bay and Burnett, 24/9/53–30/12/54, QSA/CCL/35/889 and 1/1/55–13/12/57, QSA/CCL/30/11

Letterbook of W.H. Wiseman, 5/2/55–30/5/60, QSA/CCL/7/61

Colonial Secretary: In Letters, 1860–1890, the QSA/Col/A files and the Special Bundles Relating to the Aborigines, QSA/Col/139–QSA/Col/144

JAMES COOK UNIVERSITY LIBRARY, TOWNSVILLE

Microfilm collection of the Joint Copying Project of Colonial Office Files re New South Wales, Tasmania and South Australia. Especially useful were the files: New South Wales, Original Correspondence, 1838–1849 and Queensland, Original Correspondence 1861–1900

Other Manuscript Sources

MITCHELL LIBRARY

Papers of Sir George Arthur, especially vol. 19, Letters received 1827–28, MSS A/2179, vol. 20, 1829–30, MSS A2180 and vol. 28 Aborigines, 1825–37, MSS A2188, Tasmanian Aborigines, MSS A612

Papers of G.A. Robinson, especially vol. 14

Port Phillip Protectorate, 1839–40, MSS A7035

Port Phillip Protectorate: Correspondence 54–57a and other papers, 1839–49, MSS A7075–7078–2

Port Phillip Protectorate, Official Reports, 59–61, 1841–49, MSS A7078-MSS A7082

J.D. Lang, Papers, 20, MSS 2240

W. Gardner, Productions and Resources of the Northern Districts of NSW, 2 vols, 1842–54, MSS A176/1, A176/2

William Thomas Papers, especially his journal for 1844–47, uncatalogued MSS 214/2 and 3

E.J. Eyre, Autobiographical of Residence and Exploration in Australia, 1832–39, MSS A1806

Diary of John Gilbert, 18/9/44–22/6/45, MSS A2587

Jesse Gregson Memoirs, MSS 1382

A. Le Souef, Personal Recollections of Early Victoria, MSS A2762

Reminiscences of Mr James Nesbit, MSS A1533

A.C. Grant, Early Station Life in Queensland, MSS A858

Telfer, Reminiscences, MSS A2376

J. Backhouse, G. Walker, Report of a Visit to the Penal Settlement, Moreton Bay, MSS B706

H.W. Best Diary, 20/9/62–15/4/63 MSS B515/1

Arthur Bloxham Diary, May-July 1863, MSS B515/1

Andrew Murray, Journal of an Expedition 1859–1860, MSS 736

R.B. Mitchell, Reminiscences 1855–66, MSS B575

J. Raven, Reminiscences of a Western Queensland Pioneer, MSS A2692

Bibliography

J.F. Stevens, Histories of Pioneers, MSS 1120
Borwick Transcripts, Series 1, Boxes 49−53
J. Backhouse, G. Walker, Reports, MSS B707
Rev. W. Bedford, Papers 1823−43, MSS A76
J.E. Calder, Papers, MSS A597
J. Gunther, Journal 1836−65, MSS B504
J. Gunther, Correspondence and Notes on New South Wales Aborigines, MSS A1450
J. Gunther, Lecture on the Aborigines, MSS B505
Hassall Correspondence, MSS A1677
D. Matthews, Papers, MSS A3384
J. Orton, Letterbook, MSS A1719
R. Sadlier, Papers, MSS A1631
T.H. Scott, Letterbooks, MSS A850
L.E. Threlkeld, Papers, MSS A382
R. Windeyer, On the Rights of the Aborigines of Australia, MSS 1400

Tasmanian State Archives
Van Diemens Land Company Papers, Letters and Despatches, 1828−46, VDC 5/1−7

Battye Library, Perth
Constance Norris, Memories of Champion Bay or Old Geraldton, Q994.12/GER
L.F. Clarke, West Australian Natives: My Experiences With them, PR 2766
Mr William Coffin, Oral History Tape, PR 9893
Reminiscences of Mr F.H. Townsend, PR 3497
Report of the Rev. John Smithers re the Swan River Aborigines, 1840, PR 1785a
Extracts from the Diary of Lieut. G.F. Dashwood in Perth, September 1832, PR 956/FC
Diary of Dr S.W. Viveash, QB/VIV
F.F.B. Wittenoom, Some Notes on his Life QB/WIT
Journals of Trevarthon C. Scholl, 1865−66 QB/SHO
L.C. Burgess: Pioneers of Nor'-West Australia, PR 40
N.K. Sligo, Reminiscences of Early Westralian Goldfields, Q 994.1/SLI

State Library of South Australia
Letters Written by John Mudge...whilst a trooper at Pt. Lincoln and Mt. Wedge, 1857−60, SAA 1518
J.B. Bull Reminiscences 1835−94, SAA 950
Extracts from the Diary of Mary Thomas, SAA 1058M
Simpson Newland, The Ramingaries (Encounter Bay) Tribe of Aborigines, A571/A4
Resolution of the Bush Club, 9/5/1839, A546/B8
Papers of George Taplin, SAA 186/1/1−6. Journal, Letters Received, Lecture on Narrinyeri Tribe, History of Port Mackay

La Trobe Library, Melbourne
W. Thomas, Brief Remarks on the Aborigines of Victoria, 1839, 7838Lt
Journal of Patrick Coady Buckley, 1844−1853, 6109, Box 214/7
Diary of Neil Black, typescript, September 1839−May 1840, Box 99/1
Foster Fyans Reminiscences, 1810−1842, 6940
W. H. Hovell, Remarks on a Voyage to Western Port, 7/11/26−25/3/27 CY, 8, 1/32 c
The Journal of Francis Tuckfield, 655
The Papers of James Dredge—Notebook, 421959; Letterbook, 421961
H. Meyrick, Letters to his family in England, 1840−47, 7959

Oxley Library, Brisbane
Archer Family Papers, including Durundur Diary, 1843−44, Some Letters Mainly from Australia, 1835−55

Diary of Captain G. Griffin at Whiteside, 1/1/47–16/5/49, OM72–42
Letter of T.W. Wells to H.C.A. Harrison, 24/10/61 OM66/2/f2
Reminiscences of Mrs Adelaide Morrison OM69/8/f1
Robert Hamilton, Diary at Mt Auburn Station, 18/11/61–3/9/62, OM68/28/Q2
Harry Anning, Thirty Years Ago, OM172/123
Archibald Meston Papers, OM64/17

AUSTRALIAN NATIONAL LIBRARY
Hagenauer Letterbooks, MSS 3343
Microfilm of Australian Joint Copying Project
Church Missionary Society Records, FM4 1453–1523
  James Gunther, Letters 1837–42, Journals, 1837–40
  John Handt, Letters 1830–43, Journals 1832–41, Report 1835
  William Porter, Letters 1838–41, Journal 1838
  William Watson, Letters 1832–42, Journal 1832–37, Reports 1832–40
Methodist Missionary Society Records FM4 1398–1421
  Correspondence—In: Australia, 1812–26, 1827–36, 1837–42
London Missionary Society, FM 338–445
  Australian Letters 1798–1855
  Australian Journals 1800–1842 including W. Shelley, R. Hassall, L. E. Threlkeld
Mathew Hale Papers, FM4/1063

RHODES HOUSE OXFORD
Papers of the Anti-Slavery Society, MSS British Empire S22
Letterbook of J.P. Phillips, 1850–54, MSS Australia S1

Newspapers

NEW SOUTH WALES
Atlas, 1844–1845
Australian, 1824, 1840–41, 1848
Colonist, 1837–1839
Empire, 1851–52, 1855–58
Hunter River Gazette, 1841–42
Maitland Mercury, 1843–1850
Morning Chronicle, 1844
Sydney Gazette, 1803–1830
Sydney Morning Herald, 1834–1850 (*Sydney Herald* before July 1842)

TASMANIA
Colonial Times, 1825–1831
Hobart Town Courier, 1827–1831
Hobart Town Gazette, 1819–1825
Launceston Advertiser, 1829–1831
The Tasmanian, 1827–1828

WESTERN AUSTRALIA
Geraldton Express, 1886–1890
Inquirer, 1840–1851, 1864–67
Northern Public Opinion, 1893–1898
Pilbara Goldfields News, 1897–1898
Perth Gazette, 1833–1840

Bibliography

SOUTH AUSTRALIA
Adelaide Examiner, 1842–1843
Adelaide Observer, 1844–1849
Port Augusta Dispatch, 1877–1880
South Australian Register, 1839–1844
Southern Australian, 1838–1840

VICTORIA
Geelong Advertiser, 1840–1844
Portland Gazette, 1845–1847
Portland Guardian, 1842–1843
Portland Mercury, 1842–1844
Port Phillip Gazette, 1838–1846
Port Phillip Herald, 1840
Port Phillip Patriot, 1841–1842

QUEENSLAND
Burnett Argus, 1863
Cairns Post, 1885–1888
Colonist, (Maryborough) 1884–1888
Cooktown Courier, 1874–1879, 1888
Cooktown Herald, 1874–1877
Cooktown Independent, 1888–1891
Croydon Golden Age, 1896, 1898
Darling Downs Gazette, 1858–1859
Herberton Advertiser, 1884–1885
Hodgkinson Mining News, 1877–1888
Mackay Mercury, 1868–1880
Maryborough Chronicle, 1860–1880
Moreton Bay Courier, 1846–1862
Moreton Bay Free Press, 1852–1859
North Australian, (Brisbane) 1856–1865
North Queensland Telegraph, 1888
Peak Downs Telegram, (Clermont) 1876
Port Denison Times, (Bowen) 1867–1883
Queenslander, 1866–1900
Queensland Figaro, 1885
Queensland Guardian, 1861–1863
Queensland Times, (Ipswich) 1864–1866
Ravenswood Miner, 1871–72
Rockhampton Bulletin, 1865–1876
Torres Strait Pilot, 1897–1907
Wide Bay and Burnett News, 1881–1884
Wide Bay and Burnett Times, 1859–1860
Wild River Times, (Herberton) 1886–1889

NORTHERN TERRITORY
Northern Territory Times, 1873–1883, 1887–1889, 1890–1895

MISSIONARY JOURNALS
The Colonial Intelligencer or Aborigines Friend, 1847–1848, 1867–1871
The Aborigines Friend, 1852–1858, 1863–1865, 1878–1882

Frontier

The Colonial Intelligencer, 1874–1878
Missionary Notes of the Australian Board of Missions, 1895–1905
Kirchliche Mitteilungen, (Church News) 1886–1900
Newspaper Cutting Books on the Aborigines and related topics in Oxley Library, Mitchell Library, State Library of South Australia

A number of the papers listed above were used for periods other than for those specified. But they were in such cases only consulted for a few issues at any one time. Numerous other papers were used for an issue or two but they have not been listed. Reference has been made to a few of these in the endnotes.

Research Theses

Attwood, B.M., Blacks and Lohans: A Study of Aboriginal-European Relations in Gippsland in the Nineteenth Century, PhD, La Trobe, 1985

Allingham, A.J., 'Taming the Wilderness': The First Decade of Pastoral Settlement in the Kennedy District, BA Hons, James Cook, 1976

Beckett, J., A Study of a Mixed Blood Aboriginal Minority in the Pastoral West of New South Wales, MA, ANU, 1958

Bell, D., From Moth Hunters to Black Trackers. An Interpretive Analysis of the Black and White Experience, BA Hons, Monash, 1975

Bickford, R.A., Traditional Economy of the Aborigines of the Murray Valley, BA Hons, Sydney, 1966

Biskup, P., Native Administration and Welfare in Western Australia 1897–1954, MA, West Australia, 1960

Brayshaw, H., Aboriginal Material Culture in the Herbert–Burdekin District, PhD, James Cook, 1977

Bridges, B., Aboriginal and White Relations in New South Wales 1788–1855, MA, Sydney, 1966

Blundell, V.J., Aboriginal Adaption in North West Australia, PhD, Wisconsin, 1975

Brown, R.B., A History of the Gilbert River Goldfield, 1869–1874, BA Hons, James Cook, 1974

Bury, W.R., The Foundations of the Pt McLeay Aboriginal Mission, BA Hons, Adelaide, 1964

Critchett, J.F., A History of the Framlingham and Lake Condah Aboriginal Stations, 1860–1918, MA, Melbourne, 1980

Christie, M.F., Race Relations between Aborigines and Colonists in Early Victoria, 1835–86, PhD, Monash, 1978

Crawford, I.M., William Thomas and the Port Phillip Protectorate, MA, Melbourne, 1967

Curthoys, A., Race and Ethnicity: A Study of the Response of British Colonists to Aborigines, Chinese and non-British Europeans in N.S.W. 1856–1881, PhD, Macquarie, 1973

Denholm, D., Some Aspects of Squatting in New South Wales and Queensland, 1847–1864, PhD, ANU, 1972

Desailly, B., The Mechanics of Genocide, MA, Tasmania, 1978

Eckermann, A.K., Half-Caste, Out Caste, PhD, Queensland, 1977

Evans, G., Thursday Island, 1878–1914, BA Hons, Queensland, 1972

Evans, K., Missionary Effort Towards the Cape York Aborigines, 1886–1910, BA Hons, Queensland, 1969

Evans, R., European–Aboriginal Relations in Queensland, 1880–1910, BA Hons, Queensland, 1965

Gale, F., A Study in Assimilation: Part Aborigines in South Australia, PhD, Adelaide, 1956

Graves, A.A., An Anatomy of Race Relations, BA Hons, Adelaide, 1973

Bibliography

Haebich, A., A Bunch of Cast-Offs: Aborigines of the South-West of Western Australia, 1900–1936, PhD, Murdoch, 1985

Hardley, R.G., Some of the Factors that influenced the Coastal Riverine and Insular Habits of the Aborigines of South-East Queensland and Northern New South Wales, BA Hons, Queensland, 1975

Harrison, B.W., The Myall Creek Massacre, BA Hons, New England, 1966

Hartwig, M.C., The Coniston Killings, BA Hons, Adelaide, 1960

Hartwig, M.C., The Progress of White Settlement in the Alice Springs District and its Effect on the Aboriginal Inhabitants, 1860–1914, PhD, Adelaide, 1965

Hocking, B., Native Land Rights, LLM, Monash, 1970

Hoskin, G., Aboriginal Reserves in Queensland, BA Hons, Queensland, 1968

Jenkin, G., The Aborigines Friends' Association and the Ngarrindjeri People, MA, Adelaide, 1976

Johnston, S.L., The New South Wales Government Policy Towards the Aborigines, 1880–1909, MA, Sydney, 1970

Kirkman, N., the Palmer River Goldfield, 1874–1884, BA Hons, James Cook, 1984

Krastins, V., The Tiwi: A Culture Contact History of the Australian Aborigines on Bathurst and Melville Islands, 1705–1942, BA Hons, ANU, 1972

Loos, N.A., Aboriginal-European Relations in North Queensland, 1861–1897, PhD, James Cook, 1976

Loos, N.A., Frontier Conflict in the Bowen District, 1861–1874, MA Qualifying, James Cook, 1970

McGrath, A., We Grew Up the Stations, PhD, La Trobe, 1983

McGregor, R., Settling the Black Question: Aborigines in the East Kimberley, BA Hons, James Cook, 1985

Milich, C., Official Attitudes to the South Australian Aborigines in the 1930s, BA Hons, Adelaide, 1967

Murray-Prior, J., Women Settlers and Aborigines, BA Hons, New England, 1973

O'Kelly, G.J., The Jesuit Mission Stations in the Northern Territory, 1882–1899, BA Hons, Monash, 1967

Pearson, M., The MacIntyre Valley: Field Archaeology and Ethnohistory, BA Hons, New England, 1973

Pedersen, H., Pigeon: An Aboriginal Rebel, BA Hons, Murdoch, 1980

Prentis, M.D., Aborigines and Europeans in the Northern Rivers of New South Wales, 1823–1881, MA, Macquarie, 1972

Rosewarne, S., Aborigines in Colonial Queensland, MA, Melbourne, 1976

Rule, M., Relations between the Aborigines and Settlers in Selected Areas of the Hunter Valley, BA Hons, Newcastle, 1977

Russo, G.H., Bishop Salvado's Plan to Civilize and Christianize the Aborigines, 1846–1900, MA, Western Australia, 1972

Ryan, L., The Aborigines in Tasmania, 1800–1974, PhD, Macquarie, 1976

Sabine, N., An Ethnohistory of the Clarence Valley, BA Hons, New England, 1970

Shelmerdine, S., The Port Phillip Native Police Corps as an Experiment in Aboriginal Policy and Practice, 1837–1853, BA Hons, Melbourne, 1972

Shepherd, B.W., A History of the Pearling Industry of the North-West Coast of Australia, MA, Western Australia, 1975

Smith, P., Yarrabah, 1892–1910, BA Hons, James Cook, 1981

Taylor, J.C., Race Relations in South East Queensland, BA Hons, Queensland, 1967

Taylor, N., The Native Mounted Police of Queensland, 1850–1900, BA Hons, James Cook, 1970

Thorpe, W., Archibald Meston and the Aborigines: Ideology and Practice, 1870–1970, BA Hons, Queensland, 1978

Walker, J.A., Aboriginal-European Relations in the Maryborough District, 1842–1903, BA Hons, Queensland, 1975

Waller, K.G.T., The Letters of the Leslie Brothers in Australia 1834–54, BA Hons, Queensland, 1956

Willmott, J., The Pearling Industry in Western Australia, 1850–1916, BA Hons, Western Australia, 1975

Contemporary Books, Articles and Pamphlets

Archer, T., *Recollections of a Rambling Life*, Yokohama, 1897

Arden, G., *Latest Information with Regard to Australia Felix* etc., Melbourne, 1840

Atkinson, J., *An Account of the State of Agriculture and Grazing in New South Wales*, London, 1826

Austin, R., *Journal of Assistant Surveyor R. Austin*, Perth, 1855

Backhouse, J., *A Narrative of a Visit to the Australian Colonies*, London, 1843

Bagehot, W., *Physics and Politics*, London, 1872

Balfour, H., 'On the Method Employed by the Natives of N.W. Australia in the Manufacture of Glass Spear Heads', *MAN*, 1903

Barnard, J., 'Aborigines of Tasmania', *AAAS*, Z, 1890

Bartlett, T., *New Holland*, London, 1843

Barton, R.D., *Reminiscences of an Australian Pioneer*, Sydney, 1917

Bennett, M.M., *Christison of Lammermoor*, London, 1927

Bennett, S., *The History of Australasian Discovery and Colonization*, Sydney, 1867

Beveridge, P., *The Aborigines of Victoria and Riverina*, Melbourne, 1889

Beveridge, P., 'On the Aborigines Inhabiting the...Lower Murray, Lower Murrumbidgee, Lower Lachlan and Lower Darling', *Journal of Royal Society of New South Wales*, 17, 1883

Bolderwood, R., *Old Melbourne Memories*, Melbourne 1884

Bond, G., *A Brief Account of the Colony of Port Jackson*, Oxford, 1806

Bonwick, J., *The Last of the Tasmanians*, London, 1870

Bonwick, J., *Port Phillip Settlement*, London, 1883

Bonwick, J., 'The Australian Natives', *JAI*, 16, 1887

Bradley, W., *A Voyage to New South Wales, 1786–92*, Sydney, 1969

Braim, T.H., *A History of New South Wales*, 2 vols, London, 1846

Breton, W.H., *Excursions in New South Wales, Western Australia and Van Diemens Land*, London, 1833

Bridge, T.F., *Letters from Victorian Pioneers*, Melbourne, 1898

Brock, D.G., *To the Desert With Sturt*, Adelaide, 1975

Brown, P.L. (ed.), *The Narrative of George Russell*, London, 1935

Bull, J.W., *Early Experiences of Life in South Australia*, Adelaide, 1884

Bulmer, J., 'Some Account of the Aborigines of the Lower Murray, Wimmera and Maneroo', *Proceedings Royal Geographical Society of Victoria*, 1, 5, March 1888

Bunbury, H.W., *Early Days in Western Australia*, London, 1930

Burkitt, A.N., 'Observations on the Facial Characteristics of the Australian Aborigines', *AAAS*, 18, 1926

Byerley, F.J., *Narrative of an Overland Expedition*, Brisbane, 1867

Byrne, J.C., *Twelve Years Wanderings in the British Colonies*, 2 vols, London, 1848

Calder, J.E., *The Native Tribes of Tasmania*, Hobart, 1875

Calvert, A.F., *The Aborigines of West Australia*, London, 1894

Campbell, J., *The Early Settlement of Queensland*, Brisbane, 1936

Carnegie, D., *Spinifex and Sand*, London 1898

Carrington, G., *Colonial Adventures and Experiences*, London, 1877

Carron, W., *Narrative of an Expedition of the late Assistant Surveyor Mr E.B. Kennedy*, Sydney, 1849

Chester, E., Early Days in Albany: Reminiscences of Mr E. Chester', *WAHS*, 1, 1931

Bibliography

Chewings, E., *Back in the Stone Age*, Sydney, 1936

Collins, D., *Account of the English Colony of New South Wales, 1798–1804*, 2 vols, London, 1802

Crawford, J.C., 'The Diary of James Coutts Crawford', *South Australiana*, 1, 2, 1964, 1965

Curr, E., *An Account of the Colony of Van Diemens Land*, London, 1824

Curr, E., *The Australian Race; its origin, languages, customs*, 4 vols, Melbourne, 1886–1887

Curr, E., *Recollections of Squatting in Victoria*, Melbourne, 1883

Daly, D., *Digging, Squatting and Pioneering Life in the Northern Territory of South Australia*, London, 1887

Darwin, C., *Journal of Researches* etc., London, 1839

Davenport, S., 'Letters of Samuel Davenport 1842–1849', *South Australiana*, 6, 10, 1967, 1971

Dawson, J., *Australian Aborigines; the languages and customs of several tribes of Aborigines in the Western District of Victoria*, Melbourne, 1881

Dawson, R., *The Present State of Australia*, London, 1830

De Brebant Cooper, F., *Wild Adventures in Australia and New South Wales*, London, 1857

De Satge, E. and O., *Pages from the Journal of a Queensland Squatter*, London, 1901

Devanny, J., *Travels in North Queensland*, London, 1951

Doyle, M. (ed.), *Extracts from the Letters and Journals of George Fletcher Moore*, London, 1834

Dredge, J., *Brief Notices on the Aborigines of New South Wales*, Geelong, 1845

Dumont D'urville, M.J., *Voyage de la Corvette L'Astrolabe*, Paris, 1830

Dunnett, J.S., 'Evaluation in Australia', *Empire Review*, 14, 1907–1908

Durack, P.M., 'Pioneering in the East Kimberleys', *WAHS*, 2, 14, 1933

Easty, J., *Memorandum of the Transactions of a Voyage from England to Botany Bay*, Sydney, 1965

Eden, C., *My Wife and I in Queensland*, London, 1872

Eipper, C., *Statement of the Origin, Condition and Prospects of the German Mission to Aborigines at Moreton Bay*, Sydney, 1841

Eyre, E.J., *Journals of Expeditions of Discovery*, 2 vols, London, 1845

Fenwick, J., 'Diary of John Fenwick', *Queensland Heritage*, 2, 3, November, 1970

Field, B., *Geographical Memoirs of New South Wales*, London, 1825

Finlayson, Pastor, 'Reminiscences', *RGSSA*, 4, 1902–190

Fison, L. & A.W. Howitt, *Kamilaroi and Kurnai*, facsimile edition, Oosterhout, 1967

Flinders, M., *A Voyage of Terra Australis*, 2 vols, London, 1814

Fraser, J., *The Aborigines of New South Wales*, Sydney, 1892

Fremantle, C.H., *Diaries and Letters of Admiral Sir C. H. Fremantle*, London, 1928

Froggatt, W.W., 'Notes on the Natives of West Kimberley, North West Australia', *Proceedings of Linnean Society of New South Wales*, 3, May 1888

Giles, E., *Australia Twice Traversed*, 2 vols, London, 1889

Gillen, F.J., 'The Natives of Central Australia', *RGSSA*, 4, 1898–1901

Grant, J., *The Narrative of a Voyage of Discovery*, London, 1803

Gray, R., *Reminiscences of India and North Queensland*, London, 1913

Grey, G., *Journals of Two Expeditions of Discovery*, 2 vols, London, 1841

Gribble, J.B., *Black but Comely: Aboriginal Life in Australia*, London, 1884

Gribble, J.B., *Dark Deeds in a Sunny Land*, Perth, 1905

Griffith, C., *The Present State and Prospects of the Port Phillip District*, Dublin, 1845

Hall, T., *A Short History of the Downs Blacks*, Warwick n.d.

Hale, M.B., *The Aborigines of Australia*, London, c.1889

Harris, A., *Settlers and Convicts*, 2nd edition, Melbourne, 1954

Hawker, J.C., *Early Experiences in South Australia*, Adelaide, 1899

Haydon, G.H., *Five Years Experience in Australia Felix*, London, 1846

Haygarth, H.W., *Recollections of Bush Life in Australia*, London, 1848

Henderson, C.C., 'The Mutation Theory of Evolution in History', *AAAS*, 13, 1912

Henderson, J., *Excursions and Adventures in New South Wales*, 2 vols, London, 1851

Henderson, J., *Observations on the Colonies of New South Wales and Van Diemens Land*, Calcutta, 1832

Hives, F., *The Journal of a Jackeroo*, London, 1930

Hodgen, M.T., *Early Anthropology in the Sixteenth and Seventeenth Century*, Philadelphia, n.d.

Hodgkinson, C., *Australia: From Port Macquarie to Moreton Bay*, London, 1845

Hogson, C.P., *Reminiscences of Australia*, London, 1846

Horne, G & G. Aiston, *Savage Life in Central Australia*, London, 1924

Hovell, W., 'Journal of a Journey from Lake George to Port Phillip, 1824–25', *JRAHS*, 7, 1921

Howitt, A.W., *The Native Tribes of South-East Australia*, London, 1904

Howitt, R., *Impressions of Australia Felix*, London, 1845

Hull, H.M., *Experience of Forty Years in Tasmania*, London, 1859

Hunter, J., *An Historical Journal of Events at Sydney and at Sea, 1787–1792*, Sydney, 1968

Huxley, T.H., *Evidence as to Man's Place in Nature*, London, 1863

Irwin, F.C., *The State and Position of West Australia*, London, 1835

Jack, R.L., *Northmost Australia*, 2 vols, London, 1921

Jorgensen, J., 'A Shred of Autobiography', *Hobart Town Almanach and Van Diemens Land Annual*, 1838

Journals of Several Expeditions Made in Western Australia, London, 1833

Jukes, J.B., *Narrative of the Surveying Voyage of HMS Fly*, London, 1847

Kennedy, E.B., *The Black Police of Queensland*, London, 1902

Kennedy, E.B., 'Extracts from the Journal of an Exploring Expedition into Central Australia', *JRGS*, 22, 1852

Kennedy, E.B., *Four Years in Queensland*, London, 1870

King, P.P., *Narrative of a Survey of the Inter-tropical and Western Coast of Australia*, 2 vols, London, 1827

Kirby, J., *Old Times in the Bush in Australia*, Melbourne, 1894

Kittle, S., *A Concise History of the Colony and Natives of New South Wales*, Edinburgh, 1816

Knight, J.J., *In the Early Days*, Brisbane, 1895

Labillardiere, M., *Voyage in Search of La Perouse, 1791–1794*, London, 1800

Landor, E.W., *The Bushman or Life in a New Country*, London, 1847

Lang, G.S., *The Aborigines of Australia*, Melbourne, 1865

Lang, J.D., *Queensland*, London, 1861

Lawrence, W., *Lectures on Comparative Anatomy*, London, 1819

Leichhardt, F.W.L., *The Letters of F.W. Ludwig Leichhardt*, collected, translated and edited M. Auroussean, 2 vols, Cambridge, 1968

Lindsay, D., *Journal of the Elder Scientific Exploring Expedition, 1891–2*, Adelaide, 1892

Lloyd, G.T., *Thirty-three Years in Tasmania and Victoria*, London, 1862

Loyau, G.E., *The History of Maryborough*, Brisbane, 1897

Lubbock, J., *Pre-Historic Times*, London, 1865

Lumholtz, C., *Among Cannibals*, London, 1889

Lumholtz, C., 'Among the Natives of Australia', *Journal of American Geographical Society*, 21, 1889

MacAllister, D., 'The Australian Aborigines', *Melbourne Review*, 3, 1878

McCombie, T., *Essays on Colonization*, London, 1850

McCombie, T., *The History of the Colony of Victoria*, Melbourne, 1858

McCrae, G.C., 'The Early Settlement of the Eastern Shores of Port Phillip Bay', *Victorian Historical Magazine*, 1, 1911

Bibliography

MacGillivray, J., *Narrative of the Voyage of HMS Rattlesnake*, 2 vols, London, 1852

Mackaness, G. (ed.), *Fourteen Journeys Over the Blue Mountains of NSW, 1813–41*, Sydney, 1965

Mackay, R., *Recollections of Early Gippsland Goldfields*, Traralgon, 1916

McKillop, D., 'Anthropological Notes on the Aboriginal Tribes of the Daly River, North Australia', *RGSSA*, 5, 1893

McKinlay, W., *McKinlays Journal of Exploration*, Melbourne, 1862

McLaren, J., *My Crowded Solitude*, Sun Books edition, Melbourne, 1966

McLean, J., 'Police Experiences with the Natives', RGSSA, 6, 1902–1903

MacPherson, A., *Mount Abundance*, London, 1897

Major, T., *Leaves from a Squatters Notebook*, London, 1900

Mann. J.F., *Eight Months with Dr Leichhardt*, Sydney, 1888

Mathew, J., *Eaglehawk and Crow*, London, 1899

Mathew, J., *Two Representative Tribes of Queensland*, London, 1910

Melville, H., *The History of the Island of Van Diemens Land*, London, 1835

Merivale, H., *Lectures on Colonization and Colonies*, 2nd edition, London, 1928

Meston, A., *Geographical History of Queensland*, Brisbane, 1895

Meyrick, F.J., *Life in the Bush, 1840–47*, London, 1939

Mitchell, T.L., *Journal of an Expedition into the Interior of Tropical Australia*, London, 1848

Mitchell, T.L., *Three Expeditions into Eastern Australia*, 2 vols, London, 1834

Moore, G.F., *Diary of Ten Years Eventfull Life of an Early Settler in West Australia*, London, 1884

Moore, G.F., *A Descriptive Vocabulary of the Language in Common Usage Amongst the Aborigines of West Australia*, London, 1842

Morgan, J., *The Life and Adventures of William Buckley*, London 1967 edition, edited C.E. Sayers

Morrell, J., *Sketch of a Residence Among the Aborigines of North Queensland*, Brisbane, 1863

Morris, E.E., *A Dictionary of Austral English*, London, 1898

Mudie, R., *The Picture of Australasia*, London, 1829

Newland, S., *Memoirs of Simpson Newland*, Adelaide, 1928

Newland, S., 'The Parkinjees or the Aboriginal Tribes on the Darling River', *RGSSA*, 2, 1887–1888

Newland, S., 'Some Aborigines I Have Known', *RGSSA*, 1894–1895

Nicolay, C.G., *The Handbook of Western Australia*, London, 1896

Nott, J.C. & G.R. Gliddon, *Types of Mankind*, London, 1864

Ogle, N., *The Colony of Western Australia*, London, 1839

Oxley, J., *Journals of Two Expeditions into the Interior of New South Wales*, London, 1820

Paine, D., *The Journal of Daniel Paine 1794–1797*, edited R.J. Knight & A. Frost, Sydney, 1983

Palmerston, C., 'Diary of Christie Palmerston', *Queensland Heritage*, 1, 8, May 1968

Parker, E.S., *The Aborigines of Australia*, Melbourne, 1854

Parker, K.L., *The Euahlayi Tribe*, London, 1905

Peron, M.F., *A Voyage of Discovery to the Southern Hemisphere*, London, 1809

Petrie, T., *Reminiscences of Early Queensland*, Brisbane, 1932

Pitt-Rivers, A.C.F., *The Evolution of Culture*, Oxford, 1906.

Pitts, H., *The Australian Aborigines and the Christian Church*, London, 1914

Plomley N.J.B. (ed.), *Friendly Mission: the Tasmanian Journals and Papers of George Augustus Robinson, 1829–1834*, Hobart, 1966

Porteus, S.D., 'Mentality of Australian Aborigines', *Oceania*, 4, 1933

Pridden, W., *Australia, Its History and Present Condition*, London, 1843

Pulleine, P. & H. Woolard, 'Physiological and Mental Observations on the Australian

Aborigines', *Proceedings Royal Society of South Australia*, 54, 1930

Ramsay-Smith, W., 'The Place of the Australian Aboriginal in Recent Anthropological Research', *AAAS*, 11, 1908

Reilly, J.T., *Reminiscences of Fifty Years Residence in West Australia*, Perth, 1903

Richardson, A.R., *Early Memoirs of the Great Nor-West*, Perth, 1914

Richmond, F., *Queensland in the 'Seventies': Reminiscences of the Early Days of a Young Clergyman*, Singapore, 1927

Ridley, W., *Kamilaroi and Other Australian Languages*, 2nd edition, Sydney, 1875

Robarts, N., 'The Victorian Aborigine As He Is', *AAAS*, 14, 1913

Robertson, W., *Cooee Talks*, Sydney, 1928

Rolleston, H.D., 'Description of the Cerebral Hemispheres of an Adult Australian Male', *JAI*, 17, 1887

Ross, J., 'The Settler in Van Diemens Land Fourteen Years Ago', *Hobart Town Almanack*, 1836

Roth, H.L., *The Aborigines of Tasmania*, 2nd edition, Halifax, 1899

Roth, W.G., *Ethnographical Studies Among the North-West-Central Queensland Aborigines*, Brisbane, 1897

Rusden, G.W., *History of Australia*, 3 vols, London, 1883

Russell, H.S., *The Genesis of Queensland*, Sydney, 1888

Sadlier, R., *The Aborigines of Australia*, Sydney, 1883

Schurmann, C.W., *Vocabulary of the Parnkalla Language*, Adelaide, 1844

Searcey, A., *In Australian Tropics*, London, 1907

Searcey, A., *In Northern Seas*, Adelaide, 1905

Semon, R., *In the Australian Bush*, London, 1899

Shann, E.O.G., *Cattle Chosen*, London, 1926

Shenton, E., 'Reminiscences of Perth 1830–1840', *WAHS*, 1, 1, 1927

Siebert, O., 'Sagen Und Sitten Der Dieri Und Nachbarstämme in Zentral-Australien', *Globus*, 47, 1916

Sinnett, F., *The Rush to Port Curtis*, Geelong, 1859

Smith, C., *The Booandick Tribe of South Australian Aborigines*, Adelaide, 1880

Smyth, A.B., *The Journal of Arthur Bowes Smyth, 1787–1789*, edited P. Fidcon, Sydney, 1979

Smyth, R.B., *The Aborigines of Victoria*, 2 vols, Melbourne, 1876

Spencer, H., 'Comparative Psychology of Man', *JAI*, 5, 1876

Spencer, H., *The Principles of Sociology*, London, 1876

Spiller, G., 'The Mentality of the Australian Aborigines', *The Sociological Review*, 6, 1913

Stevenson, J.B., *Seven Years in the Australian Bush*, Liverpool, 1880

Stokes, J.L., *Discoveries in Australia*, 2 vols, London, 1846

Streeter, E.W., *Pearls and Pearling Life*, London, 1886

Stuart, J.M., *Explorations Across the Continent of Australia 1861–1862*, Melbourne, 1863

Sturt, C., *Narrative of an Expedition into Central Australia*, 2 vols, London, 1849

Sturt, C., *Two Expeditions into the Interior of Southern Australia*, 2 vols, London, 1833

Sutherland, A.G., *Victoria and Its Metropolis*, Melbourne, 1888

Sutherland, G., *Pioneering Days: Across the Wilds of Queensland*, Brisbane, 1913

Taplin, G., *The Narrinyeri, their Manners and Customs*, Adelaide, 1878

Taplin, G. (ed.), *The Folklore, Manners, Customs and Languages of the South Australian Aborigines*, Adelaide, 1879

Taunton, H., *Australind*, London, 1903

Teichelmann, C.G., *Outlines of a Grammar, Vocabulary and Phraseology of the Aboriginal Language of South Australia*, Adelaide, 1840

Tench, W., *Sydney's First Four Years*, Sydney 1961 edition introduced by L.F. Fitzhardinge

Threlkeld, L.E., *An Australian Language*, Sydney, 1892

Threlkeld, L.E., *Australian Reminiscences and Papers*, edited N. Gunson, Canberra, 1974

Tuckey, J.H., *An Account of a Voyage to Establish a Colony at Port Phillip*, London, 1805

Bibliography

Turnbull, J., *A Voyage Round the World* etc., 2nd edition, London, 1813

Vogan, A.J., *The Black Police*, London, 1890

Vogt, C., *Lectures of Man*, London, 1864

Wake, C.S., 'The Mental Characteristics of Primitive Man, as Exemplified by the Australian Aborigines', *JAI*, 1, 1872

Walker, J.B., *Early Tasmania*, Hobart, 1902

Wallace, A.R., 'Mr Wallace on Natural Selection Applied to Anthropology', *Anthropological Review*, 16, 1867

Wallace, A.R., 'The Action of Natural Selection on Man', *Half Hours with Modern Scientists*, New Haven, 1873

Warburton, P., *Journey Across the Western Interior of Australia*, London, 1875

Ward, A., *The Miracle of Mapoon*, London, 1908

Welsby, T., *Collected Works*, 2 vols, Brisbane, 1907

West, J., *History of Tasmania*, 2 vols, Launceston, 1852

Westgarth, W., *Australia Felix*, Edinburgh, 1848

Westgarth, W., *Australia*, Edinburgh, 1861

Westgarth, W., *A Report on the Condition, Capabilities and Prospects of the Australian Aborigines*, Melbourne, 1846

Westgarth, W., *Tracks of McKinlay and Party Across Australia*, London, 1863

White, C., *An Account of the Regular Gradation in Man*, London, 1799

Widowson, H., *The Present State of Van Diemens Land*, London, 1829

Willshire, W.H., *The Aborigines of Central Australia*, Adelaide, 1891

Wilson, T.B., *Narrative of a Voyage Round the World*, London, 1835

Windsor-Earl, G., 'On the Aboriginal Tribes of the North Coast of Australia', *JRGS*, 16, 1846

Windsor-Earl, G., *Enterprise in Tropical Australia*, London, 1846

Withnell, J.G., *The Customs and Traditions of the Aboriginal Natives of North-Western Australia*, Roebourne, 1901

Wild, J.J., Outlines of Anthropology, *AAAS*, 1, 1889

Wood, K.M., 'A Pioneer Pearler—Reminiscences of John Wood', *WAHS*, 2, 12

Woods, J.D. (ed.), *The Native Tribes of South Australia*, Adelaide, 1879

Worgan, G.B., *Journal of a First Fleet Surgeon*, Sydney, 1978

Young, S.B., 'Reminiscences of Mrs Susan Bundarre Young', *JRAHS*, 8, 1923

Zillman, J.H.L., *Past and Present Australian Life*, London, 1889

Recent Books, Articles

Allen, J., 'The Archaeology of Nineteenth Century British Imperialism', *World Archaeology*, 5, 1, June 1973

Anderson, C., 'Aboriginal Economy and Contact Relations at Bloomfield River, North Queensland', *Australian Institute of Aboriginal Studies Newsletter*, 12, September 1979

Anderson, R.H., 'The Effect of Settlement upon the New South Wales Flora', *Proceedings, Linnean Society of New South Wales*, 66, 1941

Bach, J., 'The Political Economy of Pearl Shelling', *Economic History Review*, 14, 1, 1961

Baker, S.J., *The Australian Language*, Melbourne, 1966

Barwick, D., 'Coranderrk and Cumeroogunga' in T. Epstein (ed.), *Opportunity and Response*, London, 1972

Basedow, H., *The Australian Aboriginal*, Adelaide, 1925

Bates, D., *The Passing of the Aborigines*, London, 1938

Bennett, M.M., *The Australian Aborigines as a Human Being*, London, 1930

Bern, J., 'Ideology and Domination', *Oceania*, 50, 2, December 1979

Berndt, R.M. 'A Preliminary Report of Fieldwork in the Ooldea Region', *Oceania*, 13, 1942–43

Berndt, R.M., 'Surviving Influence of Mission Contact on the Daly River', *Neue Zeit-*

schrift Fur Missionswissenschaft, 8/2−3, 1952

Berndt, R.M. & C.H., *Arnhem Land: Its History and Its People*, Melbourne, 1954

Berndt, R.M. & C.H., *From Black to White in South Australia*, Melbourne, 1951

Biskup, P., *Not Slaves, Not Citizens: The Aboriginal Problem in Western Australia 1898−1954*, St Lucia, 1973

Blainey, G., *Triumph of the Nomads*, Melbourne, 1975

Black, J., *North Queensland Pioneers*, Townsville, n.d.

Bridges, B., 'The Colonization of Australia: A Communication', *Teaching History*, November 1977

Bridges, B., 'The Aborigines and the Land Question in New South Wales', *JRAHS*, 56, 2, June 1970

Bridges, B., 'Pemulwy: A Noble Savage', *Newsletter of the Royal Australian Historical Society*, 88, 1970

Bridges, B., 'The Native Police Corps, Port Phillip District and Victoria 1837−53', *JRAHS*, 57, 2, June 1971

Broome, R., *Aboriginal Australians*, Sydney, 1982

Chase, A.K. & J.R. Von Sturmer, 'Mental Man and Social Evolutionary Theory', in G.E. Kearney et.al., *The Psychology of Aboriginal Australians*, Sydney, 1973

Christie, M.F., *Aborigines in Colonial Victoria*, Sydney, 1979

Corris, P., *Aborigines and Europeans in Western Victoria*, Canberra, 1963

Coutts, P.J. et al, 'Impact of European Settlement on Aboriginal Society in Western Victoria', *Records of the Victoria Archaeological Survey*, 4, August 1977

Cribbin, J., *The Killing Times: The Coniston Massacre 1928*, Sydney, 1984

Davies, M., 'Settlers and Aborigines at Port Lincoln 1840−45', *South Australiana*, 18, 1979.

Docker, E.C., *Simply Human Beings*, Brisbane, 1964

Donaldson, I. & T., *Seeing the First Australians*, Sydney, 1985

Evans, R. et al, *Exclusion, Exploitation and Extermination*, Sydney, 1975

Farwell, G., *Land of Mirage*, London, 1950

Frost, A., 'New South Wales *terra nullius*: the British denial of Aboriginal land rights', *HS*, 19, 1981

Gale, F., *A Study of Assimilation: Part Aborigines in South Australia*, Adelaide, 1964

Gardner, P., 'The Journals of De Villiers and Warman', *Victorian Historical Journal*, 50, 1979

Gardner, P., 'The Warrigal Creek Massacre', *JRAHS*, 66, 1980

Gill, A., 'Aborigines, Settlers and Police in the Kimberleys 1887−1905', *Studies in Western Australian History*, 1, 1977

Green, N., 'Aboriginal and Settler Conflict in Western Australia, 1826−1852', *The Push from the Bush*, 3, May 1979

Green, N., *Broken Spears: Aborigines and Europeans in the southwest of Australia*, Perth, 1984

Gunson, N. (ed.), *Australian Reminiscences and Papers of L.E. Threlkeld*, Canberra, 1974

Haddon, A.C., *Head Hunters: Black, White and Brown*, London, 1932

Hallam, S., *Fire and Hearth*, Canberra, 1975

Hamilton, A., 'Blacks and Whites: The Relationships of Change', *Arena*, 30, 1972

Hamman, J., 'The Coorong Massacre', *Flinders Journal of Politics and History*, 3, 1973

Hancock, W.K., *Australia*, Jacaranda edition, Brisbane, 1960

Hasluck, A., 'Yagan the Patriot', *WAHS*, 7, 1961

Hasluck, P., *Black Australians*, Melbourne, 1942

Haynes, B.T., *West Australian Aborigines, 1622−1972*, Perth, 1973

Hercus, L., 'Tales of Nadu-Dagali (Rib-Bone Billy)', *Aboriginal History*, 1, 1, 1977

Hughes, I., 'A State of Open Warfare', *Lectures on North Queensland History*, second series, Townsville, 1975

Bibliography

Hutchison, D.E. (ed.), *Aboriginal Progress: A New Era?*, Perth, 1969

Inglis, J., 'One Hundred Years of Point Macleay, South Australia', *Mankind*, 5, 12, November 1962

Loos, N.A., *Invasion and Resistance*, Canberra, 1982

Markus, A., *From the Barrel of a Gun*, Melbourne, 1974

May, D., *From Bush to Station*, Townsville 1983

McBride, I. (ed.), *Records of Time Past*, Canberra, 1978

McMahon, A., 'Tasmanian Aboriginal Women as Slaves', *THRA*, 23, 2, June 1976

The Mapoon Story According to the Invaders, Sydney, 1975

Mulvaney, D.J., 'The Ascent of Man: Howitt as Anthropologist', in M.H. Walker, *Come Wind, Come Weather*, Melbourne, 1971, pp.285–312.

Mulvaney, D.J. & J. Golson, *Aboriginal Man and Environment in Australia*, Canberra, 1971

Mulvaney, D.J., *The Pre-history of Australia*, revised edition, Ringwood, 1975

Murray-Smith, S., 'Beyond the Pale: The Islander Communities of Bass Strait in the Nineteenth Century', *THRA*, 20, 4, December, 1973

Olbrei, E. (ed.), *Black Australians: The Prospects for Change*, Townsville, 1982

Reid, G., *A Nest of Hornets: The Massacre of the Fraser Family at Hornet Bank Station, Central Queensland, 1857*, Melbourne, 1982

Reynolds, H., 'Jimmy Governor and Jimmie Blacksmith', *Australian Literary Studies*, 9, 1, May 1979

Reynolds, H., 'The Unrecorded Battlefields of Queensland', *Race Relations in North Queensland*, Townsville, 1978

Roughsey, D., *Moon and Rainbow*, Sydney, 1971

Rowley, C.D., 'Aborigines and Other Australians', *Oceania*, 32, 4, 1962

Rowley, C.D., *The Destruction of Aboriginal Society*, Melbourne, 1972

Rowley, C.D., *The Remote Aborigines*, Melbourne, 1972

Rowley, C.D., *Outcasts in White Australia*, Melbourne, 1972

Ryan, L., 'The Struggle for Recognition: part Aborigines in Tasmania in the Nineteenth Century', *Aboriginal History*, 1, 1, 1977

Spencer, B., *Native Tribes of the Northern Territory of Australia*, London, 1914

Spencer, B., *Wanderings in Wild Australia*, 2 vols, London, 1928

Spencer, B. & F.J. Gillen, *Across Australia*, London, 1912

Spencer, B. & F.J. Gillen, *The Arunta*, London, 1922

Spencer, B. & F.J. Gillen, *The Native Tribes of Central Australia*, Dover edition, New York, 1968

Stanner, W.E.H., *After the Dreaming*, Sydney, 1969

Thorpe, O., *First Catholic Mission to the Australian Aborigines*, Sydney, 1949

Threadgill, B., *South Australian Land Exploration, 1856–1880*, Adelaide, 1922

Tindale, N.B., 'A Survey of the Half-Caste Problem in South Australia', *RGSSA*, 42, 1940–41

Wade-Broun, N., *Memoirs of a Queensland Pioneer*, Sandgate, 1944

Walker, M.M., *Come Wind, Come Weather*, Melbourne, 1971

Watson, D., *Caledonia Australis: Scottish Highlanders on the Frontiers of Australia*, Sydney, 1984

Wegner, J., 'The Aborigines of the Etheridge Shire' in H. Reynolds (ed.), *Race Relations in North Queensland*, Townsville, 1979

Willey, K. *Boss Drover*, Adelaide, 1971

Woolmington, J., *Aborigines in Colonial Society, 1788–1850*, Melbourne, 1973

Wright, J., *The Cry for the Dead*, Melbourne, 1981

Yarwood, A.T. & M.J. Knowling, *Race Relations in Australia*, North Ryde, 1982

Index

Index

ABORIGINAL SOVEREIGNTY

Reflections on race, state and nation

HENRY REYNOLDS

Since Federation, Australians have thought of themselves as one sovereign nation. But what of the original Australians? Are they nations within?

Aboriginal Sovereignty is a provocative study of the relations between indigenous Australians and mainstream society. It presents a bold new interpretation of Aboriginal political development. It challenges us to consider that the Mabo decision is not the boundary at which the recognition of indigenous rights must cease.

1 86373 969 6

DISPOSSESSION

Black Australians and white invaders

HENRY REYNOLDS

Aboriginal and immigrant Australians have shared this continent for 200 years. Nineteenth-century writers were aware of the importance of the Aboriginal presence, but when the colonists began to write their own history the Aborigines were erased from the account. Recently, this 'history' has been overturned as we rediscover the role of Aborigines in our past.

This fascinating collection of documents, in which our forebears speak for themselves, is compiled by a leading authority on white–Aboriginal relations. It challenges the general reader to reinterpret our past.

ILLUSTRATED

1 86448 141 2

IN THE AGE OF MABO

History, Aborigines and Australia

EDITED BY BAIN ATTWOOD

The High Court's 1992 Mabo decision has provoked much controversy in contemporary Australia. As the ruling has increasingly become the subject of intense debate throughout the community, the implications of Mabo have shifted from the law to history, politics and culture.

Mabo was underpinned by the emergence of a new field of knowledge called 'Aboriginal history'. This book discusses the far-reaching outcomes of Aborigines presenting their histories, not only for the law and the disciplines of history, archeology and anthropology, but also for the politics of identity.

Contributors include Deborah Bird Rose, Henry Reynolds, Tim Murray, John Morton, Andrew Markus, Rosemary Hunter and Richard Broome.

1 86373 841 X

INVASION TO EMBASSY

Land in Aboriginal politics in New South Wales

HEATHER GOODALL

We should have land, this is our land. We are hungry for our land.

MILLI BOYD
Woodenborg, 1972

Invasion to Embassy challenges the conventional view of Aboriginal politics to present a bold new account of Aboriginal responses to invasion and dispossession in New South Wales. At the core of these responses has been land: as a concrete goal, but also as a rallying cry, a call for justice and a focal point for identity.

Invasion to Embassy is unique in presenting New South Wales Aboriginal history as a history of activism, rather than a saga of passivity and victimisation. In telling this engrossing story, Heather Goodall reveals much about white Australians—not only as oppressors, but as allies and as newcomers who must in turn sort out their relations to the land.

ILLUSTRATED

1 86448 149 8

TERRIBLE HARD BISCUITS

A reader in Aboriginal history

EDITED BY VALERIE CHAPMAN AND PETER READ

A fine beginning for those intent on understanding the colonial past that shaped black and white Australia.

RICHARD BROOME

Terrible Hard Biscuits introduces the main themes in the history of Aboriginal Australia: the complexity of Aboriginal–European relations since 1788; how Aboriginal identity and cultures survived invasion, dispossession and dislocation; how indigenous Australians have survived to take their place in today's society.

Contributors include Isabel McBryde, Henrietta Fourmile, Bob Reece, Philip Clarke, Lyndall Ryan, Richard Baker, Heather Goodall, Peter Read, Bowman Johnson, Andrew Markus, Elspeth Young and Scott Robinson.

ILLUSTRATED

1 86373 964 5

FOR THE RECORD

160 years of Aboriginal print journalism

EDITED BY MICHAEL ROSE

. . . a unique overview of the history of our use of the print media in our attempts—from the loftiest to the humblest—to get the message out.

JOHN NEWFONG
Australia's first Aboriginal professional print journalist

Michael Rose has brought together examples of Aboriginal journalism from a wide range of Aboriginal and mainstream publications. He includes articles from early activists and others who used newspaper and magazine journalism in their fight for justice. It includes an eye-witness account of a Maralinga atomic bomb test in the 1950s, Kevin Gilbert's passionate call for a formal treaty between Aboriginal people and the Australian government, and Noel Pearson's commentary on the High Court's Mabo decision.

ILLUSTRATED

1 86448 058 0

CONTESTED GROUND

Australian Aborigines under the British Crown

EDITED BY ANN MCGRATH

Both indigenous and non-indigenous Australians have a lot to learn about each other before reconciliation between the two peoples can be realised. This book will go a long way towards achieving that end.

PAUL BEHRENDT

Contested Ground provides a comprehensive and up-to-date account of the processes and experiences which shaped the lives of Aboriginal Australians from 1788 to the present. It integrates eye-witness accounts, oral histories and historical research to present the first colony-by-colony, state-by-state history of white–Aboriginal relations.

Contributors include Heather Goodall, Richard Broome, Henry Reynolds, Dawn May, Peggy Brock, Sandy Toussaint, Peter Read and Maykutenner (Vicki Matson-Green).

ILLUSTRATED

1 86373 646 8

ABORIGINAL AUSTRALIANS

Black responses to white dominance

Second edition

RICHARD BROOME

This book tells the history of Australia from the standpoint of those who were dispossessed, the original Australians. Surveying two centuries of Aboriginal–European encounters, it reveals what white Australia lost through unremitting colonial invasion and tells the story of Aboriginal survival through resistance and accommodation. It traces the Aboriginal journey from the margins of colonial society to a more central place in modern Australian.

Aboriginal Australians first appeared in 1982 and has won a wide readership. This new enlarged edition brings the story up to the mid 1990s.

ILLUSTRATED

1 86373 760 X